"Kanika Batra's *Worlding Postcolonial Sexualities: Publics, Counterpublics, Human Rights* is a tour de force of LGBTQI history, this time refreshingly tracing related southern activism, which is shown to take creative and sometimes arcane paths that lead to increased LGBTQI consciousness and visibility. The comparison across southern activist spaces breaks with the currently dominant colonized understanding of 'internationalism'."

Joan French, *Institute of Gender and Development, University of the West Indies at Mona, Jamaica*

"*Worlding Postcolonial Sexualities* is a shining new gem in comparative studies. In a refreshing shift beyond the established canons, narratives, and genres of postcolonial, feminist, and queer studies, Batra reveals how feminist and LGBTQ newsletters, magazines, and journals in Jamaica, India, and South Africa, published between the late 1970s and late 1990s, created counterpublic spaces for articulating and defending sexual rights, while tracing the emergence of these print cultures and organisational networks from the global South into transnational spheres as vibrant, alternative, relational, and intersectional forms of feminist and queer history and coalition."

William J Spurlin, *Professor of English and Vice-Dean, Brunel University London, UK*

"Kanika Batra brilliantly uses queer journalism in Jamaica, India, and South Africa to analyze counter discourses and the growing visibility of LGBTQ+ resistance. It answers the urgent question of how alternative queer histories and practices have become agents of postcolonial change and, equally importantly, how they develop transnational South-South connections. This deeply insightful book is a must-read for anyone interested in 'worldmaking,' feminism, queer politics, and social change."

Premilla Nadasen, *Professor of History, Barnard College, Columbia University, New York, USA, author of* Household Workers Unite

"Kanika Batra's *Worlding Postcolonial Sexualities*, builds on her book on postcolonial drama published in 2011, taking her research into an under-studied area of English-language magazines published from the late 1970s to the mid- 1990s. This book is remarkable in analyzing feminist and queer activism in connection with each other. Batra asserts astutely that the separation of feminist from gay issues in not productive in India, Jamaica, South Africa, scenarios that are different from activism for sexual rights for gays and lesbians in Europe and North America. Rather, in these Global South locations, activist groups attempt to gain space and raise awareness against sexual violence via legislative struggles as well as feminist activism and publications. Such efforts work towards social change in the arena of sexual inequalities. This book, in combining studies of gender and sexuality with those of space and region as increasingly important in our global perspectives in comparative studies, brings new archival material into transnational gender and globalization studies."

Ketu H. Katrak, *Professor of Drama, University of California, Irvine, USA, author of* Politics of the Female Body

WORLDING POSTCOLONIAL SEXUALITIES

Worlding Postcolonial Sexualities demonstrates how late twentieth-century postcolonial print cultures initiated a public discourse on sexual activism and contends that postcolonial feminist and queer archives offer alternative histories of sexual precarity, vulnerability, and resistance.

The book's comparative focus on India, Jamaica, and South Africa extends the valences of postcolonial feminist and queer studies towards a historical examination of South-South interactions in the theory and praxis of sexual rights. Analyzing the circumstances of production and the contents of English-language and intermittently bilingual magazines and newsletters published between the late 1970s and the late 1990s, these sources offer a way to examine the convergences and divergences between postcolonial feminist, gay, and lesbian activism. It charts a set of concerns common to feminist, gay, and lesbian activist literature: retrogressive colonial-era legislation impacting the status of women and sexual minorities; a marked increase in sexual violence; piecemeal reproductive freedoms and sexual choice under neoliberalism; the emergence and management of the HIV/AIDS crisis; precariousness of lesbian and transgender concerns within feminist and LGBTQ+ movements; and Non-Governmental Organizations as major actors articulating sexual rights as human rights. This methodologically innovative work is based on archival historical research, analyses of national and international policy documents, close readings of activist publications, and conversations with activists and founding editors.

This is an important intervention in the field of gender and sexuality studies and is the winner of the 2020 Feminist Futures, Subversive Histories prize in partnership with the NWSA. The book is key reading for scholars and students in gender, sexuality, comparative literature, and postcolonial studies.

Kanika Batra is Professor of English at Texas Tech University. She writes on and teaches transnational feminist and queer studies, postcolonial literature, and comparative literature. She is the author of *Caribbean Poetry: Derek Walcott and Edward Brathwaite* (2001) and *Feminist Visions and Queer Futures in Postcolonial Drama* (2011).

SUBVERSIVE HISTORIES, FEMINIST FUTURES NWSA PRIZE

The *Subversive Histories, Feminist Futures* book prize is in collaboration with the National Women's Studies Association.

Edited by Janell Hobson, the series exemplifies original research in feminist histories that "subvert" dominant and normative patterns of historical narrative by centering women, gender, and feminist politics. Prize winners represent the best of scholarship that delves into women's histories, queer histories, people of color histories, and reclamations of non-western world.

2020

Winner:
Worlding Postcolonial Sexualities
Publics, Counterpublics, Human Rights
Kanika Batra

Runner Up:
Afro Native Women's Survivance
Reanae McNeal

https://www.routledge.com/Subversive-Histories-Feminist-Futures-NWSA-Prize/book-series/FEMFUTURES

WORLDING POSTCOLONIAL SEXUALITIES

Publics, Counterpublics, Human Rights

Kanika Batra

Routledge
Taylor & Francis Group

LONDON AND NEW YORK

First published 2022
by Routledge
2 Park Square, Milton Park, Abingdon, Oxon OX14 4RN

and by Routledge
605 Third Avenue, New York, NY 10158

Routledge is an imprint of the Taylor & Francis Group, an informa business

British Library Cataloguing-in-Publication Data
A catalogue record for this book is available from the British Library

Library of Congress Cataloging-in-Publication Data
Names: Batra, Kanika, 1972- author.
Title: Worlding postcolonial sexualities : publics, counterpublics, human rights /
Kanika Batra.
Description: Abingdon, Oxon ; New York, NY : Routledge, 2021. | Includes
bibliographical references and index.
Identifiers: LCCN 2021011838 (print) | LCCN 2021011839 (ebook) |
ISBN 9780367772161 (hardback) | ISBN 9780367772109 (paperback) |
ISBN 9780367772161 (ebook) | ISBN 9781000430097 (adobe pdf) |
ISBN 9781000430127 (epub)
Subjects: LCSH: Sexual rights–Developing countries. | Sexual rights–Press
coverage–Developing countries. | Sexual minorities–Developing
countries. | Sexual minorities in mass media. | Human rights
movements–Press coverage–Developing countries. | Postcolonialism.
Classification: LCC HQ65.5.D44 B37 2021 (print) |
LCC HQ65.5.D44 (ebook) | DDC 305.3–dc23
LC record available at https://lccn.loc.gov/2021011838
LC ebook record available at https://lccn.loc.gov/2021011839

ISBN: 978-0-367-77216-1 (hbk)
ISBN: 978-0-367-77210-9 (pbk)
ISBN: 978-1-003-17030-3 (ebk)

DOI: 10.4324/9781003170303

Typeset in Bembo
by Taylor & Francis Books

For Rich

CONTENTS

FIGURES

ACKNOWLEDGEMENTS

I began dreaming about *Worlding Postcolonial Sexualities* over 15 years ago amid doctoral research which led to a previous book on postcolonial drama. While this was not an easy project to complete, it has sustained me for many years amid the demands of work and life. Elusive sources, unfamiliar contexts, teaching, administration, family health, a global pandemic, and other events interrupted the progress. In retrospect, these challenges also energized me in ways that I could not have anticipated a decade ago.

Thanks are due to many people on three continents. From India, the Department of English, University of Delhi, Malashri Lal, Sumanyu Satpathy, Shormishtha Panja, and Christel Devadawson for opportunities to reconnect with graduate students at my alma mater. To my friends and former colleagues for facilitating interactions with students in many parts of India: Kuntal and Munish Tamang from Motilal Nehru College; Jitender Gill, Swati Pal, Namita Sethi, and Rita Sinha from Janki Devi Memorial College; Smita Jha and Nagendra Kumar from the Indian Institute of Technology, Roorkee; Anurag Kumar, Monika, and Bhushan Sharma from Shri Mata Vaishno Devi University in Jammu. I would also like to thank Ashok Row Kavi and Vivek Anand for conversations about *Bombay Dost*.

From Jamaica and Toronto, Honor Ford-Smith provided invaluable assistance in all things Sistren. Joan French, formerly of Sistren and UNDP, shared important publications related to the Caribbean women's movement and heroically established a digital archive of Caribbean feminist materials. Honor and Joan offered extensive comments on draft versions of this work. Joan Ross-Frankson kindly made time to talk about her editorship of *Sistren* magazine. My research visits to Kingston over the past decade have also led to connections with the indomitable women from Women's Media Watch and the Tambourine Army. Thanks to Hillary Nicolson and Taitu Heron for their important work on gender-based violence in Jamaica. Thanks to Judith Wedderburn who arranged a valuable session with members of Women's

Media Watch to talk about the origins of the organization. I will forever cherish the memory of participating in a small way in the staged reading of Carole Lawes, Honor Ford-Smith, and Eugene Williams' powerful *Song for the Beloved* and conversations with women from various communities in and around Kingston.

In South Africa, immense gratitude to the dedicated staff of GALA, Johannesburg. Gabriel Hoosain, and Anthony Manion from GALA sourced the archives, helped with suggestions, and held conversations about queer politics. Conversations with Anthony clarified many aspects of early gay liberation in South Africa. GALA librarian Carol Preston helpfully looked for missing page numbers for the reference list. Henk Botha kindly agreed to talk about *Link/Skakel* and introduced me to Johannesburg and its environs. Shamim Meer generously discussed the origins and aims of *Speak* magazine over a wonderful Indian-South African meal. My gratitude also to Thevan Harry from the KwaMuhle Museum in Durban for leading me to important sources about women's activism in the city during the 1980s and 1990s.

In the United States and Canada, many friends and mentors helped with suggestions and timely readings of drafts. Matthew Chin's scholarship on Jamaican sexualities and his willingness to share materials exemplifies academic generosity. I thank him for many conversations and a careful reading of sections of the book. Thomas Glave read and commented on one of the earliest articles that kickstarted this book. He has been very kind in recognizing my work which owes much to his own inspiring writing on the queer Caribbean. Ketu Katrak's pioneering research on African literature and culture inspires as much as her friendship sustains. Ketu embodies academic open-heartedness and feminist solidarity that teaches by example. Gaurav Desai's rigorous scholarship on African literature and his dedicated service to the profession are always inspiring. I am grateful for his assistance with this project over the past decade. Feroza Jussawalla is a mentor to scholars from all parts of the world. I am indebted to her friendship and support over the years. Sincere thanks to Pallavi Rastogi and Sangeeta Ray for sharing their insights on early versions of the introduction. Maryse Jayasuriya and Brian Yothers are the most generous of friends. I appreciate their commitment to literary studies and student success, their unfailing kindness, and timely assistance with this work. One of the joys of completing this book is that it allows me to collaborate with Maryse on a new project. I am incredibly lucky to be collaborating with dedicated feminist DH scholars on the Orlando Women's Writing Project. Katherine Binhammer, Susan Brown, Karen Bourrier, Pat Clements, Corrinne Harol, Kathryn Holland, and Isobel Grundy teach by their dedication and commitment to women's literary expression.

Thank you also Purabi Panwar, Renuka Bisht, and Sonal Sena for continued connections with Delhi. Not only are they the best dinner and texting buddies, Rajender Kaur, Gaura Shankar Narayan, and Nira Gupta-Casale keep me grounded with their friendship and unflagging encouragement. Laura and Ken Baake, Ken and Elyn Patterson, SaraLee and Bill Morris, Marc and Sally Wilson embody quiet, sustained, supportive friendships.

Closer to home, I had the happy responsibility of directing the Comparative Literature program at Texas Tech for four years while working on this book. The annual symposium and lecture series provided opportunities to learn from various disciplines. Visits from postcolonial colleagues and friends who made symposium happen were incredible learning opportunities. Thank you, Gaurav Desai, Hopeton Dunn, Honor Ford-Smith, Neville Hoad, Ketu Katrak, Harveen Mann, Anuradha Marwah, William Spurlin, Sangeeta Ray, Ileana Rodriguez, and Shu-mei Shih for contributing your time and expertise to the symposium. Many of the ideas that made their way into this book originate from your important contributions to the field.

My colleagues at Texas Tech provided a collegial institutional network so crucial for research. Nesrine Chahine, Roger McNamara, Jennifer Snead, Yuan Shu, and Rich Rice read and offered their comments on parts of this book. Bruce Clarke and Sam Dragga were the most supportive of chairs. With patience, good humor, and his own example, Bruce persuaded me that it is possible to be an active researcher while taking on administrative responsibilities.

Thanks also to my doctoral students Kerry Manzo, Kenna Neitch and to the English Department office staff Junaita Ramirez, Quita Melcher, and Ashely Olguin who took on some of the onerous tasks connected to administration to free up my time. A special thanks to Kerry and Kenna whose work is a reminder for continued advocacy of interdisciplinary research in traditional English literature departments. Doctoral student Shayla Corprew's assistance in the final stages of this book was invaluable. As these students embark on their own career paths, we find ways to share sources, opportunities, and ideas to make the long and sometimes lonely research paths manageable and joyful.

Sabbaticals in 2013 and 2019–2020 and several timely scholarship catalyst and humanities grants from Texas Tech University ensured that I had the time and resources to complete this project. Crucial resources were provided by a generous short-term fellowship at the Harry Ransom Center, University of Texas at Austin in 2016 and a Bienecke Library Fellowship at Yale University in 2018. My thanks to the African Literature Association for the 2018 Abioseh Porter Prize for Best Article in African Literary Studies awarded to Chapter 6 of the book that first appeared in the journal *Postcolonial Studies*. Thanks also to the National Women Studies Association for awarding the book manuscript the NWSA-Routledge prize 2020.

Early versions of some chapters were published in journals. Sections of Chapter 2 appeared in *Small Axe: A Caribbean Journal of Criticism*. A version of Chapter 4 appeared in *Signs: Journal of Women in Culture and Society*. A version of Chapter 6 appeared in *Postcolonial Studies*. The materials from *Jamaica Gaily News* are reproduced with permission from Larry Chang and the Digital Library of the Caribbean. Joan Ross-Frankson, Joan French, and Sistren Theatre Collective kindly allowed me to use *Sistren* materials. Images and articles from *Manushi* are reproduced with permission from Madhu Kishwar, from *Bombay Dost* with permission from Ashok Row Kavi and the Humsafar Trust, from *Link/Skakel* and *Exit* with permission from Henk Botha and the Gay and Lesbian Memory in Action, and from *Speak* with the kind consent of Shamim Meer. The beautiful cover image for the book is a generous gift from Manjula Padmanabhan. I am thrilled that her art lends its brilliance to my work, much as her writings have illuminated the ideas I have explored over the years.

My family supports me in ways impossible to list here, though I will try. Bindu and Kim care for my parents in India and ensure that my visits home are comfortable and productive. Kim's work in theatre and the joy he brought into our lives as the youngest in the family are always present in my thinking and writing. Amma's reminders to finish the book were always encouraging, and her confidence in my ability to do so unflagging. Papa's cooking infused with his love for all of us sustains body and soul. Our beloved Faridabad animal person Golu, aka Golu Chand Batra, works his magic into all my visits home. Puneet and Alana complete this circle of love from Delhi to Lubbock to Toronto.

Words cannot convey how much of this book is owed to Rich who takes care of most domestic chores including caring for our beloved animal people, Googly, Holly, Cheeni and Goli, and the birds. His unconditional love and understanding in my writing moments of joy and despair allow me the luxury of intense, time-consuming research. Rich has been my companion on many journeys for this book. He has shared every success and struggle associated with it. His digital expertise has been invaluable in the collection of the material, its organization, storage, and use. I can ask for no better reader, photo editor, or book cover designer than him. I am grateful every day for the barn full of books, music, movies, laughter, students, and teachers from all over the world that he brings to our home. Rich truly embodies service above self in all that he does for me, our extended family, the university, the profession, and the community.

I have only managed to provide a glimpse of Indian, Jamaican, and South African feminist and LGBTQ+ histories despite the incredible generosity of my friends, family, interlocutors, and colleagues.

ABBREVIATIONS

AAWORD	Association of African Women for Research and Development
ABVA	AIDS Bhedbhav Virodhi Andolan
ACT UP	AIDS Coalition to Unleash Power
AIDSTAR	AIDS Support and Technical Assistance Resources
AIDWA	All India Democratic Women's Association
AIWC	All India Women's Congress
ALOEC	Asian Lesbians of the East Coast
ANC	African National Congress
ASEAN	Association of Southeast Asian Nations
AWOJA	Association of Women's Organizations of Jamaica
BD	*Bombay Dost*
BJP	Bharatiya Janata Party
BRICS	Brazil, Russia, India, China, and South Africa
CAFRA	Caribbean Association for Feminist Research and Action
CALERI	Campaign for Lesbian Rights in India
CEDAW	Convention on the Elimination of All Forms of Discrimination against Women
CLGA	Canadian Lesbian and Gay Archive
COSAS	Congress of South African Students
CTOP	Choice on Termination of Pregnancy
CUSO	Canadian University Students Overseas
DAWN	Development Alternatives with Women for a New Era
DISA	Digital Innovation South Africa
DLoC	Digital Library of the Caribbean
FEMNET	The African Women's Development and Communication Network
FEW	Forum for Empowerment of Women

GAD	Gender and Development
GALA	Gay and Lesbian Memory in Action
GASA	Gay Association of South Africa
GFM	Gay Freedom Movement
GLOW	Gays and Lesbians of Witwatersrand
HOMASIA	Umbrella organization of gay activists from South and South-East Asia
ICCPR	International Covenant on Civil and Political Rights
IGA	International Gay Association
ILGA	International Lesbian, Gay, Bisexual, Trans, and Intersex Association
ILGHRC	International Lesbian and Gay Human Rights Commission
INFOSEM	Integrated Network for Sexual Minorities
IRN	International Resource Network
IUCD	Intra-Uterine Contraceptive Device
IWM	Indian Women's Movement
JAMAL	Jamaica Movement for the Advancement of Adult Literacy
JCHR	Jamaica Council for Human Rights
J-FLAG	Jamaica Forum for Lesbians, All-Sexuals, and Gays
WE-Change	Women's Empowerment for Change
JGN	The *Jamaica Gaily News*
JLP	Jamaica Labor Party
LAGO	Lesbians and Gays against Oppression
LGBT	Lesbian, Gay, Bisexual, and Transgender
LGBTQ+	Lesbian, Gay, Bisexual, Transgender, and Queer or Questioning
L/S	*Link/Skakel*
MSM	Men who have Sex with Men
NACO	National Aids Control Organization
NGO	Non-Governmental Organization
NLRF	National Legal Reform Fund
NOW	Natal Organization of Women
NPGE	National Policy for Gender Equality
OLGA	Organization of Lesbians and Gays Activists
PNP	People's National Party
PUTCO	Public Utility Transport Corporation
RGO	Rand Gay Organization
SAARC	South Asian Association for Regional Cooperation
SALGA	South Asian Lesbian and Gay Association
SANCO	South African National Civic Organization
SAWNET	South Asian Women on the Net
SHRG	Scottish Human Rights Groups
SITA	Suppression of Immoral Trafficking in Girls and Women Act
STD	Sexually Transmitted Diseases
TARSHI	Talking about Reproductive and Sexual Health Issues

UDF	United Democratic Front
UDHR	Universal Declaration of Human Rights
UN	United Nations
UNAIDS	The Joint United Nations Program on HIV/AIDS
UNDP	United Nations Development Program
UNESCO	United Nations Educational, Scientific and Cultural Organization
UNHRC	United Nations Human Rights Committee
USAID	United States Agency for International Development
USSR	Union of Soviet Socialist Republics
UWI	University of the West Indies
WAD	Women and Development
WAND	Women and Development Unit
WCC	Women's Construction Cooperative
WGM	Wits Gay Movement
WID	Women in Development
WLUML	Women Living Under Muslim Laws
WMW	Women's Media Watch
WPJ	Worker's Party of Jamaica
WROC	Women's Resource and Outreach Center

1

INTRODUCTION

Worlding postcolonial sexualities: Archives, activism, and anterior counterpublics

> This distancing of sexuality from questions of transnational feminism or rather the practice of deploying an uninterrogated heterosexuality within transnational feminist analyses both cedes the domain of sexuality to LGBTT/queer studies and renders an incomplete story of the ways in which the racialized gendered practices of neoimperial modernity are simultaneously sexualized.
>
> (Alexander and Mohanty 2010, 37)

Some of my most vivid and perplexing memories as a teenager are of a group of gaudily dressed masculine-feminine performers clapping loudly while singing outside homes celebrating marriages and childbirth. I also remember being confused on learning that two girls, students in a Delhi University college, were expelled for public displays of affection with each other. And I wondered how it was possible that my hairdresser's husband was rumored to be sexually interested in workers at his construction company. Nobody around me used the terms transgender, lesbian, gay, or bisexual to describe *hijras*, women desiring women, men desiring men, and married men and women expressing same-sex desire in the India of the early 1980s. It was only later in the decade that feminist journals such as *Manushi* and gay magazines such as *Bombay Dost* provided Indians of my generation with a vocabulary for gender differences and sexual identities.

In this book I read feminist, gay, lesbian, and queer movement publications as activist literature to offer a feminist-queer history based on deep readings of these materials from the late 1970s to late 1990s. As documents and records of activism, these publications inscribed postcolonial genders and sexualities with cautious publicness that led to LGBTQ+ emergence from closeted enclaves to global arenas.[1] While feminist magazines have been frequently and consistently consulted as historical resources over the past few decades, postcolonial LGBTQ newsletters and magazines are infrequently used.[2] The central premise of *Worlding Postcolonial*

DOI: 10.4324/9781003170303-1

Sexualities is that postcolonial studies, offering astute analyses of folklore, mythology, literature, film, theatre, art, music, dance, and law as sites of resistance to normative codes of gender and sexuality, will be richer in considering feminist and LGBTQ print media as equally important for histories of gender and sexuality. Preceding digital modes of connection and community building, these media describe an *anteriority* of local, national, and transnational connections, insufficiently examined in postcolonial gender and sexuality studies. Engaging three global South contexts, Jamaica, India, and South Africa, my goal is to chart common grounds of feminist-queer solidarities toward decolonial futures.

The heuristic 'worlding' describes how public emergence of feminist and queer activism – in response to colonial legislative legacies criminalizing sexual minorities, neoliberal development policies, increase in social-sexual violence, health crises fueled by unsafe contraceptives and the AIDS epidemic – led to hitherto unprecedented global discussions on postcolonial sexualities in the last three decades of the twentieth century. Worlding owes its conceptual charge to literary studies,[3] international studies (Pettman 1996/2004; Tickner 2001), and urban studies (Roy 2011; Ong 2011). These accounts enable ways of seeing, learning, thinking, and knowing by diagnosing the imperialist-colonialist basis of North-South interactions, and ways to counter these by prioritizing South-South exchanges. My comparisons in this book are based on "research of an intermediate scale above the nation-state and below the world-system" (Cheah 2016, 5). The formation of feminist and queer organizational and print networks was part of a wider decolonial project to combat the colonizer-colonized relations of power/knowledge that dominated many Asian, African, and Caribbean nations and retained their hold in changed conditions of postcolonial governance. These networks played a key role in changing the direction of knowledge production about gender and sexuality. That Jamaica, India, and South Africa have some of the highest levels of violence against women and sexual minorities in the world at once complicates the task of changing the directionality of feminist-queer analysis and makes it even more imperative. The multifaceted critical purchase of worlding in this book is as follows: it describes how activists *respond* to sexualized violence, health crises, and outmoded legislation; defines how postcolonial feminists and queer activists *create* national, regional, and transnational alliances; and engages with the ways in which these concerns *emerge* in the transnational public sphere.

These actions of creation, emergence, and response enable a postcolonial feminist and queer history heeding M. Jacqui Alexander and Chandra Mohanty's important call to interrupt "unexamined heterosexuality" in transnational feminist analysis and establish the "domain of sexuality" as common ground between feminist and LGBTQ+ activists. Observing the trajectory of Southern feminist and queer movements over the past decade I felt a rising urgency to think more about this common ground. Perhaps this urgency is a reflection of the push and pull of local-global forces which lead to sexual victories *and* sexual precarities: Jamaica's history of gay liberation is all but forgotten amid accounts of rampant homophobia even as women, gays, and lesbians there struggle to achieve piecemeal legislative changes amid increased sexual violence; India's women's, gay, and lesbian movements have celebrated recent legislative gains that have not helped curb endemic and brutal rapes garnering global notoriety for the country; South Africa has emerged as a pioneer in guaranteeing gendered and sexual rights at a time when many African gay, lesbian, and women's movements face extreme social backlash and sexual violence is on the rise. Discussing select publications from each of these contexts, *Worlding Post-colonial Sexualities* addresses the following questions: What is the archival status of feminist and queer publications as activist literature within and outside their countries of origin? Why is this body of work scarcely mined in postcolonial gender and sexuality studies? What does the increasing valence of "rights" talk evinced in these publications mean for global South feminist and queer movements? How do we develop historical and cultural methods for analyzing the publics and counterpublics preceding these media and brought into being by them? And finally, what lessons do these semi-remembered counterpublics carry for us two decades into the twenty-first century?

I did not locate these archival materials amid the "dust" that Carolyn Steedman (2002) eloquently theorizes as an occupational hazard for cultural historians; I found them in personal collections, organization offices, university libraries, and, more recently, in digital forums.[4] In this introductory chapter, I begin with a broad-strokes sketch of feminist and queer concerns documented in these publications, fill in the details of socio-political contexts of activism, and finally, gloss the emerging shades and shapes of postcolonial feminist-queer coalitions towards panoramic comparisons. The chapters that follow describe the origins, form, content, and politics of newsletters, newspapers, journals, and magazines from the 1970s to the 1990s. These publications depict emerging postcolonial sexual publics in two distinct narrative forms: journalistic reportage, case histories, campaign accounts, meeting records, manifestoes, action documents (the social); and fiction, non-fiction, poetry, and drama (the literary). The publications are primarily in English, originate from urban metropolitan, multilingual locations, and serve as partial historical sources. Mine is a necessarily partial account since a comprehensive history of postcolonial sexualities demands engagement not only with activist literature in local languages from non-urban locations but also oral histories beyond the scope of my study. First, a turn to national and transnational framings of rights and development that contextualize postcolonial feminist and LGBTQ activist publications in the final decades of the long twentieth century.

Worlding sexualities in gender time

An unobstructed path from feminist to gay and lesbian to queer activism, in which social movements steadily learn from previous exclusions and march towards idea-lized inclusiveness and perfected political strategies, presents an uncomplicated but historically inaccurate map. Such a map cannot easily account for dissensions and contradictions within and between movements. Feminist and queer scholars have challenged such linearities, temporalities, and spatialities (Grewal & Kaplan 2001;

Freeman 2010; Arondekar & Patel 2016). Highlighting non-linearities, my account similarly pushes against existing historical and geographical specializations in post-colonial studies to think through feminist, gay, lesbian, and queer studies in a comparative framework.[5] The analyses offered in the chapters raise several challenging queries addressed through South-South comparisons: How does the Indian trajectory of gender and sexuality-based activism, with its oscillation between progressive and retrogressive ideologies, compare with Jamaican and South African postcolonial sexual histories? How do we account for the Jamaican state's recalcitrance on legalizing abortion and decriminalizing homosexuality when writing comparative postcolonial sexual histories? Is it valid to cite South Africa as exemplary in securing constitutional freedoms for gay and lesbian citizens despite its high rates of "corrective rape" against lesbian women and a significant section of people living with HIV/AIDS without adequate recourse to treatment? These queries disrupt neat narratives of progress from colonial domination to postcolonial liberation to decolonial futures assuring improved lives and rights for women and LGBTQ+ citizens.

Cross-border teaching, activism, scholarship, and pedagogy has influenced the comparative analyses in *Worlding Postcolonial Sexualities* that combine archival research, examination of national and international social, cultural, and legal policies, close readings of the contents of representative publications, and interviews with activists and founding editors. Revisiting "Under Western Eyes" several decades after it was first published, Chandra Talpade Mohanty sketches a curricular strategy she calls "The Feminist Solidarity or the Comparative Feminist Studies Model" based on "understanding the historical and experiential specificities and differences of women's lives as well as the historical and experiential connections between women from different national, racial, and cultural communities" that would organize syllabi around areas like sex work, militarization, environmental justice, and human rights (2003, 243). Inderpal Grewal and Caren Kaplan question "the distinctness of areas presupposed by the comparative framework" while "respecting the specificities of historical and cultural conjectures" to arrive at "new insights into the workings of gender and patriarchy across various borders rather than simply within the parameters of the state or the nation." (2001, 668–669). Over the years this book took shape, I taught several graduate courses on transnational feminist and queer studies. One iteration of the course connected feminist and queer studies to introduce two important modes of thinking and activism, their separations, and the intersectional social, political, and academic potentialities of race, class, caste, religion, gender, sexuality, and nationality. The course description emphasized the complementarity of feminist and queer approaches in responding to the AIDS crisis, sexual violence, and the sex panics of the previous decade that prefigured the emergence of queer studies in the 1990s. In retrospect, I was testing the North-South approach to gender and sexuality studies, learning from my students the ways in which these comparisons challenge assumptions about feminist and queer movements in the South, and working out how to "rewrite postcolonial gender histories of social change in conversation with studies of decolonization, anticapitalist critique, and LGBTT/queer studies in the North and the South" (Alexander & Mohanty 2010, 25).[6]

My training in literary studies, especially the work of comparatists and feminist intellectuals who deploy narrative analysis to study gender and sexuality, has been crucial in the connections between feminist and queer analyses (Apter 2010; Hemmings 2011; Lanser 2014–2015). Narrative and women's studies scholar Susan Lanser's argument that comparative studies today can be as much about "confluence" as it was about "influence" in the recent past and her call for the interconnectedness of queer and feminist critiques have been central to the analyses offered in this book:

> Modifying feminist with queer resists a feminism that would promote stable or unified, cross-cultural or cross-temporal categories of sex, gender, or sexuality. But anchoring queer with feminist reminds us that however queer we might want comparative literature – or the world – to be, heteronormative and gender-based hierarchies, inequalities, oppressions and suppressions are global phenomena, if widely diverse in configuration.
>
> (2014–2015)

Lanser's awareness of inequalities and oppressions echoes transnational feminist work in the global South which often mingles "questions of access to drinking water with those of access to antiretroviral drugs, and the languages and spaces of 'empowerment' and poverty with those of intimacies and sexualities" (Nagar & Swarr 2010, 13). Examining three configurations and terrains of struggles meant delving into social, political, and legal contexts of feminist and LGBTQ+ activism including sustained interaction with collectives and organizations. From 2008–2020, I attended meetings, observed and participated in performances, and sat in on community outreach workshops and training sessions in India, Jamaica, and South Africa. I also conducted semi-structured interviews and had numerous recorded and unrecorded conversations with activists to seek connections between the production of knowledges and "a politics of social change in favor of the less privileged people and places" (Nagar 2014, 94).

The activist literature (magazines, newsletters, newspapers, and journals) analyzed in *Worlding Postcolonial Sexualities* translate middle-class and subaltern experiences into feminist and queer analyses for a local and national readership across varying levels of literacy. Nation, location, translation, and language are useful heuristics in "engendering a map" that is "attentive to different spatializations in the construction of sexualities" (Alexander & Mohanty 2010, 36) to assess the specific impact of these publications. Benedict Anderson's important claim that the nation as an imagined community is dependent both on the emergence of print and comparisons with pre-existing forms of nationalism frames my juxtaposition of activist literature. What follows is a concise account of the rationale connecting these Southern contexts.

Jamaica achieved independence from British colonial rule in 1962, and, after a brief period of experimentation with the West Indian Federation, the island nation charted its own course of governance and development, deeply divided across class and color lines as the light-skinned, often upper- and middle-class creole populations, retained and confirmed their place within postcolonial political, legal, and educational institutions. Its two-party political system has led to clientelism, garrison politics, and increased levels of social violence during electoral transitions. Jamaica's Gay Freedom Movement (GFM), one of the earliest postcolonial sexual liberation movements, was led by light-skinned, middle-class, foreign-educated, Kingston-based professionals in the late 1970s. In the 1980s, its leaders represented nascent shifts in power from creole to black populations in Jamaica that were formalized in the 1990s. The GFM is largely ignored in most current histories of sexual activism when the country is described as one of most homophobic in the world. The late 1970s and early 1980s was a time when subaltern constituencies – black women workers, Rastafarians, Maroons, peasants, the poor, the elderly, and the uneducated – were a priority for the creole intellectual Michael Manley's People's National Party-led democratic socialist government, and the gay and lesbian and feminist movement inserted itself into the narrow spaces opening during this political moment. Subsequently, the country experimented with both capitalist and socialist forms of governance, followed by the privatization of the economy from the early 1980s onwards. Over the next decades while there were no substantive legislative changes, the Jamaican government attempted to address violence against women, gays, and lesbians through partnerships with Non-Governmental Organizations, the United Nations, and other Caribbean transnational advocacy organizations.

Indian and South African national trajectories differ significantly from the one charted above. Not only are these larger and more populous nation-states, but their political and economic prominence (as members of the five-nation BRICS group) has ensured greater scrutiny of their records on the rights of women and sexual minorities. India achieved independence from colonial rule in 1947 and has enjoyed about 75 years of democratic socialist and then free market postcolonial governance under Hindu upper caste political elite leadership, though lower caste political alliances led to a distinct shift from the 1980s onwards. The country's seven decades since independence have been characterized by sustained, and sometimes confused, attention to gender concerns in the face of continued violence against women and sexual minorities of all castes and classes, but especially vicious forms of sexualized violence against Muslims and the lower castes.[7] India's liberal democratic policies in the 1980s and 1990s, marked by insufficient attention to religious and caste differences, contextualize the galvanization of the women's and LGBTQ+ movement in the country. While this period saw strong feminist activism leading to (largely) progressive legislation,[8] middle class feminists who had become aware of religious, class, and caste differences among women were initially reluctant to take on board violence faced by gay men, lesbian women, and trans populations. Indian LGBTQ+ activists struggled for over two decades to decriminalize homosexuality, securing a legislative victory in 2018 even as the country reeled under horrific incidents of sexual violence against women and children.

Under repressive apartheid measures since the late 1940s, South Africa's twentieth-century history is one of decades of political, social, and revolutionary action against racial segregation. Though petty-apartheid principles were implicitly relaxed from the late 1980s in response to international condemnation of apartheid, censorship and militaristic controls continued during a period of increased state and intra-party violence. The 1990s were a momentous decade for South Africa as the country moved towards the end of apartheid. Even in the face of these world-historic transitions, the Gay Association of South Africa (GASA), one of the earliest gay liberation movements in the global South led largely by white, middle class South Africans, maintained a stridently apolitical stand. This was in marked contrast to sections of the South African women's movement in the same period which scrupulously connected gender concerns and anti-apartheid principles to argue for rights and civic benefits for black and colored working class women in alliance with liberal white feminists. When South Africa's history of settler colonialism and apartheid finally ended in 1994, and a democratically elected government was formed by the African National Congress, the country was the first to constitutionally prohibit discrimination on the grounds of sexual orientation. Since then, despite progressive legislation, there has been an increase in violence, especially against black gender non-conforming people.

As these brief accounts indicate, the "concept of nationality within comparative practice needs to be pressed for deeper insights about the intersection of nationalisms and sexualities" (Higonnet 1994, 159). Scrupulous attention to nation and translation can nuance postcolonial histories, polities, and legislative trajectories. Operating in multilingual, multiracial, multireligious, multiclass, and/or multicaste contexts, postcolonial activists initially published their newsletters and magazines in various languages to reach varying constituencies. Many of the publications began as vehicles of expression in Hindi, English, Jamaican creole, and Afrikaans. However, non-English versions did not last long due to lack of contributors, readers, advertisers, and inadequate financial support. Since the vocabularies of activism are increasingly both English and non-print, it is unsurprising that the non-English versions struggled even as print gave way to the digital in the late 1990s.

The publications can be situated in widening worldly circuits of activism. As an example, the gay newsletter the *Jamaica Gaily News* and the feminist magazine *Sistren* included articles in creole and standard English, serving as conduits of information and community-building for readers of varying classes and educational levels within and beyond urban Kingston. The gay newsletter circulated secretly within the Caribbean to reach European and North American organizations in modes of reciprocal exchange; the feminist newsletter circulated widely in Asia, Africa, Europe, and North America. Similarly, *Manushi* originated as a middle class women's journal from Delhi in the 1980s, and *Bombay Dost* began as an urban magazine connecting gay people and raising awareness about AIDS in the city in the 1990s. Both assiduously attempted to reach readers across the country to eventually establish pan-Indian and international South Asian diasporic, Southeast Asian, African, and North American readership. *Link/Skakel* began as a newsletter in English and Afrikaans affiliated to the Gay and Lesbians of South Africa in the 1980s, primarily for middle class, white gay men. It was distributed in Johannesburg before and after its transformation into a commercial newspaper for the gay and lesbian community, much as the women's magazines *Speak* and *Agenda* moved in and beyond their origins in Durban and Johannesburg. South African media reached a wide readership in the region including Zimbabwe, Namibia, and other African countries, and gay and women's rights groups and readers in America and Europe. Each has its own unique trajectory of local origin, national circulation, class-caste-color readership, political aims, collaboration, transnational dissemination, and in many cases, discontinuation. During the years they were in publication, they translated complex ideas about rights and justice to educate their readers.

Translation is both *translatio*, a transfer of ideas and concepts from one language, period, or narrative form to another, and, in the context of my analysis, *trans-late*, a sometimes belated recognition of the intersections of feminist and queer struggles. Facilitated by feminist and LGBTQ publications, ideas about rights and justice moved in what can, following Julia Kristeva's important conjunction of the sexual and the symbolic in "women's time," be called *gender time*. *Gender time*, like *trans-late*, describes a belated temporality in which gender factors in development priorities when it describes postcolonial women as a specific race-class-religious-caste constituency in need of assistance. Developmental concerns addressing non-Western women as deserving of basic 'rights' to food, shelter, education, employment, and health make gender legible in national and international contexts. An expansive view of human rights premised on the intersectionality of gender and sexuality and inclusive of women, gay, lesbian, and queer subjects is not easily translatable in such developmental paradigms. At the international level, differences between limited and expansive understandings of gender were prominent during the Third World Conference on Women in Nairobi (1984) and the Fourth World Conference in Beijing (1995). An account of the Non-Governmental Organizations' (NGO) forum gathering at the Nairobi conference in the short-lived South Asian lesbian newsletter *Anamika* describes the awkwardness of meetings between *khush* (gay) and straight women and vociferous objections to discussions of sexuality which left many participants angry and upset (Khayal 1986, 3). Feminists were also reluctant to discuss lesbian rights in 1995 and ultimately sexual orientation language was excluded from the final document of the UN Platform for Action (Fernandez 1999, 58). Arguing that injustice is multidirectional, feminist philosopher Nancy Fraser calls for "cross-cutting forms of the redistribution-recognition dilemma" attentive to needs and rights claims based on multiple axes of identities (1997, 33). Development in the South was translated as economic redistribution with little regard for recognition claims based on gender identities and sexual choice, thereby setting up a false opposition between economic and cultural injustice that is detrimental to "transformative remedies." (Fraser 1997, 2014).

A brief history of the development paradigm and its translations can be traced back to the United Nations Development Program (UNDP) invoked by international aid agencies for projects involving women in Southern nations in the 1960s. The beneficiary model implied in Women in Development (WID) approaches elicited strong feminist critiques that eventually led to a changed vocabulary of Women and Development (WAD) locating women as equal participants in development.[9] Critiques that WAD was inattentive to gender relations, cross-gender alliances, and divisions within classes allowed for the emergence of the modified category Gender and

Development (GAD).[10] Largely due to structures set up by international aid agencies and adopted by the UN, rights-based approaches were central within WID/WAD and in shifts to GAD. The development framework mirrored international discussions on livelihood, health, education, housing, justice, security, and political and civil society participation as fundamental human rights (Mukhopadhyay & Meer 2008, 14). Recognizing the limitations of the WID/WAD and GAD approaches, feminist analyses of gender and development have held states accountable for failing to fulfil goals developed at UN forums while acknowledging structural constraints on meeting these goals under adjustment policies dictated by lending agencies in the North (Molyneux & Razavi 2002, 2005). Precarious social and economic conditions in the South fueled by rising oil prices and debt crises of the early 1980s led to state and private disinvestment from key sectors, adversely impacting women's lives and livelihoods (Molyneux & Razavi 2002, 11). Though there are some serious attempts to analyze sexuality in relation to the differential distribution of economic and political power in GAD projects (Jolly 2000; Nagar & Raju 2003), a fuller account can be gleaned from the activist literature produced over the last three decades of the twentieth century.

Cumulatively, this body of work comprising print counterpublics presents a model of global South feminist-queer alliances based on a set of common concerns: redressing gender-based violence; providing health services such as AIDS testing, safe contraceptives, and affordable drugs; and repealing legislation criminalizing reproductive and sexual choice. These publications also reveal the ways in which postcolonial women's activism from the late 1970s to the late 1990s was connected to inter- and transnational circuits invoking human rights through UN and non-UN platforms. Organizations such as Development Alternatives with Women for a New Era (DAWN), the Caribbean Association for Feminist Research and Action (CAFRA), and the Association of African Women for Research and Development (AAWORD) played a major role in placing Southern concerns center stage within and outside the UN. Gay, lesbian, and queer activism was connected to worldly circuits initially through the International Lesbian and Gay Association (ILGA), the International Lesbian and Gay Human Rights Commission (ILGHRC), and Amnesty International. An examination of this period by DAWN states "in the throes of the struggle for sexual and reproductive rights, the challenges of integrating global economic justice (the main concern of many South governments, and organizations) with gender justice (especially sexual and reproductive rights) became apparent" (Sen & Durano 2014, 13). Considering systems of power at structural levels allows expansion of development thought and processes and a serious consideration of sexuality within these processes.

Recognizing common concerns, postcolonial feminists and LGBTQ+ activists, among them Peggy Antrobus, Beverley Ditsie, Devaki Jain, Lucille Mathurin Mair, Gita Sen, and Navi Pillay, sought to reframe discussions around gender and sexuality at UN forums. Somewhat disappointingly, the emergence of women's rights as human rights in these nations is largely a story of the postcolonial Jamaican, Indian, and South African states' indifferent implementation of laws to curb discrimination against women and effectively combat sexual violence. Sexual violence was first framed as a human rights issue through the 1979 UN Convention on the

FIGURE 1.1 A poster from an organization involved in Women in Development Initiatives in India in the personal collection of the author.

Elimination of All Forms of Discrimination against Women (CEDAW). Discussing women's rights as human rights, Charlotte Bunch describes efforts to integrate women's rights into development, and the growing interest in violence against women as a health and development issue (1990, 494). Bunch is among the earliest feminist scholars to indicate how the human rights community can incorporate gender perspectives and interrelations between sex, race, class, nation, age, and sexual preference to "expand the terms of their work" (1990, 497). While India and Jamaica were original signatories to CEDAW in 1980, South Africa became a signatory in 1993. Feminists note that CEDAW lacks teeth and that it has the weakest implementation and enforcement mechanism of any human rights convention (Bunch 1990, 496; Oloka-Onyango & Tamale 1995, 715).

FIGURE 1.2 Cover page of an information booklet produced by the Women's Resource and Outreach Center in collaboration with the United Nations Development Fund for Women in 2008 to describe CEDAW provisions. Booklet sourced by the author from WROC in Kingston, Jamaica.

A similar situation prevailed with regards to LGBTQ+ rights, first discussed within the human rights framework in 1994 with the resolution of a landmark case by the UN Human Rights Committee (UNHRC).[11] Despite intense discussions on sexual orientation, the language was not included in the 1995 Beijing Platform for Action at the World Conference on Women.[12]

As the subsequent chapters of this book reveal, while international, multi-state framings such as CEDAW or UNCHR are crucial sites of broad human rights demands, the conventions and resolutions are not internationally binding and are observed more in breach than promise. Despite frequent setbacks, feminist and queer collectives rely on human rights or a broad rights discourse to world postcolonial sexualities in three inherently transnational ways. First, they participate in communicative multilateral and intergovernmental political arenas such as the UN and regional political solidarities in Africa, South Asia, and the Caribbean. Second, they are key actors in transnational solidarity and advocacy networks such as AAWORD, DAWN, WLUML, and others. And finally, they form broad national coalitions to solicit public support, such as the Jamaica Forum for Lesbians, All-Sexuals, and Gays' work with Women's Empowerment for Change (J-FLAG-WE-Change), Talking about Reproductive and Sexual Health Issues (TARSHI) in India, and the Organisation of Lesbian and Gay Activists (OLGA) in the anti-apartheid United Democratic Front (UDF). Using print as a crucial mode of communication, postcolonial feminists and LGBTQ+ activists imagined translational, transnational, and transformational counterpublics. Reading about the imaginative ways in which they pressed their claims, including street demonstrations, community drama, multigenerational conversations, recruiting allies, creating music, video, and film, sustained the difficult work of writing *Worlding Postcolonial Sexualities*.

Moving on to the key ideas explored in the title of my book, I turn to surveying Western conceptualizations of publics and counterpublics, feminist and queer revisions of these concepts, and their applicability to the project of worlding sexualities.

Publics, counterpublics, and human rights ink[13]

German philosopher Jürgen Habermas's macro-historical account of the role of print in creating a "world of readers" or "the public" in seventeenth century Europe has assumed canonical status in Western thought (1961/1991, 26). Habermas conceptualizes the emergence of a bourgeois public sphere but does not adequately consider distinctions between classes and differences in social status of those participating in European venues and spaces for discussion such as coffee houses, salons, and debating societies. Habermas emphasizes rational debates on "areas of common concern" with the state, and establishes the idea of a public as inherently inclusive (1961/1991, 37). On this view, special interest associations transform the liberal conception of the public sphere. Nancy Fraser disputes this conceptualization of the bourgeois public sphere to argue that differences in social status made some sections of the population unequal participants in the Habermasian discourse community.

Especially for women and racially marked populations, the public sphere was not inclusive. Habermas thus fails to examine "other nonliberal, nonbourgeois, competing public spheres" (Fraser 1997, 74). In highly stratified societies, subordinated groups such as women, workers, people of color, and gay and lesbians constituted "alternative publics" that Fraser describes as "*subaltern counterpublics*." Members of these groups "invent and circulate counterdiscourses" allowing them to "formulate oppositional interpretations of their identities, needs, and interests" (Fraser 1997, 81). Fraser's views on counterpublics allow for contestations and non-egalitarian tendencies within and beyond them. Fraser connects counterpublics to participatory democracy through ideas of recognition, redistribution, and representation to foreground bivalent or multivalent identities such as working class lesbian women or transgender sex workers. Further, observing that the framework for an articulation of the public sphere in Habermas's recent work as well her own remained Westphalian or nation-oriented, Fraser has recently offered a "post-Westphalian" model that is cognizant of transnationality and trans-territoriality allowing for comparisons between Southern movements for gender and sexual justice (2014).

These reinterpretations of Habermas have inspired nuanced feminist and queer analyses of publics and counterpublics. Jocelyn Olcott, for instance, argues for the centrality of Fraser's feminist counterpublics in describing how the International Women's Year (IWY) 1975 marked a growing awareness among Western and postcolonial feminists about the importance of media representation to further the women's movements (2012). Focusing in particular on language and competing "first-world vs third-world" politics of two "innovative" but widely contested media efforts set up in the US, Women International Network News and Hotwire IWY, Olcott concludes:

> Following IWY, efforts to create feminist counterpublics – both by informing the common sense created by mainstream media and by creating alternative media – became a core strategy of transnational women's movements particularly in the efforts leading up to UN conferences in the 1990s.
>
> (2012, 43)

For Fraser, feminist counterpublics

> comprised the agitational wing of a radical mass social movement – emancipatory, anti-systemic, and committed to structural change. Dedicated at once to external propaganda and to internal consciousness-raising, these were discourse arenas in which members of a subordinated gender learned to speak for themselves and to talk back to power.
>
> (2014, 138)

Taking its cue from this body of work, *Worlding Postcolonial Sexualities* examines feminist and LGBTQ publications as alternative media or counterpublic discourse arenas that enabled feminist-queer voices to be heard in national and international forums.

Acknowledging Fraser's and other feminist contributions to public sphere theory, queer theorist Michael Warner describes publics as self-organized relations among attentive strangers, characterized by personal and impersonal modes of social address, which are nevertheless riddled with contradictions. In Warner's opinion the reflexive circulation of discourse that characterizes a public as a social space has a specific temporality (2002, 67–87). Warner proposes a further modification of Habermas's ideas informing a critical analysis of gender and sexuality by suggesting that some publics are defined by their tension with a larger public, because their discussions "contravene the rules obtaining in the world at large, being structured by alternative dispositions or protocols" and that these kinds of publics can be labeled "counterpublics" (2002, 56). Like Fraser, Warner is deeply invested in the world-making potential of counterpublics, especially since these may not replicate the logic and rationality of dominant publics but instead offer alternative ways of being and belonging. To support this overly optimistic reinterpretation Warner analyses how the public sphere facilitates debates over gender and sexual relations and allows new forms of embodiment and social relations to emerge (2002, 54). In sum, Fraser argues for changing the terms on which gender is discussed in the public sphere, and Warner expresses the queer hope of enlarging stranger-socialities to transform the gendered and sexual rationalities of the dominant public. Since both Fraser and Warner describe largely Euro-American counterpublic forms, any extension of these ideas begs the question: What are the most effective strategies and venues for postcolonial publics to articulate their rights claims and what counterpublic forms emerge from this effort?

Seyla Benhabib's interventions offer a possible answer to the question posed above. Benhabib deploys cosmopolitanism to think through human rights across borders, offering a Habermasian perspective on a communicative discourse-centric model of democracy. She proposes a post-Westphalian "jurisgenerative" framework to "expand the meaning and reach of law" in global civil society. With this expansion in place, she urges us to think how the "effects of human rights declarations and treaties enable new actors" including women, ethnic, religious, and linguistic minorities "to enter the public sphere, to develop new vocabularies of public claim-making, and to anticipate new forms of justice to come in processes of cascading democratic iterations" (Benhabib 2011, 15). Much like Habermas's ideal of citizen participation in public debate, this exegesis emphasizes "communicative freedom" in ways that do not adequately consider power differentials or the dangers of public claim-making in certain contexts. Despite this, Benhabib's heartfelt appeal to human rights in our troubled times is a salutary reminder of the value of "cascading democratic iterations" in the public sphere to create opinion and pressure on the state. Working in close cooperation with national and international legislative structures, feminist-queer activist literature is an instance of democratic iteration that emerged as a powerful agent of social change.

As postcolonial democracies, India, Jamaica, and South Africa are impacted by social, political, economic, and, in times of COVID-19, medical and health challenges that exacerbate social tensions including increases in sexual violence. One of

the goals of this book is to examine feminist and queer activist literature as facilitating democratic iterations with the awareness that democracy is a messy business,
riddled with class, race, caste, religious, gender, and sexual disparities, and that
counterpublics are not immune to the push and pull of political and social power.

From subaltern to locational counterpublics

Fraser, Warner, and Benhabib make urgent claims based on the (sometimes idea-
lized) circulation of ideas in the public sphere. Ideas, as we well know from Michel
Foucault, circulate amid and despite constraints on their emergence. Despite these
constraints, postcolonial feminist and queer invocations of human rights reflect
hopeful visions of change. Emerging postcolonial feminist and queer alliances can
finesse human rights and subalternity anew though interlinked axes of gender and
sexuality. Important revaluations of Italian thinker Antonio Gramsci's views on
subalternity and articulation are useful in such a finessing.[14] Revisiting the subaltern
project, Gayatri Spivak rethinks the critique of gender she initially articulated in
"Can the Subaltern Speak?" to express disappointment that the subalternists are
"now engaged in postcolonial exercises away from the subaltern classes" and that
there is no attempt in this practice to "question the political strategy that appro-
priates the disenfranchised" (2005, 477). For Spivak, this would involve "the active
scrupulous and vigilant contamination of historiography from the constative
through the disciplinary performative into the field of historical possibility of what
we can only call the present" (2005, 484). Looking over the magazines, newsletters, and journals that are my primary sources, I learned that charting gender
exclusively through feminist publications could lead to a heteronormative view of
sexual rights; similarly, charting sexuality through LGBTQ publications can foreground a homonormative cisgender gay male perspective that may be oblivious to
other forms of difference. In the Spivakian spirit of "vigilant contamination" my
goal is to amplify lesbian and trans voices to counter the heteronormative and
homonormative perspectives sometimes reflected in my primary materials. I am
arguing that worlding sexualities involves considering feminist and LGBTQ publications as *anterior counterpublics* to map the terrain of a feminist-queer coalitional
politics relevant for the twenty-first century.

Worlding Postcolonial Sexualities considers various aspects of subalternity. Race,
class, Christianity, and notions of respectability deeply impact Jamaican social
structures and perception of gender and sexuality; caste, religion, and class are often
key factors in Indian social formations; and in South Africa, race, class, language,
and ethnicity emerge as constitutive to a politics of gender and sexuality. Addressing
the race-class debates in South Africa, Stuart Hall describes articulation as a political
conjoining of race and class (1980). Although Hall does not mention gender and
sexuality as the modalities in which race and class may be lived and experienced, in
later writings he considers the relevance of Gramscian thought for an open-ended
politics that encompasses cultural, ethnic, sexual, and other forms of identity (1988).
Following Hall, the gendered and sexualized subject needs to be simultaneously

articulated within women's, gay, lesbian, and queer movements where "articulation provides a mechanism for shaping intervention within a particular social formation, conjuncture or context" (Slack 1996, 113). Within late twentieth and early twenty-first century social formations the process of worlding sexualities involves a broad coalition of sexually disenfranchised groups including those located away from urban metropolitan centers of consumption and activism; transvestites, transsexuals, trans-gender, "third genders"; and those marked by race, class, religion, and caste, besides being sexually stigmatized. Despite limited evidence of organizational or political alliances within these materials, reading gay, lesbian, queer, and feminist activist literature together *can* lead to a comprehensive non-exclusionary of sexual activism. Together these works mark the "field of historical possibility" that is the future of postcolonial feminist and queer activism.

Marcus Green reminds us that for Gramsci, subalternity was a matter of degree rather than innate social, economic, or political positioning. Once subaltern groups become conscious of their social position, they can organize and struggle to trans-form this position. When applied to readers who perceived themselves as subaltern in terms of their gender, sexual, racial, class, caste, and/or religious positions, this is an important observation. And though the degree of their participation in feminist or queer activism varied, many of these readers participated in print-mediated communities through their letters, articles, poems, autobiographical pieces, and short stories. If the aim of participative organization is, according to Gramsci, the transformation of the state and its oppressive social relations, these groups could only cease being subaltern in a transformed state (Green 2002). The print media analyzed in *Worlding Postcolonial Sexualities* articulates varied ways of participation and gestures to possible transformations achievable through progressive social poli-cies and legislation by making demands on the state and building public support across cities, townships, and other non-urban areas.

As the cover image from *Speak*, a Durban-based South African women's maga-zine indicates, cities provided media technologies, personnel, readers, writers, and access to state structures. My analyses in the subsequent chapters emphasize *locational* over *subaltern* counterpublics. Often the city emerges as a key player in the myriad expressions of sexuality when a specific area fosters sexual communities: Hillbrow as a bohemian whites-only gay area in Johannesburg, South Africa that was transformed into a mixed race gayborhood in the 1980s–1990s; Gateway of India and Grant Road as popular cruising spots in Mumbai, India; and the rela-tively safe social spaces for middle class gay men and lesbian women in New Kingston, Jamaica.[15] Accounts of public life in these cities when read with anthropological, political, and historical analyses situate emergent sexualities in specific geographies. Caribbean scholars study gendered and sexual violence in Kingston, Jamaica to clarify the connections between violent urban masculinity and sexuality from the 1970s to the present (Gray 2004; Thomas 2011). In urban slums gun ownership "reinforced heterosexual notions of manliness and the image of male potency" (Gray 2004, 239). Another reading focuses on communities in Kingston to outline how and why the body has become a site of social conflict.

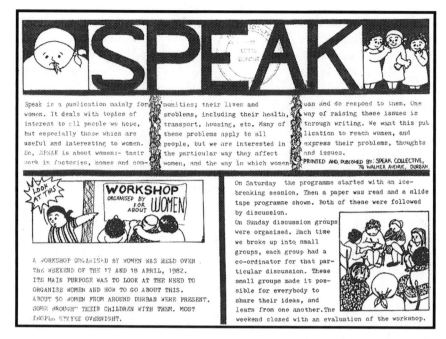

FIGURE 1.3 Cover page from the first number of *Speak* magazine published from Durban, South Africa. Image courtesy of Shamim Meer and the magazine archive of Digital Imaging South Africa.

Directing attention to normative gender and sexual coding, this scholar observes that "anxieties about the transnational tend to be expressed through attempts to regulate the sexual" to conclude that "sexuality marks the limit point of Jamaicanness – and thus of the transnational space of Jamaica – as there is no space for sexual alterity within a Jamaican experience, migrant or not" (Thomas 2011, 15, 165). Jamaican women's and LGBTQ+ movements have worked to promote sexual awareness and sexual health from the 1970s to the present to create a space for "sexual alterity." In the absence of any formal recognition of Jamaican gay and lesbian histories, creating space for such discussions has involved compiling textual evidence. One of the earliest essays on the subject uses a combination of memory and oral history to assert the presence of lesbians – described by local residents as "man royals" and "sodomites" – on the island (Silvera 1992). More recently, anthologies of gay and lesbian writing from the Caribbean document the existence and persistence of gay and lesbian relationships in urban and rural areas despite pervasive hostility (Glave 2008; Glave 2013).

From India, accounts of Bombay and Delhi analyze social and political conditions which made these cities conducive to feminist and queer activism and vulnerable to fundamentalist and nationalist orthodoxies. A magisterial survey of the transformation of Bombay to Mumbai describes the ways in which the Hindu nationalist party, Shiv Sena, strives to "expand the boundaries of male sexuality" by linking masculinity to violence against religious minorities (Hansen 2001, 93). Additionally, as in Jamaica, sexual policing involves castigating upper and middle class gay and lesbian life choices as "Westernized" by pointedly ignoring working class and *dalit* (literally downtrodden or lower caste) sexualities. Ethnographic work on gay, lesbian, and queer presence in Delhi accounts for the emergence, continuation and/or dissipation of gender and sexuality-based activism (Bacchetta 2002; Dave 2012). Indian scholars and activists have scrupulously documented same-sex love in literature and history to chart the continuity of non-hetero-normative social arrangements and cultural traditions (Thadani 1998; Vanita & Kidwai 2001). Through these works, "sodomy is recovered amid a stretch of archival evidence, threaded together by claims to diverse temporalities and spatialities that make it constitutively Indian and not an extension of Western influence or behavior" (Arondekar 2009, 173). These materials were strategically employed in a petition to decriminalize homosexuality filed by the Naz Foundation in 2001 against the government of India.

South African writings on inner-city Johannesburg describe the transformation of the area from an exclusively white space to a gay neighborhood, and eventually an immigrant locale (Parnell & Mabin 1995; Morris 1999; Landau 2006). One study observes that "Johannesburg faces the challenge of turning around an endemic culture of violence. This requires further reflection on masculinity and its relationship to sexual violence" (Reid & Dirsuweit 2002). These connections between race, sexuality, and violence are also explored through situated ethnographic work on gay, lesbian, and trans lives in Soweto, Cape Town, and small towns in South Africa (Tucker 2009; Swarr 2012a, 2012b; Reid 2013). Unlike Johannesburg, Durban does not have a long history of feminist and queer urban analysis, though accounts of Indian women's associations in the city allow us to see how forms of publicness intersect with women's social organizations (Vahed & Waetjen 2010). As in India and Jamaica, landmark anthologies *The Invisible Ghetto* (Krouse 1993) and *Defiant Desire: Gay and Lesbian Lives in South Africa* (Gevisser & Cameron 1995) compile essays, life-narratives, interviews, and photographs documenting sexual diversity.[16]

The brief review of methods and disciplinary protocols employed in feminist, gay, and lesbian studies offered here reinforces that sexual histories are often assembled from "fragmentary" sources (Pandey 2006). Arranging the fragments into formalized archives imposes an "imaginary" unity on

> pieces of time to be assembled, fragments of life to be placed in order, one after the other, in an attempt to formulate a story that acquires its coherence through the ability to craft links between the beginning and the end.
>
> (Mbembe 2002)

Sometimes these fragments are not preserved in optimal archival spaces such as libraries, museums, community centers, organization offices, digital collections where the narrative may acquire coherence. Reading these materials for political aspirations and political limitations, I offer a necessarily *selective* view. For instance, in pointing to the absence or minimal presence of lesbians and trans subjectivities in gay newsletters at a time when there were no postcolonial publications exclusively for lesbians or trans populations, I suggest *one* possible way to read the multiple worldings offered by the archives. These newsletters, newspapers, magazines, and journals document feminist and LGBTQ+ aspirations of change from illegality to legality, violence to survival, disease to resilience, and no rights to human rights.

Archival worldings

Despite the relatively recent history of sexual activism in many formerly colonized nations, the emergence and circulation of activist literature means that the archive is rapidly expanding and developing. This section describes the conversations enabled and suppressed in feminist and queer archives when they are read together. Much of the activist literature has been systematically archived and validated and the remainder is being collected, archived, and digitized as I write.

In a famous deconstructive formulation, Jacques Derrida mentions how the archive both promises and calls into question a coming of the future (2006, 36). Elizabeth Povinelli observes: "Archival power authorizes specific forms of the future by domiciling space and time, the here and now relative to the there and then; us as opposed to them" (2011, 150–151). Following Antoinette Burton's invocation of archive stories, one story about postcolonial archives of sexuality begins with legacies of colonial legislation. Article 377 of the Indian constitution punishing "unnatural sexual acts" was a nineteenth-century statute in force until 2018. After two decades of activist efforts, it was "read down" in 2009 to decriminalize homosexuality, and then reinstated in 2013 pending an appeal against this decision. In 2018, a landmark judgement by the Supreme Court of India finally declared the law unconstitutional "in so far as it criminalizes consensual sexual conduct between adults of the same sex." Section 76 of the Jamaican constitution sentences those convicted of the "abominable crime of buggery" to ten years in prison. Despite efforts by gay rights advocates, there is little possibility of it being removed.[17] Till the 1990s, the apartheid government in South Africa could convict people under the 1969 Immorality Amendment Act, which amended a 1957 act prohibiting sexual relations between different races, including sexual relations between men under the age of 19 and sexual activity between men at a "party," where party was defined as more than two people. The Equality Clause, guaranteeing non-discrimination based on sexual orientation, was enshrined in the South African constitution in 1996, ensuring that gay and lesbian people no longer lived under the threat of imprisonment.

Another archive story is the emergence of postcolonial feminist collectives and their collaborations. The Indian women's movement managed to push for progressive legislation on marital and domestic rights in the 1970s and 1980s in the wake of extreme forms of violence including dowry deaths, rapes, and abductions. During these decades the Jamaican women's movement allied with other

Caribbean and international feminist organizations to publicize violence against women and children including rape, incest, and domestic abuse, to secure rights within and outside matrimony by using family courts. The South African women's movement was closely associated with anti-apartheid efforts as it sought to secure reproductive choice by demanding legal reform from the apartheid state; the Women's Charter for Effective Equality was proposed as a guide for securing women's rights in the post-apartheid era. These publications are a historical record of incipient and sometimes reluctant feminist alliances with gay and lesbian struggles.

Given this recent and contested history, it is no surprise that the activist literature documenting these struggles is not readily accessible. During the last two decades of the twentieth century, feminist, gay, and lesbian media was often hampered by lack of financial support from publishers and advertisers, low circulation figures, and in some cases, the need for secrecy to protect its subscribers and purchasers. Research accessibility to these materials involves circuits of mobility and, in many cases, the flow of materials has taken a global turn. Copies of the newsletters and magazines discussed in *Worlding Postcolonial Sexualities* are available in select collections in Africa, South Asia, and the Caribbean but are better preserved and more easily available in Euro-American repositories. Some are in special collections in The Hague, the Gerber/Hart Gay and Lesbian Library and Archives in Chicago, the Northwestern University Libraries in Evanston, the Library of Congress, and the Canadian Lesbian and Gay Archives, largely due to the foresight and international connections of founding editors and scholars. The feminist publications *Manushi, Sistren, Agenda,* and *Speak* are available digitally; the gay, lesbian, queer publications *Link/Skakel, Exit,* and *Bombay Dost* are not yet digitized. Navigating multimodal archival routes in various parts of the world is a sobering reminder that it is not easy to reverse the direction of knowledge production and transmission from North-South to South-South relationalities.

Though the archives are sometimes carefully preserved, often they are woefully neglected. One instance of this neglect is the *Jamaica Gaily News* (*JGN*) which was not available in any library in Jamaica and the wider Caribbean till 2019. The *JGN* was founded in 1978 and operated as an underground publication till 1984 when it was discontinued due to financial and organizational hurdles. After 1984, the materials related to the production of the newsletter and a set of its copies was stored by individuals in Jamaica (Chang 2011). The existing papers were eventually brought over to the US by Thomas Glave, a Jamaican-American academic and activist. After years of seeking institutional support in the US, the Caribbean International Resource Network established a partnership with the digital Library of the Caribbean and the collection of select organizational documents related to the *JGN* and the GFM was born in 2010. However, the only physical holdings of *JGN* that I know of are part of the International Lesbian and Gay Association (ILGA) collection at The Hague and the Canadian Lesbian and Gay Archive (CLGA). This is because the GFM had reciprocal exchange arrangements with ILGA and *The Body Politic*, the first Canadian gay magazine, whose papers were the basis of the CLGA (Batra 2010).[18] Anthropologist Matthew Chin spent several years collecting the complete set of the *JGN* from archives in Canada and Europe, and from personal collections in Jamaica (2019a, 2019b). Chin generously shared his collection with researchers and the Caribbean International Resource Network (IRN), and the materials became publicly available in October 2020.

The gay newsletters and magazines allow us to read a marginal lesbian presence that can be supplemented with feminist sources. Initially gay "sistahs" did not involve themselves in the nascent and underground Gay Freedom Movement (GFM) in Jamaica in the1970s because they feared familial and societal repercussions. Despite editorial exhortations, women's participation in the GFM remained low, even as women of all classes and sexual orientations were involved in the feminist movement in Jamaica. Much like the movement for gay rights, the movement for women's rights was perceived as fundamentally Western in orientation, making the emergence of openly lesbian personal or activist connections dangerous, especially in the 1990s. Some of the founding members of the feminist theatre collective, Sistren, were lesbian and were out to fellow members, through the group had consciously steered clear of any representation of lesbian sexuality in their drama and in *Sistren* magazine. *Sistren* magazine when read with the *JGN* reveals a tentative articulation of non-heteronormative desires and support for gays and lesbians, providing a contrapuntal account of the history and politics of sexuality in the country (Chapters 2 and 3).

Trikone, Anamika and *Shamakami*, connecting the South Asian and diasporic LGBTQ+ community, were founded in the US in the late 1980s. Copies are available in North American university libraries. In India organizations such as the Humsafar Trust and Lesbian and Bisexuals in Action (LABIA) have ensured that activist literature and organizational documents are available for consultation, at least within the country. *Bombay Dost* (*BD*), India's first gay magazine, was first published bilingually in English-Hindi in 1990 by its founding-editor Ashok Row Kavi. *Scripts*, India's first lesbian magazine, established by Stree Sangam (now Lesbians and Bisexuals in Action or LABIA), appeared in 1998. As in the case of *JGN*, many of these materials originated and circulated privately for fear of censorship. Even as a "registered newsletter," *Dost* editors had to be careful of "the looming danger from anti-social elements." Additionally, the editorial collective made a conscious decision not to mail the publication to its readers but to market it through select bookshops, vendors, or post boxes to preserve the anonymity of its largely closeted readership (*BD* 1992a). Despite optimal conditions of preservation and access, the magazine had a sporadic record of publication with interruptions in 2002 and 2010, marking a gap in information about gay and lesbian activism during this period. It resumed publication in a glossy overtly commercial format in the 2010s but ceased publication some years later.

Though it strived to be lesbian and trans-inclusive, *BD* was primarily a gay men's magazine focused on AIDS awareness and prevention. At first it included regular contributions by Indian lesbians (Amita & Preeti 1991). Married lesbians wrote infrequently for and to the magazine as the only available means of connection with other lesbians. In contrast, journals such as *Manushi* enabled women to express their concerns about sexual and reproductive autonomy, employment rights, and legal empowerment, though one of the editors actively eschewed the descriptor 'feminist' (Kishwar 1990). From the late 1990s onwards, the women's movement in India was compelled to consider the position of lesbian women within its fold, partly because the controversy over Indo-Canadian filmmaker Deepa Mehta's 'lesbian' film *Fire* served as a tipping point (see Chapter 4). Even overly cautious magazines such as *Manushi* focused on the controversy, as in Madhu Kishwar's scathing review of the film and the spate of responses on the now defunct web forum South Asian Women on the Net (SAWNET) in 1999. *Manushi*'s later numbers cover lesbian and trans lives largely though articles, short stories, and film reviews (Chakravarty 2004; Vanita 2004). Subsequently lesbian magazines such as *Scripts* and *Gaysi* in India and *Shamakami* in the Indian diaspora created lesbian feminist counterpublics that now include queer zines, graphic fiction, blogs, websites, and social media interactions.

In contrast to the problems encountered in Jamaica and India, South Africa has had a consistent, less disrupted gay and lesbian media since the 1980s. *Link/Skakel*, the official newsletter of the Gay Association of South Africa (GASA), first appeared in 1982. From 1985 onwards it was converted to *Exit*, described as an independent newspaper not connected to any gay organization. *Exit* continues in tabloid style and its print and online publication ensures a wide African and international readership. The complete set of the newsletter and the magazine are meticulously preserved at the Gay and Lesbian Memory in Action (GALA), formed in 1997 as a part of the South African Historical Archives in Johannesburg. GALA has independent offices and several full-time employees, including an archivist and a librarian, to manage its holdings which are readily accessible to the public and to researchers. *Link/Skakel* and *Exit* targeted a predominantly white South African gay readership with minimal attention to lesbian women. These are sporadically addressed in South African women's magazines of the 1980s and 1990s. One such publication, *Agenda*, established by a group of women academics at the University of Natal in Durban in 1987 was explicitly feminist in its self-description. In 1991 *Agenda* published a number titled "Sexual Politics" with a some articles which addressed alternative sexualities (Mina 1991; Nicol 1991). Later there were frequent reports on gay and lesbian matters including the impact of AIDS on the community and on black lesbian identities in townships.

This brief account of archival encounters indicates different modes of documentation and preservation which make feminist materials more visible than LGBTQ publications. Too, in many LGBTQ publications examined in this book, gay men's concerns dominate over those of lesbian and trans people, reiterating Ann Cvetkovich's important reminder that "the history of any archive is a history of space, which becomes the material measure of the archive's power and visibility as a form of public culture" (2003, 245). Thus "as more institutionalized archives develop gay and lesbian collections, it will be increasingly important not to forget the more queer collections and strategies of the grassroots archives" (Cvetkovich 2003, 245). As predominantly English language and intermittently bilingual publications, the activist literature in *Worlding Postcolonial Sexualities* complicates Cvetkovich's important reminder of the divide between "institutionalized" and "grassroots" archives. Mainstream institutions such as public and university libraries in Europe and North America now eagerly acquire grassroots queer archives even as institutions in the South battle space restrictions, personnel constraints, and contested ideas of archival priorities. Though GALA is an exception in this regard, its precarious institutional location became clear in 2013 when the magazines and newsletters I had easily accessed the year before were unavailable for consultation. GALA holdings had been moved out of the William Cullen Library at the University of Witwatersrand where they had been housed since the 1990s and indefinitely relocated to temporary storage. In Jamaica, the afterlives of the *JGN* illustrate that it is sometimes an uphill task to preserve LGBTQ+ archives and to find institutions interested in acquiring them in their countries of origin. *BD* and *Scripts* are selectively preserved in-house and have also found a place in some South Asian libraries. Where preservation is an urgent concern, differentiation between grassroots and institutional archives is somewhat unviable. Activist literature stands to reap the benefits of preservation and access by securing a place in institutionalized archives. *Worlding Postcolonial Sexualities* claims that till all these sources are available in digital formats and easily accessible, research on materials of the recent past demands the same time and commitment as is involved in looking through dusty archives. This book has attempted to assemble and organize a varied palette of feminist and queer sources to draw a rainbow-hued postcolonial sexual history.

Speaking of archives, activism, rights, and counterpublics, the book could have been structured in many ways. The arrangement finally chosen is based on the three contexts with two chapters each on Jamaica, India, and South Africa analyzing representative feminist and LGBTQ publications.

Part I, Abeng, challenging depravation invokes the abeng horn used by Jamaican maroons as a call to arms to describe the democratic socialist moment that created conditions for feminist activism and gay and lesbian emergence. **Chapter 2** contends that recent efforts by organizations like Jamaica Forum for Lesbians All-Sexuals and Gays to redress legal and social discrimination against sexual minorities continue the efforts of the Gay Freedom Movement in the 1970s and 1980s to create an imagined community existing under the shadow of violence, discriminatory laws, and the AIDS pandemic. The goal is to describe how GFM's underground newsletter the *Jamaica Gaily News* fulfilled the dual purposes of socialization and activism for the gay and lesbian community. My claim is that the print-mediated community generated by the GFM allows us to present a revisionary account of Kingston, Jamaica as a liberationist-activist rather than virulently homophobic space. **Chapter 3** is on the newsletter/magazine *Sistren* published by the Sistren Theatre Collective from the 1970s to the 1990s. The contents of the magazine reveal that while the women's movement advocated legislative reform to address rampant sexual violence, activists steered clear of making any direct connections with sexual choice and orientations. Presenting these as health concerns enabled a detailed, though indirect, discussion on sexual choice within these magazines without inviting opprobrium from readers or the governmental machinery in Jamaica and other Caribbean nation-states.

Part II, Azadi, emerging freedoms uses azadi, a nationalist rallying call for freedom from British colonial oppression, to examine how Indian feminist, gay, and lesbian print media created publics and counterpublics. **Chapter 4** begins by discussing how independent journals such as *Manushi* furthered the Indian Women's Movement (IWM) by presenting new ways of articulating gender and sexuality from the 1980s. Here I contend that the IWM's sustained focus on sexual violence in the last decades of the twentieth century prepared the ground for a cautious articulation of sexual rights, including non-normative sexuality, primarily on the grounds of a comparable violence and reclamation of geographic, institutional, typographic, judicial space in ways similar to the women's movement in Jamaica and the larger Caribbean. **Chapter 5** is on the cultural reach of emergent LGBTQ publications, specifically India's leading gay magazine *Bombay Dost*'s projected audience and possibilities of a coalitional sexual politics in the 1990s. *Bombay Dost*'s minimal representation of lesbians can be compared with diasporic publications such as *Anamika, Trikone,* and *Shamakami*. Similarly, *Bombay Dost* and its associated Non-Governmental Organization (NGO) Humsafar's minimal focus on at-risk transgender populations is in contrast to Humsafar's extensive outreach work on AIDS with MSM (men who have sex with men). My contention is that the gay male focus of the worldings attempted by *Bombay Dost* made it somewhat irrelevant for a new generation of queer activists who actively sought feminist and transgender alliances.

Part III, Amandla, embodying power evokes the African National Congress' anti-apartheid exhortation, amandla or power, to examine South African activist literature during anti-apartheid resistance. **Chapter 6** examines the controversial trajectory of legal reform and political change initiated by the gay movement in South Africa to claim urban and national space without challenging racial segregation. Gay liberation literature under apartheid lagged behind important shifts in sexual activism. The primary archive used is *Link/Skakel*, the official newsletter of the Gay Association of South Africa (GASA), which soon became a mainstream gay newspaper called *Exit*. The analysis reviews critical debates around the term Afropolitanism to describe how the development of a gay and lesbian subculture in Johannesburg was influenced by models of gay consumerism and activism in the North. It demonstrates how the North-South direction of comparison and the exclusivist racial and gendered assumptions were challenged by a 'queer Afropolitanism' connecting racial and sexual liberation, articulated first by lesbians in GASA and later the Gays and Lesbians of Witwatersrand (GLOW). **Chapter 7** describes the ways in which the feminist magazines *Speak* and *Agenda* contributed to an ongoing discussion of gender and sexuality initiated by black South African lesbian and gay organizations such as GLOW and the Organization of Lesbians and Gays Activists (OLGA) founded during this period. A cultural history of gender and sexuality in South Africa reveals not the expected tensions between feminist and LGBTQ+ activism (as in India or Jamaica) but rather an initially hesitant and then a more confident engagement with women's sexuality during politically turbulent times. These feminist magazines focused on AIDS as impacting gay, lesbian, *and* heterosexual populations of all races in the contexts of sexual violence and reproductive choice. Thus, they addressed race and class disparities as fundamental but also saw gender parity and sexual equality as crucial to establishing a new South Africa.

The Coda situates these publications in twenty-first century feminist and LGBTQ+ activist geographies. Digital archives such as the relatively recent Caribbean International Resource Network (IRN), the well-established Digital Innovation South Africa (DISA), and the short-lived India Network for Sexual Minorities (Infosem) allow iterations of print counterpublics analyzed in *Worlding Postcolonial Sexualities* as instances of feminist and queer world-making and world-shifting.

Notes

1 I use LGBTQ+ when discussing sexual and gender identities and activism and LGBTQ when discussing print media published from the 1970s to the 1990s. Publications such as the *Jamaica Gaily News, Link/Skakel* and *Exit* predate the adoption of queer as a descriptor of sexual and political identity. Despite its unwieldiness, LGBTQ helps me avoid anachronistically labeling the gay and lesbian magazines as queer.

2 The importance of feminist magazines as historical sources is implicit in Nandita Gandhi and Nandita Shah's overview of the Indian women's movement (1993), Honor Ford-Smith's account of funding and organizational democracy in the Jamaican Sistren Theatre Collective (1997); and Shireen Hassim's analysis of South African women's organization (2006). Among the accounts that consult global South LGBTQ magazines as sources are Jyoti Puri (2002), Ketu Katrak (2006), Ruth Vanita (2007), Daniel Conway (2009), and Matthew Chin (2019a, 2019b).

3 One of the earliest uses of the concept was by Gayatri Spivak (1985) who turns to archives of the imperial past to describe how the "Third World" was "worlded" as "ethnicist and primitivist." Spivak exposes the epistemic violence in these attempts by reading the imperial construction of Rani of Sirmur along the axes of gender, race, and class.

Edward Said elaborates on these ideas by describing nineteenth century British fiction's embeddedness in the "world" of imperial power and colonialist expansion (1993).

More recently, the heuristic has been deployed by literary and cultural critics in the context of American studies and world literature. Pheng Cheah, though primarily concerned with a literary-philosophical exploration of the concept, offers a useful direction involving "the thick transnationalism of transregional networks" facilitating "research of an intermediate scale above the nation-state and below the world-system" to offer "immanent resources for resisting Northern- and Western-centric capitalist globalization" (2016, 5). For Rob Wilson, worlding "as a critical practice enacts openings of space, time, and consciousness to other values and multiple modes of being" and "a worlded criticism seeks new and emergent connections to and articulations with region, place, area, and trans-regional forms" (2019, 128–129).

While I engage most directly with urban studies approaches to worlding in this book, literary critical and international studies scholarship focusing on non-Western (con)texts helped hone my analysis.

4 In the introduction to *Archive Stories: Facts, Fictions and the Writing of History*, Antoinette Burton (2005) mentions that the "idiom" of the archive has expanded to include online sources. For discussions of queer archives see also Ann Cvetkovich (2003), Judith Halberstam, (2005), Allison Bechdel (2012), and Gayatri Gopinath (2018). Feminist-queer

theorizations of the colonial archive include accounts by Anjali Arondekar (2009) and Ann Laura Stoler (2009).

5 I arrive at this project from a disciplinary training in Postcolonial Studies and Comparative Literature. Comparative literary studies historically engaged literature from two or more national or linguistic contexts, Postcolonial literary studies is sometimes premised on area-based specializations in African, Caribbean, or South Asian literature.

6 Important work on sexualities in Africa, the Caribbean, and South Asia brings together voices from many different disciplines. See for instance the essays in Ruth Vanita's edited anthology *Queering India* (2002b), Mikki Van Zyl and Melissa Steyn's *Performing Queer* (2008), and Faith Lois Smith's *Sex and the Citizen: Interrogating the Caribbean* (2011).

7 India was shocked into renewed acknowledgement of violence against lower caste women in September 2020. The horrific gang rape and murder of a 19-year *dalit* woman from Hathras, Uttar Pradesh, by four upper caste men made national and international headlines. Despite complaints to the police, the perpetrators were not arrested for over ten days. Upon her death in a Delhi hospital, the woman was cremated by the police without her family's consent to prevent an autopsy report.

8 Some of this legislation been retrogressive. The controversy over women's rights versus minority rights came to a head in the Shah Bano case involving Muslim women's right to maintenance after divorce. The 1986 Muslim Women (Protection of Rights on Divorce) Act enacted legislation curbing the rights of divorced Muslim women to seek maintenance under the common (rather than personal, that is, religion-based) laws. Subsequently, with the rise of the Hindu majoritarian government, defense of women's rights has become a ploy for curtailing the rights of religious minorities.

9 Revisiting the debates over WID/WAD during and after the UN Decade for Women (1975–1985), the general opinion is that "WAD is regarded as contesting WID claims that women have been excluded from development" (Saunders 2002, 7).

10 GAD "prescribed" several changes in the WID project: bringing men into the process of development so that structural causes of women's subordination could be addressed; integrating women and development into all projects and programming or "gender mainstreaming"; and emphasizing participatory government by recognizing the diversity of women's experiences and their needs (Jaquette 2017, 247).

11 The *Toonen vs Australia* case resulted in Australia repealing Tasmania's criminalization of gay sex. The United Nations Human Rights Committee ruled that such criminalization violated the International Covenant on Civil and Political Rights which included sexual orientation under its anti-discrimination provisions.

12 In 2011, South Africa proposed that the Office of the UN High Commissioner for Human Rights draft a resolution documenting "discriminatory laws and practices and acts of violence against individuals based on their sexual orientation and gender identity." Led by South African feminist Navi Pillay, a frequent contributor to *Speak* and *Agenda* (see Chapter 7), these efforts culminated in a landmark UN report documenting human rights violations based on sexual orientation and gender identity. The report can be accessed at: www.ohchr.org/Documents/Issues/Discrimination/A.HRC.19.41_English.pdf

13 The title of this section refers to Joseph Slaughter's important book, *Human Rights, Inc: The World Novel, Narrative Form, and International Law* (2007). One of the key strands in Slaughter's argument is an account of the 1960s as the UN Development Decade. The beneficiaries of this decade were countries of the global South, the so-called "developing" economies, some of which are now in strong economic positions. In Slaughter's view: "As the discourse of development has claimed a greater stake in the discourse of human rights, their lexicons have become almost synonymous and functionally interchangeable in the legal formulae of international human rights" (2007, 211). This is an astute assessment of the crisscrossing paths of development and human rights talk.

14 Gramsci's influence on postcolonial studies via the differing trajectories of subaltern historiography and cultural theorists like Stuart Hall has been analyzed as post-Marxist. More recently, it has been the subject of polemical debates following Timothy

Brennan's scathing review of Neelam Srivastava and Baidik Bhattacharya's edited collection *The Postcolonial Gramsci* (2012).

15 Often institutional and academic contexts such as universities provide momentum to pioneering feminist publishing and activism. This was the case with the University of Delhi in India, the University of the West Indies, the Jamaica School of Drama, and the University of KwaZulu-Natal in Durban.

16 Gay and Lesbian Memory in Action (GALA) has played a major role in public discussions of sexuality through its community outreach and publications programs. *Sex and Politics in South Africa* edited by Neville Hoad, Karen Martin, and Graeme Reid (2005) contains essays, personal testimonies, and rebuttals interspersed with photographs of archives held at GALA. GALA also published *Trans: Transgender Life Stories from South Africa*, edited by Ruth Morgan, Charl Marais, and Joy Rosemary Wellbeloved (2009).

17 Citing the example of South Africa, the Jamaica Forum for Lesbians, All-Sexuals, and Gays (J-FLAG) submitted a parliamentary petition to amend the Constitution to include non-discrimination on the basis of sexual orientation. The petition was rejected in 2001 but the parliamentary committee suggested repealing the Buggery Law. As of today, the law remains on the books, though another appeal by J-FLAG's Education and Outreach Office has been filed.

18 I looked at these in 2005 while on a research trip to Toronto in search of material on the feminist theatre group Sistren Theatre Collective. A brief account can be found in my article (Batra 2010) "'Our Own Gayful Rest: A Postcolonial Archive." *Small Axe: A Caribbean Journal of Criticism 14.1*: 46–59. My grateful thanks to Matthew Chin for diligently collecting the full set of the *Jamaica Gaily News* and making it available to community activists in Jamaica and to scholars outside the country.

PART I

Abeng, challenging depravation

2

"BETTA MUS CUM"[1]

Jamaica as the 'problem-space' of gay and lesbian liberation

Jamaican dancehall's sporadic advocacy of sexual violence is a tired (and tiring) cultural narrative. Even as artists like Buju Banton, Beenie Man, and Elephant Man walked back their overt homophobia by written or verbal statements apologizing for their "murder music" of the 1990s and early 2000s, others like Shaggy joke away and deny violence against gay, lesbian, and trans people (2015), or, like Sizzla Kalonji, continue to declare that homosexuals have no place in the country (2015). Late in 2019, openly gay dancehall artist Demaro dropped the video of his catchy single "Mi Readi" on the Internet, loudly announcing, "Yo, mi readi/tell everybody get readi/Jamaica rudebwoy comin tru real heavy/Straight to the top, non-stop dat smaddy." Scholarly opinion on homophobia in dancehall has been divided between commentators who perceive its causal connection to anti-gay violence (Chin 1999; Glave 2000; Gutzmore 2004), cultural critics who examine the relationship between violent, patriarchal heterosexual masculinity as structured in contrast with "effete" homosexuality (Hope 2010), and those who read dancehall as socially radical and its artists' violent talk as "cathartic" rather than causal (Cooper 2004a, 145–178). While Jamaicans' perceptions of non-normative sexualities since dancehall's anti-gay violence came to attention have gradually shifted to a grudging acceptance, there is no national consensus on how culturally embedded anti-gay expression impacts those who await legal, social, and cultural respect. Like Demaro, Jamaica has been "worldwide readi" to affirm the rights of its LGBTQ+ citizens for many decades.

Literary clues first led me to an almost forgotten history of gay and lesbian liberation in Jamaica. Turning over the pages of *The Gayley News*, Ian Kaysen pretends to ignore his friend Dale's concern about the unnamed condition taking a toll on his health, slowly reducing him to "a small gathering of bones" in Patricia Powell's novel about gay men. Reading what seems to be the pen friend section of a privately circulated magazine that existed in Jamaica from 1978 to 1984, at first facetiously named *The Toilet Paper* and then the *Jamaica Gaily News* (*JGN*), Dale sarcastically remarks on Ian's

DOI: 10.4324/9781003170303-3

calculated indifference to his illness: "You'd think how sick you are, you'd have your Bible open instead" (Powell 1994, 65). Powell, a Jamaican American lesbian writer, was aware of the existence of the Gay Freedom Movement (GFM) through its newsletter, the *Jamaica Gaily News* (*JGN*) in the 1970s. The newsletter title most directly puns on *The Jamaica Daily News*, a paper published at that time. It also evokes leading national dailies *Daily Gleaner* (now *The Gleaner*) and *Daily Observer* (now *The Observer*) where articles and readers' letters continue to debate homosexuality. The novel describes social and self-inflicted violence on gay men and lesbian women and their efforts to forge a community amid the pressures of making a living in Jamaica.

I was amused at Powell's reference to *Gayley News*, thinking it was a witty quip on generic newspaper titles. Some days later an announcement on the Jamaica Forum for Lesbians All-Sexuals and Gays website about a proposed archive of the *Jamaica Gaily News* (*JGN*) caught my attention. Tracing these archival holdings to the Canadian Lesbian and Gay Archives (CLGA), my previously planned trip to

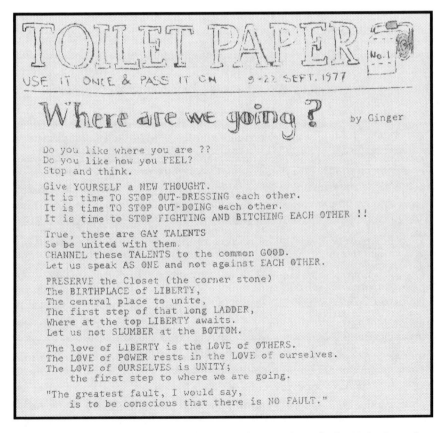

FIGURE 2.1 Section of the cover page of the first number of *The Toilet Paper*, later renamed the *Jamaica Gaily News*. Image courtesy of Larry Chang, Matthew Chin, and the *JGN* Digital Archive at the Digital Library of the Caribbean.

Toronto for research on Jamaican women's drama in the 1970s and 1980s suddenly took a new direction. The theatre group, Sistren, active around the same time as the GFM, performed plays about women's sexuality outside the framework of "respectable" domesticity.[2] These all-female performances led to Sistren being labeled "sodomites" by its conservative and sometimes hostile audiences. Thinking through these connections between stigmatized sexualities and feminist performances, I explore the accidental convergences between feminist, lesbian, and gay conversations initiated by Sistren and the GFM in the Jamaican public sphere in this and the following chapter. Phillip Pike's 2002 documentary *Songs of Freedom: Compelling Stories of Courage and Hope by Jamaican Gays and Lesbians* puts faces to many of the names in the *JGN* archive and provides a succinct account of the GFM's struggles and successes. Conversations with Larry Chang, Jamaican gay rights advocate and GFM founder, and communication with activists and scholars from Jamaica over the years have been crucial to my assessment of the significance of the GFM within postcolonial sexual activism.

Recent analyses of Jamaican and/or Caribbean gay activism acknowledge the history of GFM-*JGN* led gay and lesbian organization in the country. However, some studies focusing on the recent past think of Jamaican sexuality-based activism in largely presentist terms. For instance, the International Lesbian, Gay, Bisexual, Trans, and Intersex Association (ILGA) inaccurately reported on the 2015 gay pride events with the headline "Jamaica Ready for its First Pride Ever," based on inputs from J-FLAG. There was no acknowledgement of J-FLAG's links with the GFM which had organized Pride events from 1978 to 1984 (ILGA, 2015). Similarly, outlining the circumstances that resulted in the death of 16 gay inmates of a Kingston prison in 1997, Lawson Williams writes in an informative and passionate piece that the formation of J-FLAG in 1998 "constituted the *first* significant political and institutional attempt to address homosexual issues in Jamaica" (2000, 107, emphasis added). While J-FLAG is the first forum to *openly* address homosexuality in Jamaica, the groundwork for this activism was laid by the GFM, an account we can glean from the pages of the *JGN*.

Self and community-assertion were the cornerstones of Jamaican social and cultural policies empowering subaltern constituencies comprising black women, working classes and peasants of all colors, children, the illiterate, health compromised, and older people in the late 1970s (Nettleford 1972, 1979). Though its leaders were light-skinned, middle-class Kingston-based professionals, the GFM adapted this model of self and community assertion to gender identity and sexual orientation. The movement's activities can be read through the plan of national cultural action mapped in Jamaican educator, dancer, and cultural theorist Rex Nettleford's writings. I am aware of the irony in this reading since there has been sustained speculation on Nettleford's sexuality over the years. Though he was not part of the GFM's sphere of social and political activities, his ideas and influence on Jamaican cultural policies in the 1960s–1970s as special advisor to Michael Manley is undeniable. During this period, gay men and lesbian women's "smadditisation" (Nettleford's term for the consciousness of being somebody) reflected the growing confidence of ordinary Jamaican citizens despite continuing racial and class disparities in the country. Moreover, while the GFM's efforts at gay liberation were implicitly in dialogue with the Jamaican state, the organization did not count on statist measures to redress stigmatization of homosexuality; rather it attempted to create the conditions for public discussions of sexual choice. As a sexual counterpublic, the GFM educated Jamaicans about homosexuality through popular and mass media including television, radio, and letters to leading dailies, beyond its official newsletter.

Nettleford describes the "cultural process" in Jamaica as an "on-going recycling of effort" using the image of a banyan tree. Culture is a "growth process with the source of life beginning in the roots sending up shoots which eventually bear fruits which ripen, fall back to the roots to grow again in a never-ending regenerative process" (1979, 70). The GFM's efforts to "big up" (elevate) a despised group form the roots of this tree, J-FLAG's efforts are the shoots combating two decades of anti-gay violence, and the tree's bittersweet fruits are increased visibility and vulnerability of gay, lesbian, and trans citizens. J-FLAG shares many organizational goals and members with the GFM but faces a different set of challenges as it negotiates with the state for legislative guarantees against discrimination during a time when popular culture and international outrage have placed Jamaican homosexuality in the limelight.

This chapter closely reads the *JGN* newsletter archive – painstakingly collected, rigorously analyzed, and generously shared by anthropologist Matthew Chin – to locate the emergence of the GFM within two interpretive contexts arising out of a specific set of socio-cultural conditions in postcolonial Jamaica: the national and the transnational. The national cultural policies in the 1970s created respect for black expression in music, dance, theatre, visual arts, Afro-Caribbean religious practices, decolonized educational institutions, destigmatized non-marital family structures, children born out of wedlock, and other despised identities. The GFM-*JGN*'s affirmation of gay and lesbian cultures and identities emerge in this context which, despite progressive social policies, continued to be dominated by color-class hierarchies, hegemonic masculinity, and Christianity. The transnational interpretive context for the *JGN* is the GFM's interaction with gender and sexual justice efforts outside the Caribbean, especially by North American and European LGBTQ+ organizations. It is likely that such interactions were responsible for the GFM's inconsistent and intermittent human rights claims. Two years into the movement, these claims receded in favor of education and empowerment including a focus on youth mentorship, prisoner support, health outreach, and rejoinders to religious objections against homosexuality. After the GFM's demise in 1984, sexual activism focused on HIV/AIDS education, prevention, and management with the assistance of Jamaica AIDS Support which was informally known to support sexual minorities. J-FLAG emerged in 1998 to carry forward goals of sexual liberation inspired by memories of organizational structures laid out by the GFM "elders" Larry Chang and Brian Williamson. Unlike the 1970s, there was no available map of national socio-cultural development in Jamaica in the 1990s. Conditions of uneven globalization, including Caribbean diasporic mediations, ensured that despite economic hardships, cultural production (literature, films, music, dance, theatre, arts) was not completely trammeled in neoliberalized Jamaica.

Women's studies scholars have closely studied global asymmetries reflected in the socio-legal construction of postcolonial gender and sexualities in neoliberal Caribbean states (Kempadoo 2004; Alexander 2005; Robinson 2007). Tracy Robinson (2007) includes a brief reference to J-FLAG in response to M. Jacqui Alexander's (2005) claim that Caribbean feminists must be wary of an over-reliance on the state to guarantee their rights. In Robinson's view, J-FLAG's advocacy before the Parliamentary committee set up to examine the proposed new Charter of Rights in the Jamaica Constitution acknowledged the important role of the state in guaranteeing rights. Though this advocacy was dismissed, the hearings enabled J-FLAG to "enunciate a collective vision of their imagined lives" (2007, 129).[3] The GFM's non-statist strategies of activism, including its infrequent invocation of human rights, can thus be placed in dialogue with J-FLAG's state-centered advocacy mediated by international human rights bodies such as ILGA, Human Rights Watch, and Amnesty International.

In keeping with the time frame of my study which ends before the emergence of digital activism, the analysis offered in this chapter focuses primarily on the GFM-*JGN*, and secondarily on J-FLAG. My "problem-space" or "context of argument, and, therefore, one of *intervention*" (Scott 2004, 4; 2017) is 1970s gay and lesbian emergence, a period which does not sustain either a glorification of Jamaica as the site of an early global South sexual liberationism (my previous article on the *JGN* was invested in such valorization) or disparagement as a perpetually late arrivant to the sexuality and human rights platform. Neither of these positions carries forward an urgent conversation about sexuality, especially when the geographical space is littered with tragedies of murderous violence. With Jamaica as the first of the three problem-spaces explored in this book, I begin an analysis of the ways in which feminist and LGBTQ+ negotiation of legislative, cultural, medical, and human rights claims in and through activist literature can help imagine future-oriented strategies to decolonize sexualities two decades into the twenty-first century.

Emplacements: Color, class, cultural capital

Perhaps one of the earliest postcolonial sexual liberation movements in the world, two main features of the GFM's activities immediately stand out: the unflagging volunteerism of its founders; its predominantly (though not exclusively) urban, middle class circuit of activity centering first around New Kingston, and then the larger Kingston and St. Andrew area. The founder-editor of the *JGN*, Chang, a light-skinned Chinese-Jamaican, and some of the GFM's core group members lived and socialized here. As Chang describes in an interview with Thomas Glave, he and his gay friends had their first conversation about homosexuality with straight people at a restaurant/bar in New Kingston (2012). Other popular venues mentioned in the newsletter include short-lived bars and clubs such as the Closet on Haining Road; Fanny Hill run by a GFM founder Gary Muirhead; The White

Lady in Spanish Town; The Speakeasy in Constant Spring (renamed Marshall's and Carol Heights); Maddams on West King's Road; and The Great House, likely a private residence, whose location I have not been able to ascertain. The early bars were in the heart of downtown and at Cross Roads in Kingston before new ones opened in New Kingston. New Kingston was newly constructed in the 1960s and not overly developed even into the 1980s. An enclave of upper class exclusivity with shopping plazas, hotels, banks, private schools, hospitals, theaters, nightclubs, parks, and gated residences, the area's color, class, and spatial exclusivity has been the subject of several studies (Clarke 2006; Carnegie 2014; Carnegie 2017). As a highly developed uptown, New Kingston contrasts with a dilapidated, neglected downtown, largely abandoned by big business. Charles Carnegie calls New Kingston a "zone of exception" devoid of itinerant vending and sidewalk hawking, though it is a hub of streetwalkers and "gully queens," dispossessed gay and trans youth, who emerge in the evenings and at night despite policed restrictions (2017, 145–146). To be clear, this was not a gayborhood like Hillbrow in Johannesburg, Soho in London, or Greenwich Village in New York. However, its upper and middle class gentrified environs ensured that gays and lesbians were largely ignored, or perhaps tolerated, in ways different from other densely populated predominantly black areas where gay socialization would attract more attention. The GFM's "interiorized sociality," to use Carnegie's term for daily interactions in New Kingston (2014), reflected the class and culture of its uptown origins that are my focus in this section. My analysis of gay culture and capital in the *JGN* explains the limitations of the GFM's gay liberation agenda, hampered by members' lack of initiative, lack of a permanent meeting venue, and changing socio-economic conditions in the country.

News of gay social events in Kinston was bootlegged largely through the grapevine including the *JGN* which distilled observation and information to present a surprisingly potent brew. Events covered in the *JGN* reflect the locational affiliations of GFM's key organizers and their financial status. Cash and gay cultural capital were required to access the gay clubs existing at that time. Drag balls, dance competitions, fashion shows, and theatrical entertainments, the staples of gay social and cultural life, ensured a steady clientele for the businesses. Occasionally, the *JGN* carried news about art shows, poetry readings, and film screenings at private residences. The urban professions mentioned in the newsletter run the gamut of working, middle, and upper levels, including but not limited to household help, gardening, landscaping, cooking, hairdressing, medicine, nursing, art, music, theatre and performance, exercise and fitness, tourism, the hotel industry, and of course nightclubs and bars. With new venues opening in other parts of the city, and poverty and unemployment rising in the country, changes in gay socialization included a decrease in club patronage and meetings, and increased cross-class personal and social vulnerability.

Though the relative anonymity of urban Kingston provided opportunities for employment and social interaction among gay people, it could, and often did, lead to violence.[4] A six-member committee comprising the GFM first met in the club

Closet to discuss community solutions to violence arising from "a series of fights among patrons, primarily lesbians." Listing various causes and consequences of such violence, readers wrote to the newsletter urging the importance of educating the gay "family" while maintaining secrecy to ensure its survival (Thomas 1977; Vernon 1977). Some ways of understanding this violence are proposed in Chang's interview in Phillip Pike's documentary *Songs of Freedom* (2002) and in Suzanne La Font's article "Very Straight Sex" (2001). Chang and La Font believe that the historical explanation of violence lies in understanding the dominant mode of heterosexist masculinity under colonialism when male and female slaves were agents and receptacles for reproducing slave labor. According to these views, any acknowledgement of enforced or con-sensual same-sex relations under slavery disrupted the tightly controlled reproductive economy and led to harsh reprisals. We should also consider how Afro-Caribbean moral superiority is rooted in religious beliefs and cultural traditions which denounce same-sex desire as the preserve of the Westernized elite. As in many postcolonial nations, exemplary Jamaican heterosexual morality is set up in contrast to Western homosexual immorality. It is equally possible that homophobia is sometimes tinged with either racial antagonism, envy, or fear as financially comfortable gay lives appear remarkably Western. Upscale uptown bars and clubs as scenes of gay life are many worlds away from the street, the yard, and downtown shops and bars studied as spaces of interaction between working class Jamaican men and women (Chevannes 2003). Lower and working strata queer folk including homeless gully queens, some living in street drains in New Kingston and earning their living through prostitution, are often visible and vulnerable targets of violence.

Jamaican performer, poet and dramatist Dennis Scott's remarkable play *Dog* depicts how disparities reached a tipping point during the late 1970s and 1980s when the country staggered under economic recession, cultural ferment, and political clientelism. During these years social discontent exacerbated anti-gay vio-lence, including attacks on gay clubs and bars documented in the *JGN*.[5] Maddam's was repeatedly attacked in the years the GFM was active. It was first stoned by anonymous persons interrupting a film screening, then its owners were burgled of goods worth several thousand dollars at gunpoint, and later it was fire-bombed. The Speakeasy experienced its own share of troubles when some patrons were apprehended for burglary and the police were called. While outsiders were responsible for many of these incidents, at least some were caused by disgruntled gay men denied admission, party crashers at private events, withheld or insufficient payment for sexual services, and a non-bar incident when a lesbian row ended in a person stabbing her ex-lover with an ice pick. The *JGN* regularly reported on bribery, extortion, and robbery of gay men spotted leaving clubs and bars, and, in one instance, a break-in foiled by a gay man and his partner. These led the GFM to advertise self-defense lessons and to consider a Gay Defense Force. Both ideas failed to get off the ground. The GFM archives and the *JGN* both establish a clear link between high levels of intra-gay and intra-lesbian violence and an over-investment in a club and bar culture in the absence of other meeting venues and infrequent gatherings in the homes of the founders.[6]

The general pattern of gay male conspicuous consumption was premised on leaving organizing and community formation to a select few, an attitude repeatedly attacked in the *JGN* and eventually leading to Chang's resignation as GFM General Secretary and *JGN* editor. Though the GFM considered gay owned clubs, restaurants, and shops as essential to the growth and vitality of the community, it often called out their management for exploiting and abusing patrons. An early article lambasts the management of Maddam's for their financial exploitation of its gay clientele on the flimsy pretext of losses caused by rowdiness and infrequent attendance (Johnson 1980, 3). Suggestions offered to its new owners included the idea of a "psychological contract, i.e. the process of reciprocation" between the management and its patrons involving publicity, entertainment, and other services to the gay community (Johnson 1980, 9). The bars were thus endangered and precariously positioned cultural spaces – scenes of culture, capital, conviviality – representing contradictory ideas of a community, sustained, on the one hand, by partying and boogying, and on the other, by calls to volunteer. The GFM's acknowledgement of the necessity of clubs and bars sits uneasily with its exhortation to think beyond partying and its condemnation of exploitative club owners:

> Many are finding it increasingly difficult to make ends meet and have had to reduce their expenditure, and even in some cases, limit it to the bare necessities. It is a hard fact of life. It is incumbent on those who can spend on entertainment, therefore, to make more effort to support the clubs and take up the slack, as it were.
>
> (*JGN* 1978f, 3)

This call to cash-rich members to patronize clubs and bars during lean times underlines the dilemma that while bar culture was inaccessible to most people, there was no permanent venue for meetings and organization.

In a move beyond the bars into other social spaces, the *JGN* suggested "alternative activities and groupings" to involve those who did not or could not afford to frequent bars (*JGN* 1978g, 3). An early article by Glen McDaniel under the pen name Aquarius presents the call to political action not as a choice but a question of existence: "For survival, we must take time out from the daze of boogying, camping and bitching to think and then to ACT" (Aquarius 1978, 5). In subsequent newsletters, the recurring problem of inaction and involvement is addressed more directly as a politics of shame and blame to enforce participation. Providing several dictionary definitions of "apathy" as "indifference," "lack of desire for activity," an "insensibility to suffering," and a "passionless existence," Chang's hard-hitting editorial attempts to extend interiorized gay male socialities beyond partying and cruising (*JGN* 1978h, 3).

These calls can be understood in the context of volunteerism as a socially and culturally recognized virtue in Jamaica (Nettleford 1979, 124–125; Robotham 1998). As a quasi-criminalized community, the GFM's need to maintain secrecy did not allow for cultural legitimacy or dedicated spaces available to other Jamaican social and cultural institutions of the period – among them the Tivoli Gardens

Center in West Kingston, the Count Ossie Rastafarian Center, the Jamaica Folk Singers – which had cultivated longstanding relationships between voluntary workers and state officials (Nettleford 1979, 125). The Manley era and its program of cultural action has been described as one of the peaks of voluntarism in the country:

> Youth clubs and women's groups were formed, thousands of persons volunteered to give literacy classes in JAMAL, new sports activities were supported while community and other organizations flowered. Later in the decade of the 1970s this vision, though it continued to inspire voluntarism, was riddled with the pervasiveness of class differences exacerbated by the national economic conditions.
>
> (Robotham 1998)

For Robotham, these differences led to a "shallow concept of market society...the idea that each person is to seek his or her own benefit and the society will take care of itself" (1998). Robotham's description of "*manufacturing* volunteerism" is evident in the ways in which the GFM acknowledged the labor of its founders with awards for their service, perhaps hoping this might encourage people to dedicate their time and energy to the organization. In the absence of formalized structures and spaces it was enormously difficult to organize the publication of the magazine and cultural, social, and outreach activities. The *JGN* documents in the Caribbean IRN point to the labor-intensive work of securing, editing, typesetting, mimeographing, and securing printing supplies for the newsletter.

Besides publishing the *JGN*, other volunteer initiatives arising out of the GFM's calls were the Prison Outreach Program, the Gay Youth Group, and the Gay Health Clinic. Over the years, the prison outreach program maintained regular communication with gay prisoners in Catherine District Prison, offering them material and psychological support. The members sent gifts and supplies to the gay prisoners at Christmas and New Year and discussed rehabilitation upon their release. The youth group involved GFM representatives, school students, and interested adults who met at the Speakeasy, extending the bar as a community space. (*JGN* 1978i, 1978j). A Gay Community Health Clinic was organized at the Speakeasy in November 1978 in response to the spread of sexually transmitted diseases. Follow up actions included a VD testing service and referrals to gay doctors (*JGN* 1978k, 1978l). An article on sexual health advised "sexually active persons" to undergo a blood test every six months, cautioned against self-medication, discussed reasons why members of the community were shy of attending public health clinics, and advocated for a "gay-oriented health care system at least as it relates to sexually transmitted diseases" (*JGN* 1978m, 1). The 9 March 1979 newsletter announces that the clinic had reopened at Maddam's to offer a range of services at a very nominal fee (*JGN* 1979c, 1). Placing information about the health of the community in the context of the Gay Youth Movement, the *JGN* also addressed misinformation about the initiation of young people into "corrupt" or "pervert" sexual choices and lifestyles (*JGN* 1978j, 3). The group combined its educational and health care programs by talking with trainee nurse practitioners to clear "misconceptions as to the prevalence, causes and behaviour of gays" (*JGN* 1984a, 2). Reaching prisoners, young people, and those who required health services, these interconnected initiatives at once reflected national upliftment programs in the cultural policy of the decade and refracted in rainbow hues its sphere of activities in Jamaica.

As the GFM acquired a structure and a constitution and expanded its activities, it keenly felt the lack of a dedicated space (*JGN* 1981a, 1981b).[7] The two years when several clubs temporarily or permanently closed their doors marked a low point in the organizational activities and a break in the publication of the *JGN*. While there is no information on arrangements being worked out for the new club, The Speakeasy's short-lived re-opening in 1984 provided a social (though not organizational) venue. The newsletter carried a report when it reopened as a bar called Marhsall's, catering to a mixed rather than an exclusively gay clientele (*JGN* 1984b). In the last newsletters published in 1984, GFM Treasurer FC and her partner's Beverley Hills home became a venue for gay pride week events including an art display, poetry, and music.[8] Facing disorganization and paucity of funds, the GFM abandoned the idea of a permanent venue for the community center to focus on its cultural educational efforts.[9]

The GFM's dilemmas and expectations invite an analysis of the faultlines of postcolonial sexual activism and similarities/differences between lesbian–gay and South-North social-sexual formations. In all social movements, including those for gay and lesbian mobilization, there are varying levels of investment in social needs versus political responsibility. The GFM sought to mitigate the effects of market society where gay dollars could buy entertainment but could not guarantee safety and social acceptance. Furthermore, in Jamaica, as in South Africa, urban bars and clubs served as spaces for gay male socializing more than they did for lesbians. In this respect Jamaican and South African social-sexual formations are closer to those in the global North than Indian formations, where late twentieth century venues of gay socialization were either house parties or rare singles nights at select clubs and discotheques. A comparison with North America, where market spaces led to "mainstreaming" of the gay and lesbian movement and the gay and lesbian bar emerged as the primary locus of the community, is instructive (Vaid 1995, Warner 2002). A more generous view of North American gay and lesbian socialization is based on the argument that within the gay and lesbian movement, "to a much greater degree than in any comparable movement, the institutions of culture-building have been market-mediated: bars, discos, special services, newspapers, magazines, phone lines, resorts, urban commercial districts" because "Nonmarket forms of association that have been central to other movements – kinship, traditional residence – have been less available for queers" (Warner 1993, xvii–xviii). There is some truth to this claim, though class, gender, and racial exclusions in gay social spaces also led to splinter groups such as the Salsa Soul Sisters, a group of "third-world" lesbians active in New York during the same years as the GFM in Jamaica. The members included authors Michelle Cliff and Patricia Powell. The Salsa Soul Sisters emerged out of lesbians' dissatisfaction with gay male social venues in New York; they chose to meet in another venue because of the racism experienced by lesbians of color in bars with a largely white, gay male clientele. Some diasporic Jamaican members of the group maintained active contact with the GFM through these years (Chin 2019a). The GFM-Salsa Soul Sisters' interactions are mentioned at least twice in the *JGN*.

To date there have been rare discussions of the postcolonial Caribbean as a site of gay activism since the focus remains on homophobia and anti-gay legislation reflecting

> metropolitan impulses that explain the absence of visible lesbian and gay movements as a defect in political consciousness and maturity, using evidence of publicly organized movements in the United States as evidence of their originary status in the West and their superior political maturity.
>
> (Alexander 2005, 28)

If sexual activism is judged by its longevity (time of activity) and publicness (sphere of influence, being out of the closet and into the streets), it will always be categorized as immature for failing to meet the criteria set by more powerful and transnationally connected actors in the global North. It is thus crucial to examine the GFM-*JGN*'s spheres of influence over the seven years of its existence. The *JGN*'s peak circulation of 250 copies allowed it to reach all over Jamaica via postal mail. Chang mentions that copies of the newsletter were sent to all major governmental agencies, and the organization kept up a media campaign by writing and responding to letters in major newspapers. Thus, it simultaneously created the conditions for and participated in a national conversation on sexuality by establishing contact with men, women, and teenagers in isolated peri-urban and rural areas, in prisons, medical establishments across Kingston and St. Andrew, information agencies like the Jamaican Broadcasting Corporation, major newspapers, and service organizations like Jaycees. Its discussions with members of the Jamaican Psychological Association and assistance to a student from the University of the West Indies collecting data for a study on gay people in Jamaica were intended to clear misconceptions about homosexuality (*JGN* 1980c). In addition, it documented Caribbean religious opinions on homosexuality, and on one occasion GFM members attended a discussion at Bethel Apostolic Church advertised as "Is Homosexuality a Way of Life?" to soon realize that the format reflected rigid Christian views which did not permit debate (*JGN* 1980d). The *JGN*'s letters and gayfriends section included contributions from men and women of all ages, classes, and racial backgrounds from the parishes of Mandeville, St. Ann, St. Mary, St. Catherine, Clarendon, and Portland.

Despite its predominantly urban middle and upper class origins, its market-oriented social emplacements, and activist deficit, the organization succeeded in generating an ongoing and unfinished national conversation on gender identity and sexual orientation. Judged by any standards, early gay activism in Jamaica was serious in its public efforts to address all colors, income levels, and sexualities to revise entrenched medical, cultural, social, religious misconceptions without mandating declarative identity politics for its members.

Embodiments: "Smadditised" socialities

Despite the GFM-*JGN*'s organizational deficit during these years, the gay community's growing confidence in its social and organizational activities contrasts with decreased economic opportunities in the country. Jamaica's policies under Manley's PNP government involved common people in cultural development, a process which led to the origins of the Sistren Theatre Collective comprising working class women first employed as street cleaners and then trained as teacher's aides. In an interview with David Scott, Nettleford restated his opinion that the 1970s "'smadditised' this country [Jamaica]. Everybody now thinks that he is somebody. At last, every Jack man, every Jinny woman, considers himself and herself to be somebody" (Scott & Nettleford 2006, 219). Cultural institutions and the spirit of voluntarism played an influential role in this process. The GFM devised its own methods of voluntary efforts breathing in the atmosphere of black cultural and social assertion. Though underground, the newsletter fulfilled Nettleford's mandate for culturally responsible media by focusing on matters that related the Jamaican experience to a "world-view" by giving "each Jamaican of whatever social origin an opportunity for a positive point of contact with this society" (1972, 131). Additionally, GFM-*JGN* countered misinformation in mainstream media, maintained a correspondence network to combat social isolation, and affirmed gay self-worth to readers of Jamaica's national newspapers.

"Smadditisation" or individual self-worth has yielded rich interpretations that gloss the situation of those denied personhood based on race, class, gender, or sexual orientation (Mills 1997; Heron 2003). Philosopher Charles Mills elaborates on self-worth largely in the context of race to assert that "the theory appropriate to sub-persons must necessarily be different in many ways from the theory of those who have casually taken personhood for granted" (1997, 61); feminist development scholar Taitu Heron develops these ideas in relation to space, class, and ethnicity to state that "the lack of justice maintained in the status quo means a continued denial of legitimate space to exist as *smaddy*" (2003, 509). These ideas allow us to read gay and lesbian self-assertion in the face of sexual sub-personhood, a form of subalternity that does not exclusively focus on either class or color, but instead relies on multivalent identities. Countering non-white devaluation involves recovering and revalorizing the body and language in the process of "smadditizin'," collective, militant assertion, requiring overcoming resistance against a group's personhood, but also "achievement of a socioeconomic type as a basis of respect" (Mills, 1997, 64). Smadditisation can also occur in the form of "a resort to auxiliary spaces of the creative imagination and auxiliary spaces of the dance, the roadside, the veranda, and the yawd" (Heron 2003, 509). When these were/are unavailable, other spaces such as bars, clubs, homes, and indeed print, enabled *emplacement* of gay and lesbian personhood – though temporary, sometimes riddled with frivolity, violence, and instances of exploitation – that allowed the emerging community to stake a cultural claim in Jamaican society. Beyond the Kingston bar culture, the newsletter and GFM news in mainstream media reached all parts of the island to insist the relationality of gay personhood on those who tried to deny or wish it away.

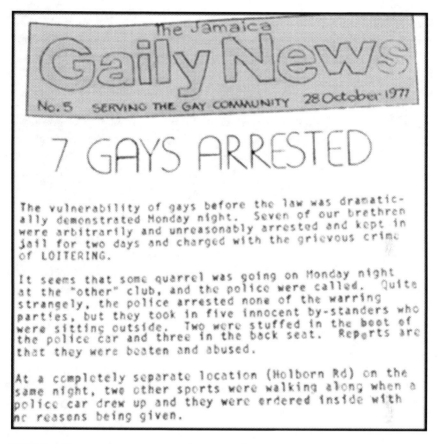

FIGURE 2.2 Section of a report on police intimidation and harassment of gay men that appeared in the *Jamaica Gaily News* in 1977. Image courtesy of Larry Chang, Matthew Chin, and the *JGN* Digital Archive at the Digital Library of the Caribbean.

This part of my argument builds on *real and imagined forms of smadditisation* by closely reading short stories, personal reflections, and prose pieces appearing in the *JGN* from 1978 to 1984. These forms disrupt the private-public dichotomy regulating (hetero)sexuality as a private concern while denying gay and lesbian people privacy by criminalizing specific sexual acts, as in the Jamaican Offences against Persons Act which makes "buggery" a crime. Whereas gay men and lesbian women were/are frequently subjected to verbal insults ("battyman," "chi-chi man," "mampala," "sodomites," "man-royals"), extortion, blackmail, and bodily attacks, none of the gay male fiction in the *JGN* is about violent encounters between gay and straight people, though it does narrate internalized gay homophobia. The couple of lesbian narratives appearing in the magazine focus on reciprocal, nurturing relationships.

Over the years of its publication, the *JGN* followed the format of popular Euro-American gay magazines by encouraging its readers to submit creative pieces. This yielded a lot of poetry, some poignant and heartfelt autobiographical accounts, a few maudlin and self-indulgent narratives, and several sexually explicit contributions. In prose features such as "Personally Speaking" by Aquarius, and "Gay Notes" by Nicholson, writers focused on sex roles, fantasies, gay appearances, fashion choices, and, later, mentoring young people in a responsible, non-sexual manner. These features adopted first-person, conversational modes with the authors presenting themselves as experienced gay men concerned about younger, inexperienced gays. For lesbians, UWI student Donna Smith aka Milady's regular column, "Girl Talk," described coming-of-age experiences, family dynamics, religious experiences, friendships, and lesbian desire in the first-person autobiographical mode.

The author, a Jamaican law student in Barbados, continued writing for the *JGN* while studying for her degree. Her connection with the GFM was initiated upon reading Chang's 1977 letter to *The Gleaner*. This was how she learned of a gay and lesbian community: "So, I came out. But not until I had been made aware of the fact that I was not alone in Jamaica" (Milady 1979a, 6). She wrote to the *JGN* to express her candid opinion on some of its contents. In a conversation on the inauguration of the *JGN* archive, Smith, who now lives in South Africa with her partner, remembered eagerly waiting for copies of the *JGN* which she secretly consumed in the house she shared with her grandmother (2020). Embodying a cyclical relationship of reader-writer-reader, Smith/Milady's fiction, poetry, and letters undoubtedly enabled at least some lesbian women to connect with the community judging from the lesbians seeking love and companionship in the gayfriends section of the newsletter.

At least twice during the years it was published, *JGN* announced fiction contests for its readers in its characteristic irreverent style which mandated "NO B-I-T-C-H-I-N-G" among its list of rules. Though there is no information on the number of entries received or the winners of these contests, quite likely the fiction published was a result of these announcements. Some of these narratives placed characters within the limited sphere of Jamaican gay socialization and activism. Smith/Milady's story "One Last Memory" about a lesbian couple at law school together describes how one of the partners dreams of practicing law to improve the lives of gay and lesbian people in Jamaica even as she is dying of an unnamed disease. This two-part story ends with the couple dancing a waltz together at the Speakeasy (Milady 1979b, 1979c). An untitled story by Bronze describes a gay man who meets "Richard" at a club, spends a memorable night, falls in love, and falls out of love because Richard objects to his partner's involvement in the gay movement. Having seen him read the *JGN*, Richard is perplexed at his lover's involvement with others who are "blatant" about their sexuality. The story ends on a happy note with Richard accepting his lover's need for gay publicness (Bronze 1980, 4). In these narratives the protagonists are comfortable with their sexual preferences, do not feel the need to hide their identity, access social spaces where they can safely express their sexuality, possess the means and the freedom to be together, and recognize the need to improve the lives of gay men and lesbian women in Jamaica. Quite apart from the insularity and limited literary quality of these stories, they offer some of the clearest examples of smadditisation in the emerging movement. The protagonists do not experience sexual stigma, and in their references to the GFM-*JGN* they participate in feedback loops and a reflexive flow of ideas characterizing gay counterpublics circulating in special, protected venues, and in limited publications (Warner 2002, 120).

Warner's ideas on publics and counterpublics are especially helpful in the analysis of gay male fiction in the magazine. These stories run the gamut of typical submissions: narratives of seduction, explosive sexual encounters, heartache, and heartbreak. The usual. They describe interiorized gay identities by omitting social violence and stigmatization. All foreground postcolonial "stranger-socialities" as chance encounters between people from varying backgrounds – a boy running away from home in the middle of the night to escape his mother's fiancé gets a ride from a stranger who turns out to be gay, a man plans an encounter with a gay electric repairman coincidentally on a service call in his neighborhood, a teenager is willingly seduced by a debating coach with whom he has no more than a passing

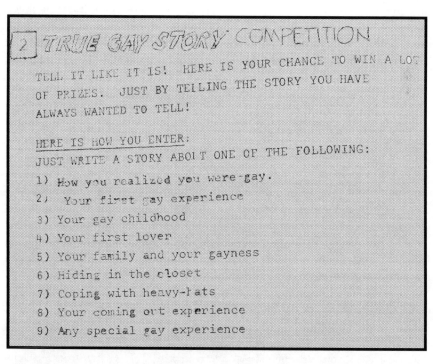

FIGURE 2.3 Section of an announcement of a short story competition in the *Jamaica Gaily News*. Image courtesy of Larry Chang, Matthew Chin, and the *JGN* Digital Archive at the Digital Library of the Caribbean.

acquaintance, and a gay male prostitute enjoys his encounters with old and young men – that disrupt neat dichotomies of the public and the private. To the extent that counterpublics facilitate a culture "in which intimate relations and the sexual body can in fact be understood as projects for transformations among strangers," these narratives describe a world-making in which "embodied sociability, affect, and play" have a defining role (Warner 2002, 122). *JGN*'s limited circulation facilitated such world-making without violent retaliation, though, since the magazine was also sent to all major governmental agencies, including the Jamaica Information Service and the Jamaican Broadcasting Cooperation, there was always the risk of censorship on charges of indecency.

While autobiographical columns and fiction were popular forms of expressing gay identity, two other forms embodied a progression from gay and lesbian to incipient queer subjectivities that made GFM-*JGN* somewhat ahead of the late 1980s and early 1990s queer moment in the United States. The writer of a column variously titled "On Di Scene" and "Pan Di Scene, Iya" by Ja Will uses the Rastafarian lingo adopted by Chang in some of his early contributions. It is thus reasonable to suppose that Chang penned the column to replace "Elsie's Closet," (a play on his initials L. C.) which commented on the scene. Since the newsletter was published fort-nightly, Ja Will takes the persona of an older, worldly Rasta man offering his opinions on gay news over the past two weeks. In one column Ja Will reiterates he is tired of the old music being played at the Speakeasy and expects "Betta mus cum," using Manley's slogan for the 1975 election campaign to comment on the quality of music being played at the bars (Ja Will 1978a, 6). The column, like the editorials, described in vivid detail the number of people at social events, their interactions with young people, the quality of entertainment, and strategies to further the movement. It also reflected on internal generational differences within the gay and lesbian counterpublic created by the GFM: "Wail pan di subjek a yoot, doouh, wen I look eena di fioocha a jus di yoot dem I si. Wen yu chek it, a dem a guh gi wi wi free-dam…. Dem a criet a sasaiati eena owa sasaiati" ["Well upon the subject of the youth, when I look in the future it is just the youth I see. When you see it, it will be them who will give us our freedom…. They have created a society within a society"] (Ja Will 1978b, 6). Noting differences within the small community, Ja Will exhorts party animals to preserve the only means of communication at their disposal: "Wen di club dem lack dung weh oonu a guh du? A ownly di paper oonu a guh av lef" ["When the clubs are locked down where will you go? It is only the paper you are going to be left with"] (Ja Will 1978c, 2). Chang's Rasta persona is at once a nod to cross-class and cross-race gay identity, a register of linguistic and cultural differences, and an assertion of print as a medium of communication, itself communicated in transcribed Jamaican patwah. In forging a generational alliance while recognizing differences of income, culture, race, and religion in the "society within a society," the persona embodies an oppositional queer aesthetics and politics that establishes racial solidarities with the Rastas as outcasts of Jamaican society but is also at odds with pervasive masculinism and homophobia in many stridently heteropatriarchal Rasta communities.[10]

A similar embodiment appears in Chang's contributions under the pseudonym "Mampala Morgan" to encourage lesbian readers and contributors.[11] "Suss-uration," (combining susu, Jamaican for confidential whispering or gossip and the standard English word conversation) by Mampala/Chang written in patwah contrasts with the tone and language of M'Lady and Yvonne's lesbian features in standard English. Like pages outlining activities of socialites and celebrities in mainstream newspapers, the Mampala's (effeminate man or a homosexual, often used as a slur) irreverent reportage of the activities of prominent members of the community raised some hackles. Despite the editorial caveat that its contents were not meant to be taken seriously, the column incurred the wrath of a reader who objected to its "bitchiness" as contributing to the low image of the community in general (*JGN* 1980e, 12). Mampala/Chang's occasionally apocryphal or playful public reportage about love, loss, change, death, romantic, and sexual liaisons outs people's activities to create a readership in the know about each other's lives. This reflexive circulation of private-public knowledge was interpreted by many as an intrusion of privacy. Thus, while sexually explicit fiction was acceptable to the readers, the (s)explicitness of Mampala/Chang's columns was objectionable because they were too close to reality.

Besides gossip, the campy androgynous persona reclaims the slur intended by Mampala – much like the word queer was reclaimed by activists – to refute the common correlation between "susu" or gossip. They announce cultural events, report on violence within and against the community, offer nuggets of advice with tongue-in-cheek reports of the various romantic, cultural, mercenary, criminal, and migratory activities: "cho man we is one big family, why we have fi tief wi one another so [Hey man, we are one big family, why do we have to thieve from one another in this way]?" (Mampala 1981a, 5). Addressing their readership after a long interval during which the newspaper ceased publication due to financial constraints, they write: "Nuff girls have come out since yuh last hear from mi, hope yuh rope een one, awrite [Enough girls have come out since you last heard from me, hope you rope in one, all right]" (Mampala 1981b, 8). These exhortations, like Milady's contributions, encourage women's involvement in the community.

Among the various forms and styles elaborating the worlds inhabited by gay men and lesbian women were erotic bordering on pornographic fiction, autobiographical disclosures, Rasta roots talk, and the Mampala's gossip. The repertoire of subjectivities, sexualities, and black/brown/yellow/white, upper/middle/working class, male/female/boy/girl/trans, respectable/flamboyant "smaddis" that this writing brings to life mark a move towards queer identities that had real-life counterparts in drag shows, beauty contests, and gender fluid performances organized by the GFM and reported in the *JGN*. Not only do these forms "redescribe nonnormative sexualities," they inscribe the "worldliness of sexuality and the conditions of the [incipient] social movement form" (Warner 2002, 18). Over the years the GFM was active, these forms took a different turn than the exhortative cultural-educational smadditisation characteristic of the early stages of the organization. I turn to human rights of the smaddis (l)inked in the newsletter and in GFM documents in the next section.

Righting/writing freedom

Chang mentioned in a personal communication that when he sent a letter to *The Gleaner* explaining homosexuality in 1977, he signed off his name as general secretary of the GFM to give the letter some legitimacy (2008). Since there was no GFM at that time, Chang's signature imagined a form that was to emerge some months later. The conditions under which GFM was launched help in understanding its multiple foci during its existence. This part of the chapter examines the GFM's local and international politics through the lens of human rights in comparison to its successor J-FLAG.

As already indicated, the GFM's emergence coincided with the precarious existence of democratic socialism in Jamaica, a middle ground intended as a "third way" between capitalism and communism. The democratic socialist experiment was introduced by Manley, leader of the People's National Party (PNP), one of the two main political parties in Jamaica. This mid to late 1970s experiment was abandoned by the end of the decade under pressure from the International Monetary Fund. The GFM continued into the early part of the next decade as a new government, headed by Edward Seaga, leader of the Jamaica Labor Party (JLP), came to power in 1980 following one of the most violent elections in Jamaica. The vocabulary of human rights acquired a legitimacy during this period in part because of President Jimmy Carter's castigation of the USSR and other Soviet bloc countries for disregarding the freedoms and rights of their citizens. US aid to foreign countries was increasingly linked to their rights record, epitomizing a politics *of* rather than a politics *for* human rights (Baxi 2008, 7). Jamaica was an unwilling and weak participant in the Cold War politics as the PNP's leanings towards Cuba made it unpopular with the United States government. Despite the global (read: US) emphasis on human rights, the category, though repeatedly mentioned in GFM documents and the *JGN*, was not used for making claims within and outside the nation-state.

The earliest reference to human rights is in the sixth number of the *JGN*, which reprints a November 1977 piece from the *Sunday Gleaner* in which the editor-in-chief Hector Wynter cites a recent Miami referendum overturning a law pledging equal rights to homosexuals. Wynter does not go into a discussion about "What makes sexual choice a human right?" Instead, he forwards the view that a right or freedom recognized as basic and fundamental cannot be destroyed because of majority opinion (*JGN* 1977, 4). The *JGN* read this as a statement supporting rights for homosexuals. In expressing the view that "minority rights can never be decided by the majority," the February 3, 1978 editorial echoes Hector Wynter's opinion. The stand illustrates a conundrum facing many postcolonial sexuality movements: the human rights framework to assert the dignity, security, and health of the population is very often against the majority opinion which considers homosexuality unnatural and abhorrent; since democracies are premised on majorities, majority opinions are not easily altered and often seep into legislative and judicial systems. Hence, in the absence of a broad national consensus guaranteeing rights, postcolonial LGBTQ+ movements must seek other ways to press minoritarian claims on the majority.

Within Jamaica, the opinions of a majority against the claims of a despised, persecuted, and criminalized minority had already been tested in relation to Rastafarians, though without directly invoking the vocabulary of human rights. A significant body of work in the previous decade, including a groundbreaking report by UWI academics M. G. Smith, Roy Augier, and Nettleford, had cleared the ground to reinstate the dignity, even nobility, of Rastafari as a mode of Afro-Caribbean existence with a unique place in mainstream Jamaica (1967a, 1967b). One way in which GFM-*JGN* made connections between a despised minority cultural identity and a despised racial minority sexuality was the *JGN*'s Rasta column analyzed earlier in this chapter. Making the Rasta-gay connection was important for the GFM on several levels: both groups were often persecuted because of their appearance, social practices, and sexual choices; both were criminalized, attacked, blackmailed, and imprisoned on charges of vagrancy and loitering; both imagined migration as a way of escaping Jamaican moralism and conservatism. Unlike gay and lesbian people, the Rastas had carved out alternative economic, social, and familial structures within Jamaica while invoking migration to Ethiopia as a desired goal. The Rastas thus presented an available model of religious, racial, and community formation that had recently been accorded some respect and recognition. While the GFM did make these connections, they were never explicit and consistent.

With the majority opinion versus minority rights dilemma unresolved, the GFM-*JGN* invoked constitutionally guaranteed rights synonymously with human rights to stake claims to publicness. During the first three years, human rights were mentioned intermittently in editorials and in Aquarius's regular column "Personally Speaking." The *JGN* addressed human rights internationally by documenting persecution of gays and lesbians in several parts of the world including Canada, Ireland, US, Iran, Greece etc. and nationally by covering incidents of violence in Jamaica. I shall examine the transnational dimension shortly; for now, I turn to the ways in which the GFM falteringly initiated the (human) rights conversation within Jamaica. Its rights claims were not addressed to a specific political party, rather the organization culled elements from the programs and agendas of both the Manley-led PNP and the Seaga-led JLP. This strategy was outlined in Ginger's article "Politics and Us" which professes an indifference to the change from the capitalist to the socialist system in the country, considering "human rights" and "human justice" as crucial non-party principles to argue for gay equality (Ginger 1977, 1). Three numbers later, JLP's "Equal Rights and Justice" campaign was called out for its lack of discussion on homosexuals (*JGN* 1978n). As the more conservative of the two parties at the time, the JLP came in for a larger share of the blame especially when one of its affiliates, the Nationalist Patriotic Movement, wrote to the GFM expressing a contradictory stance on gay rights, first by asserting that gay people "deserved" privileges enjoyed by other members of society, and then by recommending "psychiatric treatment" for them. In a strongly worded response sent to the JLP, and reprinted in the *JGN*, GFM threatened to withdraw electoral support from the JLP and its affiliates in the next elections (*JGN* 1978p, 2).

Two instances of the GFM's political distance from party and ideological affiliations stand out. The first is when members of the Jamaican Defense Force picked up five members of the community in a JLP-controlled area in Kingston on the pretext of providing them employment, only to gun them down. The incident is known as the "Green Bay Massacre" of 1978 (JGN 1978o). Long considered one of the most egregious violations of human rights in Jamaica, the JGN's response is strange to say the least. The editor castigates a member of the army who insulted the Major-General implicated in the Green Bay incident. The editorial vividly describes the feminized insults hurled at the Major General and his tearful, emotional response to the charges, but does not comment on the Major's well-known and well-publicized "governmental acquiescence" to murderous violence. This reprehensible indifference to state-sponsored murders refuses to implicate the PNP, which formed the government at the time. In the interests of political neutrality, the JGN did not take a position on the incident; however, raising it seemed important since the movement and its publication had consistently advocated human rights. The trade-offs in a politically 'neutral' position were that while the movement could not access party-based affiliations to press forward its claims, it would not be caught in the political crossfire that enveloped garrison communities in Kingston around this time. The second instance of political distancing occurred when the JGN commended the Revolutionary Marxist League of Jamaica for including a statement of support for oppressed groups, including women, gays, and black people, in one of their publications (JGN 1979d). Significantly, the statement first appeared in a publication sent by the Revolutionary Socialist League of New York, with which the Jamaican body was affiliated. As in the previous instance of political neutrality, these national-transnational circulations do not indicate the GFM's revolutionary or socialist leanings.

The GFM had always maintained international connections, most notably reciprocal publication exchanges with the Canadian gay magazine *The Body Politic*, and with North American gay and lesbian organizations. These influences are reflected in its rights claims, sexual health education programs, and pride celebrations. An undated statement titled "Gay Rights Are Human Rights" addressed to "fellow Jamaicans, in particular the more than 100,000 gays across the island" in the archives is the clearest exposition of these claims. There are two handwritten corrections on this document: first, the organization asserts "freedom of thought and conscience" but eliminates the phrase "in the practice of our lifestyles"; second, it claims "freedom of opinion and expression, including the right to equal access to mass media" by eliminating the word "any" as a qualifier for "media" and substituting it with "mass." This statement is reiterated and circulated in the JGN and the *Sunday Gleaner* to publicize the 1981 pride celebrations demonstrating that the GFM claimed and sometimes secured access to "mass" media. From the 1980s onwards it communicated with international organizations involved either in gay or lesbian rights or, more broadly, human rights advocacy. These included the International Gay Association (later renamed the International Lesbian and Gay Association) and, later, Amnesty International. The GFM decided to seek IGA membership in its early years, announcing the formation of the body in its November 24, 1978 newsletter. Perhaps due to steep fees, the membership plan could not be implemented until 1981 when the GFM became a full member with voting rights. *JGN* regularly reported on the annual conferences of the IGA and the GFM was invited to submit a report for the second conference in Barcelona read by the Canadian delegation.

Over the years, while the *JGN* continued to report on international (especially US) gay activism, it developed close international links with British and Scottish activists involved with the ILGA, which was seeking consultative status with the United Nations and pressuring Amnesty International to recognize gay prisoners of conscience. Despite taking a backseat in the GFM by then, Chang was its official representative at the third ILGA conference in Turin, Italy, his travel facilitated by a contribution from the Scottish Homosexual Rights Group. The GFM's contacts with the ILGA were crucial for its participation in transnational sexual rights advocacy and its focus on human rights was coterminous with these contacts. The ILGA and the International Human Rights Commission had some impact on the GFM's agenda and the direction of its activism, though the North American influence was more sustained as seen in the Canadian and American documents on pride, health awareness, and human rights received by the organization.

This was a period of turmoil for the organization following Chang's resignation as general secretary and editor. In an interview with Thomas Glave, Chang mentioned that his decision to step down was to give the organization a face more representative of predominantly black Jamaican society (Chang 2012). St. Hope Thomas, an Afro-Jamaican, assumed the editorship of the *JGN* in 1980, the year the GFM finalized its constitution and changed its structure hoping that assigned leadership roles and division of responsibilities would streamline functioning. Its statement of aims and objectives emphasizes that the focus was to "raise gay consciousness and awareness," "provide counselling and support," "remove homophobic prejudice and ignorance through public education," "protest anti-gay oppression," "press for the repeal of anti-homosexual laws," and "raise funds for a gay community center" (GFM 1980, 7). Once the constitution was finalized, various "action groups" produced materials and planned events that fell within their respective remits. An undated fact sheet of the organization's activities was prepared by the Involvement Group, perhaps in 1980 after the constitution was finalized. The fact sheet describes the social, political, and sexual perception as well as self-image of gay people in Jamaica (GFM "Fact Sheet"). Another undated document with the ILGA inspired logo of a lambda inside a triangle contains research on sexual minorities in Jamaica, including a brief reference to gay rights as human rights (GFM n.d. b).

Much of the research and writing in this brochure found its way into GFM/Chang's "position paper" for the ILGA conference in Turin, providing the racial, economic, and cultural background in Jamaica to contextualize the situation of sexual minorities in the country. Its findings are based on a study of gay people in the larger Kingston area where "eighty two percent are satisfied/happy with their sexuality and would not accept counselling for change" and on informed speculations about other parts of the island, "gays in Jamaica generally have a very low level of consciousness, when it comes to their rights to their sexual preference" (GFM 1981a, 6, 11). Significantly, human rights are not mentioned in this docu-ment or in Chang's notes from the conference (GFM 1981b). Despite the GFM's continued and growing connections with what Joseph Massad has disparagingly called "Gay International" (2007, 160–190) – led by bodies such as ILGA, Amnesty, and Human Rights Watch – the group decided on a path which did not explicitly focus on transnationally directed human rights advocacy. My findings reiterate Chin's important observation that,

> Although GFM's political work was deeply informed by its relationship with individuals and organizations overseas as well as by a model of "gay" sexual subjectivity, GFM members were nevertheless compelled to recognize the limits of gay modes of political action developed in places such as Britain, Canada, and the United States for achieving erotic autonomy in Jamaica.
>
> (2019a, 31)

A homegrown understanding of human rights was facilitated by the Jamaica Council for Human Rights (JCHR) formed in 1968 and funded largely by the European Union to abolish the death penalty in the country. The GFM used JCHR's brochure *Citizens' Rights: Police Powers* (1981) to summarize legal information for gay men facing harassment or blackmail. There seems to have been little contact with JCHR since it is not one of the social or cultural bodies in *JGN*'s mailing list of state officials and national organizations. The GFM's three-pronged focus during the 1980s was youth support, prisoner outreach, and health initiatives. While these established the humanity, dignity, and rights of people facing discrimination, the GFM was not overly reliant on human rights claims unlike the later efforts of J-FLAG. In part because its mission was cultural and educational in terms of encouraging the acceptance of gay lives, the GFM's efforts were less reliant on building a case against the Jamaican state nationally or internationally.

Decolonizing sexuality

J-FLAG – the acronym representing unfulfilled promises of flag independence for sexual minorities in Jamaica – originated and rose to prominence within a cultural and political climate marked by an unprecedented rise in homophobic violence. In a speech on freedom of the press and human rights, Nettleford mentions freedom of expression as a fundamental right of people of all races, classes, sexual orientation, and political affiliations. Expressing the majority versus minority dilemma, he states that "the Caribbean is fertile ground for the mushrooming of claims that would after all seek to protect the individual from excesses of terroristic minorities or the tyranny of overbearing majorities." In the same speech he breaks his characteristic silence about sexuality to mention that the majority/minority contradictions "find form in sexual issues of the moment and blasphemous libel," alluding to former Prime

Minister Seaga's insinuations about the current officeholder P.J. Patterson's homosexuality in 1993 (Nettleford 2001/2005, 32). Seaga notoriously invoked Buju Banton's "Boom bye bye" advocating death to homosexuals to hint at Patterson's sexuality. The debate resurfaced in 2005 with JLP's use of T.O.K.'s equally homophobic song "Chi Chi Man." In response, Patterson publicly declared his heterosexuality and dissociated himself from repealing the law criminalizing homosexuality.

Despite political parties' opportunistic deployment of sexuality to stir up public sentiment, J-FLAG has assiduously attempted to shape public opinion on sexual and gender diversity over the past three decades. Like the GFM, J-FLAG brought out a gay newsletter (initially titled *Hotness!* and later renamed *The Jamaica Outpost*) circulated via snail mail and its website. Like the *JGN*, this short-lived publication sought to report on events within the community and reach out to health professionals, educational bodies, law enforcement agencies, cultural institutions, and religious leadership. The similarities between the aims of the two organizations are unsurprising since some GFM members including Brian Williamson and Chang were instrumental in founding J-FLAG. The material and social exigencies encountered by the GFM have continually hindered J-FLAG during its existence: in late 2018 the building housing the organization burnt down rendering it as homeless as the GFM had been throughout its existence. Greater visibility of gay men and lesbians in Jamaica over the past three decades has led to incidents of extortion and violence, including the murder of activists like Williamson, making it imperative to combine educational efforts with rights claims addressing the socio-legal construction of sexualities in Jamaica.

GFM-*JGN*'s print-mediated community embraced rights talk to understand the Jamaican situation in relation to transnational activism largely under the aegis of the then newly formed ILGA. J-FLAG's sexual activism since its formation in 1998 – marking 50 years of the Universal Declaration of Human Rights (UDHR) and the year in which Jamaica withdrew as a State Party from the Optional Protocol to the International Covenant on Civil and Political Rights (ICCPR) – is less reliant on the ephemerality of print; it hosts a website that indicates a multifaceted political effort to work towards gay liberation and maintains an active social media presence on Facebook and Twitter.[12] J-FLAG's efforts to form a national and diasporic community enable it to press rights claims forcefully within and outside Jamaica. In its collaborations with Amnesty, Human Rights Watch, and ILGA, it provides "evidence" for transnational human rights regimes on incidents of vigilante violence against homosexuals leading to grave injury and death, police apathy to such incidents, police atrocities against gay men, sexual abuse in prisons, religious stigmatization, and rampant medical discrimination against people living with AIDS and other sexually transmitted diseases.

J-FLAG has produced an impressive body of documentation, research, and aggregative record of advocacy to challenge the Jamaican state's apathy and inaction on violence against LGBTQ+ people in the country. It has done so by pointing out glaring exclusions from the Vision 2030 plan produced by the Jamaican government, focusing on human rights, economic, and social justice in the context of "sustainable development." Its vision is coalitional, and the demand for sexual liberation is one among other demands to empower people with physical and mental disabilities, the homeless, the elderly, women, and children, and to secure economic justice for all Jamaicans (J-FLAG 2016). J-FLAG's contributions to other global forums include work on the Shadow Report on Human Rights Violations against LGBT People in Jamaica submitted to the UN Human Rights Committee in 2015 based on the research conducted by the organization over the previous decade. It is one of several signatories with three LGBTQ+ organizations and the University of the West Indies at Mona (J-FLAG et al. 2016). J-FLAG *narrates* forms of discrimination and suffering within and outside Jamaica much like the GFM did through its newsletter.

The stakes of these interventions are vastly different from the GFM era in four significant ways that characterize postcolonial sexual activism. First, when GFM expressed gay and lesbian demands for recognition and respect, the only available counterpublic was the *JGN*. This work is now accomplished through several Jamaican and diasporic forms and forums: literature about gay and lesbian lives within and outside the country by Michelle Cliff, Nicole Dennis-Benn, Patricia Powell, Staceyann Chin, Thomas Glave, Kei Miller, Marlon James; analyses by M. Jacqui Alexander, Natasha Tinsley, Rosamond King, Faith Smith, Gloria Wekker; filmic representations by Phillip Pike, Micah Fink, Selena Blake; and organizations addressing the specific needs of multiple gender identities and sexual orientations such as J-FLAG affiliates, WeChange for LBT women, Equality Youth Jamaica, and TransWave. Second, postcolonial advocacy organizations today operate in a highly volatile globalized media environment where those in the country respond to well publicized narratives of sexual disempowerment circulated by actors with little or no knowledge of local economies. A case in point is the thoughtless American campaign to boycott Jamaican products, specifically Redstripe Beer, as a symbolic gesture against homophobia. As J-FLAG pointed out in its response, the beer is produced by a Jamaican company which has always distanced itself from homophobia.[13] Another instance is the wholesale denunciation of Jamaican dancehall as homophobic disregarding its different strands of music including many queer performers. Third, rampant sexual violence against gay men, lesbian, and straight women, HIV-AIDS and other health crises have made postcolonial nation-states somewhat more responsive to the precarity of sexual minorities. Though largely crisis-oriented, some nation-states have established bodies with streams of national and transnational funding and expertise to address this precarity. Jamaica's national policy on AIDS which draws on the expertise of UNAIDS is a case in point. Finally, though painfully slow, there is a perceptible social and cultural shift. Dressed in a t-shirt in the colors of the Jamaican flag, Demaro's video shows him walking into a laundromat where drag performer Jahlove Serrano sashays to the music before the scene cuts to Demaro sitting on a street corner liming with a Rasta elder. The visual splicing indicates a scenario where racial and sexual marginalization can be countered by contingent or permanent intergenerational alliances in Jamaica as in the imagined Rasta persona Ja Will in the *JGN*.

The difference in scale and reach between the GFM and J-FLAG's human rights activism is that whereas the GFM was responding to here and now violations to redress the vulnerabilities of gay and lesbian lives, it did not (and indeed could not, given the need for secrecy), address structural state reform, focusing instead on "episodic" actions combating violence and discrimination "on a day-to-day basis in the expectation that incremental progression...in human rights culture may thus be advanced" (Baxi 2002/2008, 77). The episodic activism had an educational and cultural direction because a definitive vision for Jamaican decolonization including black cultural recognition, organicism, voluntarism, freedom of expression, and a growing sense of self-worth was available. Despite being plugged into human rights languages as "products of intergovernmental and NGO politics of desire" (Baxi 2002/2008, 35), in many ways J-FLAG's activism remains as episodic as that of the GFM. Its meticulous reports, video documentation, and media appearances document celebration, exuberance, and the push and pull of community formation amid setbacks and tragedies. J-FLAG attests to the *affective resilience of gay and lesbian lives* that is also the enduring legacy of the GFM-*JGN* archive.

It is hard to celebrate when there are so many deaths and losses to mourn. J-FLAG and its predecessor the GFM-*JGN* formed postcolonial sexual counterpublics to secure the safety, dignity, and empowerment of sexually vulnerable populations, allowing us to imagine a not-too-distant future where "betta mus cum" for LGBTQ+ Jamaicans.

Notes

1 The phrase is used in the *Jamaica Gaily News*. It riffs off Jamaican politician and People's National Party leader Michael Manley's 1972 campaign slogan "Better Must Come."

2 Sistren Theatre Collective is a Jamaican grassroots women's theatre group formed in the 1970s. It is still active. The group was formed under the auspices of the Jamaican School of Drama (JSD) headed by Dennis Scott, noted Jamaican dancer, playwright, poet, and educator.

3 Tracy Robinson's "A Loving Freedom: A Caribbean Feminist Aesthetic" is a review essay on M. Jacqui Alexander's book *Pedagogies of Crossing: Meditations on Feminism, Sexual Politics, Memory, and the Sacred.*

4 See the articles "Speakeasy Attack," *JGN* 29 (October 13), 1978a; "Editorial," *JGN* 42 (April 27), 1979a; "Speakeasy Fracas," *JGN* 43 (May 11), 1979b; "Lesbian Row Ends in Stabbing," *JGN* 23 (July 21) 1978b.

5 See the articles "DJ Held for Buggery," *JGN* 2 (January 20), 1978c; "Freed of Buggery Charge," *JGN* 19 (May 12), 1978d; "Gay Man Killed," *JGN* 25 (August 18), 1978e; "Suicide Attempts: At Home and Abroad," *JGN* 56 (January 19), 1980a.

6 Matthew Chin mentioned in a personal communication (2020) that some bars and clubs were generally open to the public though it was known that they would become "gay" bars after a certain time. There were also popular gay cruising spots where men would meet for sex (such as Tom Red Cam Road). These clubs and cruising spots were not mentioned in *JGN* but came up frequently during Chin's interviews with former GFM members.

7 In contrast to these efforts by the Kingston based GFM, the Montego Bay GFM acquired a base within months of its inception. As reported in the *JGN* article entitled "GFM Mobay Gets Own Centre" on April 4, 1980, the center was a house acquired

through the good offices of Brian Williamson. Plans included the setting up of a non-commercial club and a hostel for visitors and tourists (*JGN* 1980b).

8 The names have been anonymized because at least one individual does not want their real name to be used.

9 The last two numbers were 79 and 80 published in April/May and June 1984 respectively (*JGN* 1984c and 1984d).

10 Matthew Chin examines the connections between Rasta and gay identity by unpacking the term "gaydren," a composite of the words gay and bredren, to make important connections between race, gender, and sexual orientation. In Rasta vocabulary "the presumed subject and addressee of *bredren* is not only raced (black) and classed (poor) but also gendered (male)," in opposition to the word "sistren that is used to address women" (2019a, 30).

11 "Mampala" is Jamaican for "feminized man." The column announced this gender fluidity in the *JGN*: "Look yah nuh, os who say mi a woman? Mi is nether man nor woman, so nuh mix mi up chile [Look here now, who says I am a woman? I am neither man nor woman, so don't mix me up, child]" (Mampala 1981d, 5).

12 See www.jflag.org/

13 For details about the controversy, including J-FLAG's appeal to the protestors, see Kei Miller's (2015) blog post: https://underthesaltireflag.com/2015/07/13/if-a-gay-man-screams-in-the-caribbean-and-a-white-man-isnt-there-to-hear-him-has-he-still-made-a-sound/

3

"RIGHTS A DI PLAN"[1]

Sistren and sexual solidarities in Jamaica

In 1978, Joan Ross, longest continuing editor of *Sistren*, and the person responsible for transforming it from a newsletter to a magazine with a national, pan-Caribbean, and international circulation, wrote to *Public Opinion* denouncing harassment of gay students at the University of the West Indies. The *Jamaica Gaily News* reprinted extracts from Ross's article to talk about connections between party-based politics and sexual politics:

> At least there is one sister who uses her head and thinks for herself. She understands our position and is not prepared to react emotionally…if only Comrade Ross could get more of her colleagues in the party and the Government to see the justice and right of our case, we would be grateful. Many of us are just as socialist as the next comrade, but our distrusts of totalitarian demagogues inhibit our total commitment. In a choice between our ideology and our sexuality, our sexuality comes first for that is what we *are*, while our politics is what we choose. A very basic matter of priorities.
>
> (Gay Duncan, 1978, 5–6)

Sistren Theatre Collective, a working class women's group formed in 1977, began publishing its newsletter in 1979 around the same time as the *Jamaica Gaily News* was circulated clandestinely. Unlike the Gay Freedom Movement's wariness of politics, Sistren, which too originated amid a democratic socialist climate of social upliftment for disempowered populations, was inherently and openly political in its goal of social transformation. Though the collective was sometimes assumed to be affiliated to the People's National Party (PNP), which formed the government at the time, the party affiliations of its members spanned not just the PNP, but also the Worker's Party of Jamaica (WPJ).[2] Members of the collective advocated a broad analysis of political economy in which its popular education work involving

DOI: 10.4324/9781003170303-4

theatre, media production and analysis, academic research, and community outreach were geared toward transformative changes in the socio-economic position of women.

The collective's publication *Sistren* was initially a newsletter about its theatre work and national and international policies impacting Jamaican women, before it was reconceptualized as a magazine with a broad Caribbean focus in 1984. It was feminist in all but its name since the term was not popular in Jamaica during the 1970s. The magazine appeared about three times a year peaking at a circulation of three thousand copies. It was distributed nationally and internationally, though in the absence of formal records it is uncertain how much of the readership was international. In 2004, the building which housed Sistren in Kensington Crescent, Kingston, burnt to the ground destroying a large collection of material related to the history of the collective, among them extant copies of the newsletter. The collective is still active, but its limited scale of operations makes the process of a systematic archiving difficult to sustain. There are no copies of the newsletter (before it became a magazine) in any institutional holding in the United States or the Caribbean.[3] My account in this chapter is based on the digital archive of the magazine, conversations with members of Sistren and Women's Media Watch (WMW), and materials available at the University of the West Indies libraries. Wherever possible, I supplement this account by consulting the Caribbean Association for Feminist Research and Action (CAFRA) newsletter and the Barbados-based Women and Development Unit (WAND) publication *Woman Speak*. The Jamaican feminist archive in this chapter thus begins when the gay and lesbian one discontinues.

Activist and social movement literature such as *Sistren* are important though partial sources in understanding the regional context of Jamaican legislation on sexual rights within the Caribbean.[4] Jamaica is one among the many countries in the region which criminalize homosexuality and one of the few which has not yet legalized abortion. Sistren's community theatre, consciousness raising, and its magazine never directly connected sexual and reproductive autonomy as pressing concerns of the Caribbean women's movement. Increased political and sexualized violence during the decades Sistren was most active made its theatrical and print interventions both timely and urgent but also prevented it from addressing non-normative sexualities. In Jamaica, where women, woman-like behavior among men, and manly behavior among women are subject to heinous forms of gendered and sexualized violence, solidarities across differences are crucial to the project of worlding postcolonial sexualities through national, regional, and transnational advocacy. Demands for legislative and governmental responses to gender-based violence, health iniquities, outmoded colonial-era laws criminalizing specific sexual acts, and freedom of reproductive choice can be the basis of these solidarities, though no visible Jamaican organizations explicitly made these claims in the 1980s.[5]

Building on Chapter 2, my aim in this chapter is to establish continuities between women's, gay, and lesbian activism while making it explicit that continuity of preoccupations does not always lead to solidarities between social

FIGURE 3.1 Cover image of an early *Sistren* newsletter reporting on the collective's theatrical performances. Image courtesy of Joan Ross-Frankson, Joan French, and the Sistren Theatre Collective.

movements. Jamaica's neoliberal trajectories of development, staunchly Christian beliefs of large sections of the population, and heteropatriarchal codes are entangled with Euro-colonization and male nationalism.[6] The question I ask in relation to women's, gay, and lesbian activism is this: if identities come into being in relation to larger bio-political issues and languages of power then under what conditions does space for LGBTQ+ identities and struggles become a political possibility in Caribbean societies like Jamaica? Caribbean and Latin American decolonial feminist thought – especially Sylvia Wynter and Maria Lugones's revisions of Anibal Quijano's concept "coloniality of power" – are useful in answering this question (Wynter 1990; Lugones 2007). Too, policy documents and publications by transnational feminist organizations such as CAFRA and DAWN, housed in the Women's and Development Unit (WAND), Barbados from 1990–1996 provide a possible roadmap to Jamaican women's long, difficult, and sometimes derailed drive to securing their rights (Sen & Grown 1987). While feminist, gay, and lesbian solidarities are crucial to advance legislative and rights claims of women and sexual minorities in Jamaica and other Southern nations, there is very little evidence of such alliances in *Sistren* magazine. The minimal LGBT language in the magazine reflected the influence of middle class members of the group, especially in the numbers edited in the early 1990s. The overall trajectory of the Sistren Collective indicates that rather than name their politics as explicitly feminist or queer, members chose to work through practice and not through identity or activist categories.

"Chatting" about research

Sistren's contribution to popular theatre and community building based on personal testimonies of members has been studied for its innovative methods of collective creation. In the absence of performance records of Sistren's interventions, the magazine is an important postcolonial feminist historical source. There is, by now, a body of scholarship on class-based differences in training, education, experiences, and life circumstances of the theatre collective's core membership which facilitated as well as challenged their process of collective creation.[7] The power relationship between classes and the "educated" and "uneducated" was a real but dynamic divide that expressed itself in different cultures of communication even as the process enhanced recognition of the local language, making everyone who engaged into a learner as well as a teacher. The popular education drama methods and workshops of the collective were designed to challenge the social and language divide, as were the production of materials using comic strip formats. The range of communication approaches in the magazine reflected the group's determination to overcome racial, employment, informational, and educational divides in Jamaica. Even as the magazine reported on the group's theatrical activities within and outside the country, and announced new performances and news about its members and "friends'" research, educational, and creative activities, it was also a forum for research on Caribbean women and community activities already underway. What follows is an analysis of Sistren's conversational forays ("chats") into research and the national-transnational networks which connected and supported this work.

As women professionals drew close to Sistren as resource persons or called on the group to support their work in prisons or with AIDS patients, timely responses to this interaction emerged. One such response was Sistren Research founded by university-educated, white collar professionals Honor Ford-Smith and Joan French in 1983; it also included Joan Ross, Imani Tafara-Ama, and Hilary Nicholson (from Women's Media Watch), and several visiting international scholars. The collective "recognized the dearth of information about gender relations in Jamaica" and set up a unit to "research women's situation in Jamaica, popularize the findings, and lend support to women's groups in participatory processes" (*Sistren* 1991a, 25). Lest Sistren Research be construed as securely employed women imposing their priorities on a working class theatre group – an expedient though intellectually lazy critique prevalent in the work of at least one researcher (Smith 2008,

2013) – I reiterate that its findings did not lead to esoteric scholarship. It was cross-fertilization and dual consciousness-raising across colors and classes that developed the collective into one of the most inclusive and innovative lobbies for women's rights in the global South. Far from being an avenue of self-promotion and career advancement, Sistren Research circulated its studies and analysis among a cross-class selection of readers in Jamaica, the Caribbean, and the diaspora for opinions and advice. Among its various activities were publications on the history of women and work, illustrated booklets on sexual violence and the early Jamaican women's movement, several video productions, at least two traveling exhibitions, and many historical studies of women in political and labor struggles.

Sistren Research's landmark achievement was *Lionheart Gal: Life Stories of Jamaican Women* (1987), published to national and international acclaim. Comprising life narratives of thirteen subaltern and two middle class women from the collective, it contained accounts of their childhood, access to or denial of educational opportunities, familial and sexual relationships, work, and situatedness in urban and rural Jamaica. Louise Bennett-Coverley, whose poems popularized the use of Jamaican patwah (patois), launched the book. *Lionheart Gal* was widely reviewed in several academic and popular forums, and *Sistren* magazine carried some of these reviews. While reviewers were unanimous in their positive opinion on the format and structure, Carol Lawes specifically commented on "differences in style and rhythms of speech" of the various narratives indicating the care that had gone into "making this very readable, and…continuing efforts to standardize the writing of the Jamaican language" (1986–1987, 16). Caribbean scholar Sylvia Wynter has ascribed a "generational" quality to the autobiographical, "personal is the political" credo in which second and third wave feminism was articulated within and outside Jamaica (Wynter & Scott 2000, 137). *Lionheart Gal* illustrates this generational quality, sealing Sistren's already formidable reputation of producing theatre based on women's lived experiences to provide a model of feminist analysis that has stood the test of time. The magazine serialized extracts from the book for readers who may not have had ready access to the expensive foreign publication.

Sistren Research's work on Jamaican women activists from the early to mid-twentieth century led to a series of presentations, article-length publications, informational booklets, reports, and media productions. Ford-Smith and French's collaboration on the participation of Jamaican women in the 1938 labor uprising yielded the landmark study, "Women's Labor and Organisation in Jamaica, 1900–1938." The project was supported by Saskia Wieringa and Rhoda Reddock as part of a larger initiative exploring women's struggles and research in colonial and contemporary society, bringing together women from all part of the world, including Africa and Asia. Among these were Chaya Dattar and Nandita Gandhi who are recognized as foundational figures in the Indian Women's Movement. French and Ford-Smith sought inputs from "community group members, Sistren members, and University lecturers" to "test interest and readability at various levels" and seek the "rigours of intellectual scrutiny" (*Sistren* 1986a, 10). The research unit conducted a participatory workshop dramatizing the lives of four important figures from the early Jamaican women's movement (Amy Ashwood Garvey, Amy Bailey, Adina Spencer, and Molly Huggins) in a skit enacted by Sistren members. Couple of years later this study was the basis of a video docu-drama, *Miss Amy and Miss May*, based on the lives of Amy Bailey and May Farquharson. Since both activists were alive at the time, they had an opportunity to view the film as a moving cross-generational feminist tribute (Francis-Hinds 1990; Brown 1990). In 1996 the unit produced *The Drums Keep Sounding*, a docu-drama on the life of Jamaican performance poet Louise Bennett-Coverley. This research was accessible to readers across Jamaica and the Caribbean in the form of two booklets: *No to Sexual Violence* and *Wid Dis Ring*. When readers wrote to request access to studies conducted by the research unit, the magazine serialized Ford-Smith's literary history of the Jamaican writer Una Marson over three numbers from 1993 to 1994.[8]

Sistren's attempts to balance research-driven work with accessibility and wide reach meant that it juggled various styles of communication. The transcription of Jamaican patwah in *Lionheart Gal*, graphic booklets, and in the cartoon strip "Sista Ansa A Granny Chat 'Bout..." ensured that the magazine conveyed its analysis to academic and popular readership. In its early iterations, the comic strip by long time member, drummer, and artist Mbala was text-heavy with illustrations used to initiate (not necessarily advance) the analysis. In 1985, "Sista Ansa A Chat 'Bout De Decade," introduced the UN Decade for women. Ansa (Jamaican for "answer"), compares the historical and contemporary situation of women by drawing on her grandmother's account of times past. Speaking of the "housewifization" of post-colonial Jamaican women, Granny rejects the idea of the male breadwinner to argue for increases in the wages of female workers in the free zone. Ansa and Granny castigate UN conference planners in Nairobi for ignoring ordinary women who "neva did even know seh 1976–1985 was dedicated to the advancement of woman" since "wi neva did get no advancement." They state their demands forcefully:

> We waan di information we me hear seh dem collect in de last 10 years fi put pon toppa we experience fi build we movement. For woman ready fi move; we ready fi lead weself, and we waan well covered on all fronts so we in a better position fi win...[We want the information we heard they had collected in the last 10 years to connect with our experience to build our movement. Women are ready to move; we are ready to lead ourselves, and we want to be prepared on all fronts so that we are in a better position to win].
>
> (*Sistren* 1985a, 12)

Articulated in patwah, these views reflect the findings of an important study by DAWN which concludes that "rather than improving, the socioeconomic status of the great majority of Third World women has worsened considerably throughout the Decade" (Sen & Grown 1987, 16). From the next number Sista Ansa was an illustrated page-length feature covering Caribbean participation in international women's organizing, their role in subsistence and waged economies, experiences of infidelity, domestic, and intimate partner violence. In another comic strip, Granny makes structural connections between different aspects of the economy to convince Ansa of the links between a rally for peace and the cost of medications in the country. The narrative arc establishes that governmental expenditure on weapons led to lack of money for public health provisions, increasing the prices of medicines for common people. The artist represents then Jamaican Prime Minister, Edward Seaga, conveying to US President Ronald Reagan a decision "to cut back on education and health so that we can pay back our loan" (*Sistren* 1985b, 4). The page consistently critiqued neocolonial policies of the Jamaican state. As one of the most regular features of the magazine, it survived *Sistren*'s editorial changes after Ross-Frankson. When the magazine introduced thematic numbers – on the economic crisis, the environment, technology, sports, laws concerning women, and the family – Sister Ansa's conversations commented on these themes.

By the 1980s there was a circle of individuals and organizations labelled "Friends of Sistren," themselves involved in gender advocacy and community education. The Friends network was the impetus for Women's Media Watch (WMW) which has documented Jamaican media representations of women over the past three decades. Judith Wedderburn mentioned in a group conversation that WMW was one of the various groups for action, advocacy, and education formed out of a UNESCO-Sistren workshop, and the only one which continued to function over the years (Wedderburn and Members of WMW 2015). WMW arose as a response to sexually explicit media representations. Sistren was the first feminist organization to critique the media's objectification of women. The collective voiced objections to violence against women in ways that could not be ignored, thus bringing the matter into public discourse.[9] The magazine allows a glimpse of this multipronged emphasis (drama, workshops, and advocacy) in Sistren's objection to an advertisement by the

FIGURE 3.2 Section of the column "Sista Ansa A Chat 'Bout De Decade" that appeared in the 1985 number of *Sistren*. Image courtesy of Joan Ross-Frankson, Joan French, and the Sistren Theatre Collective.

Jamaica National Investment Promotion Bureau declaring "Your Bottom Line is Beautiful When you Make it in Jamaica" (*Sistren* 1987, 1). When the American feminist magazine *Ms* received a copy of the advertisement it condemned the sexual objectification in a letter reprinted by *Sistren*: "When things in this country have reached the stage where an organization managed by a woman can publish such an advertisement, then we have indeed 'come a long way, baby' and it has all been downhill" (McHardy 1987, 10). Undoubtedly national and international publicity led to a shaming that the Investment Promotion Bureau could ill afford. It withdrew the ad following a protest letter and a meeting between the managing director of the company and several Sistren members. This indicates there was already a feminist counterpublic of readers of the magazine. Among those commenting on media images of violence against women were Samere Tansley, a founding member of WMW. Hilary Nicholson, another WMW founder, became an important performer in the theatre collective and a researcher-writer for *Sistren*. These relationships between Sistren and WMW indicate the cross-fertilization of organizations in documenting and contesting various forms of representational and structural violence against women. I analyze some of their strategies later in the chapter.

As with the Indian collective Manushi and the South African women's collectives Speak and Agenda, active during the same years (see Chapters 4 and 7), Sistren emerged in the larger context of national and institutional discussions on gender policies. This context influences the analysis of structural factors impacting women's lives in the wider Caribbean region in the magazine. Two early articles set the tone for this analysis. Camille Lampart covered a university seminar on gender and development in the Caribbean to indicate how established formats of scholarly discussions did not encourage participation or inspire attendees. Observing that despite being very active in redressing gender and economic disparities, many women in Jamaica were still wary of the label feminist, she commends Sistren's sessions in the seminar as "rays of sunshine when we seemed to be drowning in the flood of scholarly papers" (Lampart 1987, 13). Lampart's observation about the university Women's Studies group's reluctance to be one of the focal points for the women's movement in the country explains the importance of feminist collectives in spaces outside universities and political parties. Though they closely collaborated with Women and Development units at the University of the West Indies, especially after the formation of CAFRA, Jamaican feminists also organized themselves as the Association of Women's Organizations of Jamaica (AWOJA) in 1988. Ross-Frankson's article on the Caribbean Women's Movement describes a regional meeting of CAFRA in Barbados to note that over 50 organizations were part of an umbrella body emerging out of the meeting (Ross-Frankson 1989a, 18).

CAFRA and DAWN, transnational organizations formed during the years the collective was most active, served as conduits of information for Sistren. In 1990, the DAWN Secretariat shifted to the WAND unit at UWI Barbados under the leadership of Peggy Antrobus. Appointed as Special Advisor on women by the Government of Jamaica in the 1970s, Antrobus, an early and consistent supporter of Sistren, was instrumental in founding the Bureau of Women's Affairs in the

FIGURE 3.3 Notice about withdrawal of a sexist advertisement by the Jamaica National Investment Promotion Bureau in *Sistren* magazine. Image courtesy of Joan Ross-Frankson, Joan French, and the Sistren Theatre Collective.

country. Many of her ideas on structural adjustment, its impact on women and development, and South-South women's organizing – including extracts from speeches, policy papers, and interviews – influenced the collective and find their way into the pages of the magazine. Antrobus in turn has acknowledged her enduring personal and official association with Sistren as a feminist model. Antrobus was also associated with CAFRA, Sistren's source for a pan-Caribbean perspective on legal reform impacting women and children. CAFRA provided a platform for Sistren's popular education efforts in the region and a forum for meetings and workshops leading up to the UN conference in Beijing in 1995.

The *work* of gender and sex

Bringing women's personal experiences into the public sphere, Sistren explored sexual and reproductive violence as central concerns in its life-narratives shaped into drama (Ford-Smith 1989). In later years, the collective moved to a theatre and research methodology based on broader socio-economic analysis. Sistren's gamut of concerns arising from and beyond life-narratives reimagined gender by having its female members play most male roles in the theatrical productions. The productions represented all-female communities connected through experiences of exploitative plantation practices leading to labor uprisings in the Anglophone Caribbean, the subject of Ford-Smith and French's collaborative research (*Ida Revolt inna Jonkonnu Stylee*), agricultural labor conditions of the Jamaican sugar workers (*The Case of Iris Armstrong*), Jamaican histories of rebellion (*Nana Yah*), urban domestic and factory labor reflecting the group's documentation of women's egregious work situations (*Domestick, Downpression Get a Blow*), urban violence and gang warfare in members' communities (*Muffet Inna All Wi*), housing problems faced by Jamaicans including group members (*Buss Out*), experiences of motherhood and old age based on life-stories and actual conditions in hospitals and old age homes (*Bellywoman Bangarang, QPH*), and struggles to achieve maternity benefits (*Bandoolu Version*).

Exploring multiple connotations of "wuk" (work) as means of livelihood, politicization, and sexual acts, this segment of my analysis describes the ways in which the magazine presented the collective's efforts to transform gender norms and sexual roles as necessary *work* without labeling these efforts radical or feminist. I take this deep dive into the work of gender and sexuality aware that Sistren was not able to confront the question of LGBTQ+ identities or politics either consistently or overtly. Some members of the group were wary of the label feminist and did not want to risk being taken for "sodomites." Others explored relationships with women in their private lives without publicly acknowledging these relationships. Ironically, as the group took its theatre to various parts of the Caribbean, Europe, and North America, the members were sometimes labeled man-haters and sodomites.

The magazine adapted the theatre collective's autobiographical, research, educational, and performance-based content to produce innovative features and articles on gender roles and expectations. Despite her objections to feminist autobiography (Sistren's primary method of analysis), Sylvia Wynter's ideas are crucial to understanding Sistren's goals of decolonization through its drama, community workshops, and activist literature. As part of her attempt to keep race center stage in the analysis of the "human," Wynter struggles against feminists' primary attention to gender. Wynter's ideas dislodge the colonial view of "Man" understood as the white European male exercise of power over "natives." Here is a statement from her famous afterword to *Out of the Kumbla*, a collection of essays on Caribbean women's writing:

In effect, rather than only voicing the "native" woman's hitherto silenced voice we shall ask: What is the systematic function of her own silencing both as women and, more totally, as "native" women? Of what mode of speech is that absence of speech both as women (masculinist women) and as "native" women (feminist discourse) as imperative function?

(Wynter 1990, 365)

Wynter's query is similar to Gayatri Spivak's famous question: "Can the subaltern speak?" (1988). In other words: how do privileged middle class interlocutors listen to native/subaltern women's speech? In Southern nations such as Jamaica, India, and South Africa, subalternity is often a condition of structural disadvantage involving food and shelter concerns compounded by lack of education, employment, safe housing, healthcare, pervasive violence, and denial of access to cultural institutions. Sistren's theatrical work was a mode of speech that enabled its members and audiences to listen to previously unheard voices and to develop strategies to combat subaltern silencing. The magazine continued this work. Ross-Frankson mentions that during her editorship she ensured the magazine closely replicated Sistren's methods of testimony and collective creation. She worked with contributors of different levels of literacy and writing skills to make their writing publishable (Ross-Frankson 2020). This often led to a characteristic publication format involving transcribed interviews, conversations, opinions, and comments.

Many of the experiences communicated in theatre and through the magazine were about sexual violence. Reports and articles reveal that sexual abuse of children was (and remains) endemic and frequent. Sistren's educational efforts against sexual violence included support of Teens in Action, a group formed after the rape and murder of a teenager in Seaview Gardens, West Kingston. Headed by the collective's founding member and a Seaview resident, Rebecca Knowles, the group was led by children to combat sexual abuse. Over the years it conducted workshops, discussions, and plays on sexual education, communicated between parents and children, and addressed youth unemployment and gang violence.[10] As in the case of WMW, emerging out of Sistren's political work to address the pervasive sexual objectification of women, Teens in Action embodied cross-generational, cross-class, cross-issue, and cross-community efforts.

With rampant sexual violence in domestic and public contexts, one of Sistren's major tasks was to demystify common "myths" about sexuality. Among the most pervasive was that women secretly enjoy pain during sexual encounters. Departing from its previous strategy of direct interviews, the myth was tested by surveying 20 men and 20 women. Over 50 percent of the respondents felt that "women were masochists, delighting in painful intercourse." Men equated the ability to give women sexual satisfaction with not being "saaf" (soft) (Candace 1991, 21). As noted in responses to the survey:

> Word on the streets, however, is that women "wanted it hard and stiff," and
> that a man would be seen as "saaf" if he could not "hangle de wuk" [A man
> would be seen as soft if he could not handle the work of sex].
>
> (Candace 1991, 21)

Male indifference to the "work" of women's sexual pleasure perpetuated blatant glorification of violence.

Since these beliefs were also propagated in popular culture, the magazine featured "Dancehall Culture" focusing on "slackness," or the overt, often violent, sexuality propagated in dancehall music. Marva Brown, promoter and manager of dancehall artistes, explains slackness: "My fight is when a DJ say, 'Hold down a gal and rape her because she love the rape.' That is my slackness" (Smikle 1994, 17). Caribbean critics analyze "work/wuk," in its sexual and material manifestations to indicate the proscription of female sexual pleasure in dancehall lyrics (Hope 2000; Saunders 2003). One argument about the "closely knit yet, seemingly, critically opposed discourses of economics and sexuality in Jamaican popular and national culture" examines Jamaican dancehall artist Buju Banton's advocacy of death to gay men in his song "Boom bye bye" to examine new forms of sexual proscription in Jamaica (Saunders 2003, 97). Reading these lyrics' description of oral sex as a degraded form of sex work "saaf/soft" men undertake to please women, the critic notes that many songs represent willingness to perform this kind of work as "a sure sign of man's lack of ambition (as a social or sexual worker)" who is incapable of performing other more demanding kinds of sexual work that can better satisfy a woman (Saunders 2003, 107). There is almost no reference to female pleasure in these sexual practices. Acknowledging Caribbean feminist response to homophobic and misogynist violence in the lyrics, Natasha Barnes addresses the charge that "dancehall's lyrical language harbors dangerous and hateful ideologies – paranoia about gay and lesbian sexual practices, distrust of women generally" (2006, 121) in contrast to Carolyn Cooper's reading of dancehall as a site of submerged subaltern consciousness. Cooper writes away the homophobic and misogynist violence embedded in the lyrics and in dancehall at large in the name of the culture as "*reflecting* not *propagating* violence" (2004a, 25). These crucial connections between sexuality and violence (or violence as the primary means of expressing sexuality) target women and LGBTQ+ people in equally detrimental ways. Dancehall is a complicated, heterogenous space of expression, and its culture both reflects and propagates violence.

The contrast to such violence is an *imagined* egalitarianism in the magazine in which the exceptional is presented as the desired normative, and gender parity is connected to economic imperatives. Theatrical productions and the magazine exploded the "myth of domestic bliss" through the words of women whose partners refused to take a role in daily responsibilities of cooking, cleaning, and bringing up the children, and who were often the sole earning members in their families (Ross-Frankson 1987, 3, 12). An editorial titled "Let's Rope in the Men!" cites DAWN's assessment of precarious socio-economic conditions in developing societies such as Jamaica to call for equal participation from men:

we are just going to have to demand better in this decade…we are going to have to rope in our brothers to help us do so. Our vision of the world is one in which all of us – man, woman, and pickney – have the same space in which to develop our full potential.

(*Sistren* 1990, 5)

By the early 1990s, following changes in leadership and editors Zadie Neufville and Shirley Campbell, the magazine changed its approach, moving from realistic to idealistic coverage by including short features on male allies in two regular columns titled "Acquainted" and "Can I Call you Sister."

Presenting models of gender parity, the magazine demonstrated how inequality inhibited full development of men and women's capacities. In rare cases when Jamaican men accepted equal distribution of childcare and housework responsibilities they were accused of sexual deviancy, clearly indicating that the organization of gender in the modern/colonial gender system is connected to "biological dimorphism" and "patriarchal and heterosexual organizations of relations" (Lugones 2007, 190). An article titled "Daddies that Do" addresses this by including opinions of men who share in parenting responsibilities. Lee Hall, parenting his two-year-old daughter, says that "no-one has ever called him a 'Maama-Man' but that it would not matter if they did" (*Sistren* 1989a, 15). In "Yes, Jamaican Men Can be Loving Parents," based on research by a male family planning counsellor-educator, single parent, and staff member at the University Hospital, the writer attempts to delink non-traditional gender roles from insinuations of sexual perversity: "When a father has a daughter on his lap, do observers suspect he may be finding sexual gratification? If a father is openly warm and affectionate with his boy-child, will that encourage homosexuality" (*Sistren* 1989b, 14). Bev Hanson's interview with Barry Chevannes describes how "Uncle Barry," encourages men to be "nurturers" or at least "find ways to express the nurturing role in a more dynamic way" (*Sistren* 1995a, 10–12). Fathers Incorporated, a group initiated by UWI anthropologist Chevannes, was part of a series of interrogations of Black and Caribbean masculinity and more broadly the family. Sistren ally, Owen "Blacka" Ellis, speaks about his association with Fathers Incorporated to tell the interviewer that men in active parenting roles are labeled homosexuals: "You'll find that the same group of men Sistren would call conscious men, other men call them mama man… some man because him don't box down women is considered Mama Man" (*Sistren* 1993a, 34). Sistren's male allies thus provided important (though exceptional) role models for a transformed masculinity that could accommodate nurturing roles for men, at least within heterosexual relationships.

For women, the tough economic situation often meant that they did not have the luxury of adhering to predefined gendered roles. Interviews indicated that most women were more than willing to accept work where they could find it, especially in professions dominated by men which usually brought in higher wages. A revaluation of gender was already underway through increased women's participation in non-traditional, "masculine" professions including construction, motor mechanics, engineering, computer technology, accounting, policing, parks and forest management, horse training etc. And though the magazine reports and articles do not indicate that women in these professions were labeled sexually deviant (unlike men involved in housework and childcare responsibilities), many faced hostility, aggression, and vicious competitiveness from male colleagues.

Over the years of its existence the collective analyzed the gendering of work under accelerated globalization that, on the one hand, continued exploitation of women in traditional occupations such as farming and domestic help, and on the other, led to new occupations for them in free zones or data processing. Spending time with sugar workers in rural Jamaica and listening to their stories led Sistren to develop their play *The Case of Iris Armstrong*, an acclaimed documentary *Sweet Sugar Rage*, and studies on the lives of female sugar workers. Sistren's efforts to demystify formal and informal work involved conversations in which women described physical and mental costs of repetitive labor. While the history of enslavement in Jamaica had broken down traditional sexual divisions of labor, the prevalence of sexual violence under slavery and its continuation into the twentieth century meant that labor practices were characterized on a sliding scale of respectability along class and color hierarchies. Middle class (often light skinned) women invested in homemaking or "respectable" professions such as teaching, banking, medicine, and accounting were, with rare exceptions, oblivious to blue collar work conditions. Like the sugar workers, free zone employees, factory workers, and domestic help faced slave-like labor conditions. These industries gendered female workers as docile, manageable, nimble, industrious, exploitable employees on lower wages than would be paid to men in similar conditions. Sistren was at the forefront of calls for a thorough and impartial Jamaican and pan-Caribbean governmental review of women's work in traditional and new occupations.

Steady employment and housing are crucial to the analysis of the *work of gender*. It is in this context that the group collaborated with and the magazine reported (for well over a decade) on the activities of the Women's Construction Cooperative (WCC), an organization employing women in a historically male-dominated industry. WCC was part of the Women's Housing Group set up by Sistren and the Canadian University Students Overseas (CUSO) in 1987 to provide women with employment in times of work scarcity. A feature article emphasized training opportunities, clarifying anyone could acquire those skills, and reiterating, "construction skills carry a higher wage level than working in the Free Zone or doing domestic work" (*Sistren* 1989c, 14). WCC jobs were especially valuable since housing was a major developmental concern in rapidly urbanizing Jamaica. When the demand for construction dropped, the collective initiated a repair and maintenance business strengthening non-engineered houses to withstand hurricanes. While the magazine advanced a critique of gendered division of occupations, its reports also placed WCC's training and capacity development in a cross-generational "nurturing" mode: the image of a woman worker at a construction site is juxtaposed with that of a little girl mixing cement and water to make a doll's house. The WCC women, states the reporter, have set a "fine example" for "the children of flood-stricken Clarendon, especially the little girls" (*Sistren* 1986/1987, 11). Like Sistren, the WCC ran training and development programs for women within and outside Jamaica and established a support group for women to discuss common goals, problems, and solutions for members (Rogers & Thomson 1993, 16–17). Sistren and WCC's trajectories illustrate the successes and struggles of all-women collectives engaged in important work to transform accepted gender roles in the public sphere.

Caribbean social scientists have analyzed the segregation of public versus private in terms of gender, class, and respectability (Brodber 1975; Chevannes 2001). Tracing the segregation of people and public space in Kingston, Charles Carnegies points to how the "inside" and the "outside" as "metaphoric spatial opposition provides Jamaicans a condensed, shorthand way of expressing hegemonic class distinctions." Within this schema those "born outside, living outside, and working outside bear the dishonour of – but also serve to produce – lower class status." There are lasting social implications of this spatial opposition:

> Children born to unmarried parents, and children fathered by men of higher status with working class women, were stigmatized as "outside" children as opposed to "inside" children who were born under the legal and socially valued canopy of marriage. Likewise, manual and menial labour – work done (though not exclusively) outdoors – has been devalued; as opposed to the more highly regarded white collar work performed for the most part indoors.
>
> (Carnegie 2014, 72)

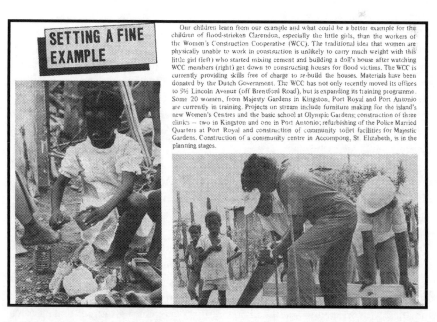

FIGURE 3.4 Report on women workers in the Women's Construction Cooperative in *Sistren* magazine. Image courtesy of Joan Ross-Frankson, Joan French, and the Sistren Theatre Collective.

Sistren disrupted these dichotomies by presenting men in care work and women in formal work to rethink gender largely in the context of waged labor, female-headed, or quasi-family cisgender structures. A fuller account demands consideration of those outside traditional waged economies, normative gender, and heterosexuality.

Sistren's research on informal commercial traders, higglers, and market women offered an evaluation of informal work. Ross-Frankson's multi-part, award-winning feature series, "Women on the Streets" interviewed prostitutes, beggars, and higglers to focus on the economic, gendered, and sexualized violence they faced. The features invite readers to rethink an easy opposition between the "yard" as the primary unit of socialization of girls and the "street" for boys that Caribbean anthropologists established in their research. The first article in the series describes the "sporting life" of two streetwalkers denied educational opportunities in childhood and financial support from men who fathered their children. Sharon, the younger of the two women, talks to the interviewer about her daily clientele: "Women check mi to. Sometimes a man and a woman will check mi and we mek love together [Women check me out as well. Sometimes a man and a woman will check me out and we make love together]" (Ross-Frankson 1985, 3). Tentatively mentioning non-heterosexual and non-monogamous desire, the article presents sex as a means of survival eschewing a discussion on morality or sexual choice: "I drive them to their block. They greet the other girls. Business is slow. Marcia looks desperately up and down the empty street. Sharon laughs and tells me the other girls think I am a client" (Ross-Frankson 1985, 12). The second article reiterates structural connections between economic, social, and sexual vulnerability. Isolyn, who begs for a living in downtown Kingston, has been brought to this condition not by a man but "a system which so easily discards those who cannot manage the race, in the name of 'budgetary constraints,' 'structural adjustment,' and 'lowering the deficit'" (Ross-Frankson 1986, 3). The articles asserted the dignity and humanity of women surviving outside waged and heterosexual marital economies.[11]

Introducing discussion on gender, sexuality and citizenship in the Caribbean, Faith Smith observes that feminists' engagement with nationalism, popular culture, reproductive and waged labor, and domestic violence in the region laid the groundwork for recent scholarship on sexuality, but that "regional feminist agendas have largely omitted nonheteronormative sexuality" (2011, 9). Addressing the analysis of gender and sexuality in the Caribbean, another scholar writes: "Caribbean counter-publics in many shapes and forms continue to work on the body, work with the body, and work the body as conduit to a collective project of liberation" (Sheller 2012, 260). There are obvious risks in the "study of 'hidden' populations such as sex workers and those engaged in same-sex relations" including gaining access, recognizing power differentials, and trust between the researcher and the subjects of her study (Lazarus 2013, 1). Despite these risks, Sistren led the way in representing sexual precarity as inextricably connected to social and economic policies through its performances and the magazine. These policies, the collective maintained, were responsible for criminalization of destitute women earning a desperate living through prostitution and begging. This analysis of work thus moved towards an interrogation of sexuality without directly invoking sexual object choice or sexual identity politics despite the clearly non-judgmental editorial perspective.

Though we cannot look to Sistren as a point of origin or continuation of the LGBTQ+ activism already underway in Jamaica by this time, the group's trajectory marks an important moment of ambivalence around the work of gender and sexuality in a deeply homophobic society. On the one hand, the group performed with lesbian groups at places like Sisterfire in the United States, had deep connections with Sister Vision, the Black and Women of Color Press in Toronto run by Stephanie Martin and the Jamaican lesbian Makeda Silvera, and some members were in queer relationships. On the other, rampant social and sexual violence meant that there were no spaces for these discussions unlike those available for discussing race and class differences. Some Jamaicans were already aware of these concerns, seeing the group's work and publications as important interpretations of gender and sexuality while making their own connections between women's, lesbian, and gay rights.

Routes to rights

Emphasizing differences between the women's and gay and lesbian movements in North America, Gayle Rubin famously stated that feminism is a theory of gender oppression but that the domain of sexuality demands another mode of theorizing. In Jamaica at a time when there was no scope for public gay and lesbian mobilization (despite the existence of underground gay and lesbian social spaces), Sistren and the larger women's movement forwarded a theory and praxis of gender and sexuality premised on revaluating work, sexual violence, and reproductive autonomy. During these years transnational feminist advocacy was changing the direction of these worldings. Rejecting neocolonial, imperialist ideas by asserting a feminist politics relevant to the global South, organizations like CAFRA and DAWN were shaping a conversation where postcolonial concerns were front and center. Because LGBTQ+ sexualities still occupied an uncertain place within these conversations, and because its members were reluctant to address the matter, Sistren was not able to analyze the connections. Responding to rampant sexual violence against women and children, the group steered clear of controversies around sexual choice for fear of potential violence, but also because its existence was precarious in the 1980s and 1990s. In 1980 death threats and threats of shooting at the theatre led to the cancellation of a performance. In 1981 the group was kicked out of the Edna Manley College following a political regime change in Jamaica. In 1982 members were attacked twice in performance. In the later 1980s and 1990s the group faced a precarious future as its funders were interested in bread and butter "development" concerns, rather than supporting the group's cultural platform which provided some scope for analysis of sexuality through its theatre work. The account I have offered claims that the contours of a feminist–queer analysis emerged not *because* of the group's conscious efforts but *despite* its scrupulous efforts to avoid any discussion of it.

During the early years of its activities Sistren collaborated with the Jamaica Council for Human Rights (JCHR), a civil society organization with a broad rights platform. Sistren's attention to the conditions of women inmates in correctional and mental health centers connected its work to the JCHR's mandate as a watchdog organization advocating constitutional and legislative reform. The magazine provides a glimpse of this work in its articles on prisons, asylums, shelters, and hospitals, critiques of inadequate facilities, rampant sexual abuse, and, in some cases, state enforced reproductive violence (through contraception injections and abortions for victims of rape) experienced by female inmates at these institutions. JCHR's success in releasing illegally detained citizens and providing legal assistance to those charged with crimes made it an important ally in Sistren's feminist justice work (Eekhoff 1991, 22). *Sistren* interviewed Florizelle O'Connor, head of JCHR, to inform its readers about the organization's interventions in cases of illegal detention and police brutality. Sistren was among the organizations JCHR contacted to seek help in publicizing police atrocities including illegal detention, torture, and assault. O'Connor wrote to delegates at a Jamaican conference on Violence Against Women (1991) asking for support on a heinous case of police brutality in which a constable brutally attacked a young woman, Pauline Mullings. Mullings, who was pregnant at the time of the attack, subsequently miscarried the twins she was expecting and faced repeated police threats after filing a case with JCHR. The magazine reprinted O'Connor's letter and an article describing legal recourses to victims of police violence (O'Connor 1991; *Sistren* 1991b).

Besides its collaboration with civil society organizations such as JCHR and WMW, another of Sistren's routes to rights was a focus on discriminatory legislation impacting women. The Jamaican Offenses Against Persons Act criminalizes abortion leading many in the country to seek illegal and medically unsupervised procedures to end pregnancies. An editorial by Ross-Frankson unequivocally states that women have a right to their bodies: "The decision to have sex goes hand in hand with deciding whether we want to have a child at this time, with this particular man" (1989b, 5). While discussing systemic problems leading to high infant mortality and post-natal depression at the Victoria Jubilee Hospital in Kingston, another article mentions reproductive choice through an anecdote. Learning about babies abandoned at the hospital, the author recounts how

> Marlon's teenage mother had him early one afternoon and by 6 o'clock that evening, she had disappeared. For this young woman, who can hardly have begun to know herself, growing Marlon was a task she simply could not cope with.
>
> (Ross-Frankson 1989c, 11)

Similarly, "Say No to Norplant" describes the adverse effects of unsupervised contraceptive implants offered to Jamaican women. Pointing to their side effects, the author observes that some symptoms "may lead some users to think they are pregnant and seek illegal abortion – further endangering their health"

(*Sistren* 1993b, 33). Connecting the right to abortion to women's mental and physical health helped deflect possible backlash from magazine readers and/or the governmental machinery.

Sistren's new editor Zadie Neufville retained the format and focus of the magazine Ross-Frankson had formalized as outgoing editor. A focus on "Women, Sexuality, and Health" (*Sistren* 1991e) under Neufville's editorship indirectly addressed sexual choices. The same number calls for legislative change on rape and other forms of sexual violence, advocates sex education to prevent teenage pregnancy and STDs including HIV/AIDS, and foregrounds women's views on their sexuality.[12] It initiated a tentative conversation on non-normative sexualities by including an article on intimate relationships that is ambiguous about whether the relationships were gay or straight (*Sistren* 1991c, 17) and an extract from Audre Lorde's "biomythography" *Zami* describing the autobiographical narrator's lesbian sexual encounter (Lorde 1991, 17). Here a conversation about women's sexuality dispelled misconceptions about women enjoying pain during sex. Those interviewed for an article titled "Woman on Being Women" talk about how they suppress their sexuality for fear of being called "whores" (*Sistren* 1991d, 38). Some years later a story about a violent man-hating "lesbian," a "pseudo boy" who desires a "real boy to love her" appeared in the magazine (Robinson 1995, 13). Reinforcing stereotypes of male homosexuality as weakness and female homosexuality as unwarranted aggression, the story is out of place amid other nuanced accounts of sexualized violence.[13] The magazine issued an apology when readers wrote to express their objections to the piece. From the early 1990s the magazine blunderingly introduced sexual identity and desire, though it was unable to advance the conversation. There were no groups led by women openly dealing with LGBT issues at the time. Sistren members demonstrated in their practice their consciousness about non-discrimination and rights of women, gay, and lesbian people, never openly addressing the matter. Non-discrimination was so intrinsic to Sistren's activities that when there was departure from it in the article stereotyping lesbianism there was a public outcry. This response brought into the limelight the collective's character and stance on the subject and testified to an already existing feminist counterpublic (in part shaped by the magazine's readership) which would not easily accept homophobia.

Related to this is the collective and the magazine's vital but irregular discussion on HIV/AIDS. During the 1990s, following an increase in AIDS-related deaths in the Caribbean in general, and in Jamaica in particular, the women's movement connected sexuality and health, like the incipient health education program of the Gay Freedom Movement. Amid alarming statistics around transmission, the magazine briefly mentions sexual orientation to dispel the perception that AIDS is a gay or "battymen" disease and to spell out the risks faced by women and their (unborn) children. "HIV/ AIDS Infections on the Increase" lists unprotected heterosexual contact as the primary source of the infection by providing statistics and recommendations for men and women to prevent transmission (*Sistren* 1991e, 29). The Health Update section publicly commended the first woman in Jamaica to openly admit she had the disease. The column later carried a positive review of "Vibes in a World of Sexuality," a play by members of the Little People and Teen Players to educate people about the pandemic (*Sistren* 1993c, 25). Though infrequent, the health section and cultural commentary directed some public attention to HIV/AIDS. Paulette Williams' *Sistren* article mentions an increasing number of babies born with the virus who rarely live beyond a few years. The obvious solution to prevent HIV transmission through contraception and legalized abortion is not presented as an option in this or subsequent articles on AIDS (1990, 26).

Several Caribbean nations have debated feminist demands for legalizing abortion over the past half century. A report on the gender development indicators for Jamaica states: "All men and women regardless of creed or race, should have access to the law for redress even from culturally differentiated gender practices" including women's access to "contraceptives and…the freedom to control childbearing if they decide to do so," and men's right to "share in the care, support, and upbringing of their offspring" (Mohammed 2000, 7–8). The 2011 amendments to the Jamaican Constitution include a Charter of Fundamental Rights and Freedoms offering similar gender-based protections as in the report but exclude sexual and reproductive choice as the basis of such protections. As the trajectory of the magazine demonstrates, women's alternative media in Jamaica historically addressed "culturally differentiated gender practices" in somewhat unequal terms; while the right to reproductive choice has been clearly expressed, the right to sexual choice has not been articulated forcefully or clearly. The influence of various denominations of Christianity in Jamaica

FIGURE 3.5 Section of a graphic dispelling common misunderstandings of AIDS in *Sistren* magazine. Image courtesy of Joan Ross-Frankson, Joan French, and the Sistren Theatre Collective.

and the reluctance of postcolonial governments to upset certain sections of the electorate makes it hard to claim either of these rights.

Changes in Jamaican laws to decriminalize homosexuality and abortion are still at the stage of futures to come. Collectives such as Sistren, even with their ambivalence on and inability to address LGBTQ+ rights, helped develop a vocabulary of rights and routes to sexual health, sexual choice, and reproductive autonomy in collaboration with other civil society groups. These can be the basis of feminist-queer solidarities.

Legislative desires

Caribbean feminist-queer solidarities are *"imagined lives"* or "the futures feminism can contribute to bring into being" (Robinson 2011, 206). In positing "imagined lives" as feminist methodology, Tracy Robinson claims that "the vibrant intellectual tradition of family studies in the Caribbean has rarely even hinted that *all intimacy and family life might not be heterosexed*" (2011, 210, emphasis added). Sistren sought to discuss gender and sexuality towards imagined "futures" in several ways: representing women's work in "masculine" domains; emphasizing male feminist affiliations; and presenting exceptional instances of transformed parenting roles and sexual relations. Sistren's theatre work and the magazine indicate that not all intimacy and family life is heterosexual. However, such is the inextricable hold of the coloniality of power over postcolonial gender norms and sexual relations – "the modern/colonial gender system" – that although it expressed a well-developed critique of violent heterosexuality, heteronormative social formations were not questioned (Lugones 2007, 189). Nor was it safe to initiate such questioning in the politically charged environment of intra-party and gang violence during the years when Sistren's performances about masculinized violence and feminist media interventions had already made the group susceptible to charges of lesbianism.

In my conversations with Jamaican scholars and activists I learned that there is a common understanding of human rights as LGBTQ+ rights, making it hard for feminists to articulate rights claims without being accused of sexual "deviancy." Since the 1980s feminist counterpublics such as Sistren and WMW have sought to shape public opinion to effect legal change. Though much of the activist literature referenced in this chapter including the magazine has ceased publication, and an explosion of digital content means that monitoring/countering media for its misogynist and homophobic representations is not an easy task, other counterpublic articulations (in theatre, music, dance, art, marches, protests, demonstrations) remain as crucial now as in the last decades of the previous century. Never calling on the Jamaican state to decriminalize homosexuality, Sistren made a strong case for the revaluation of gender and sexual roles and legalization of abortion, currently illegal under sections 72 and 73 of the Jamaica Offences Against the Person Act, the same act used to persecute homosexuals under sections 76, 77, 78, and 79.[14]

Sistren and the Hannahtown community women's landmark performance *Slice of Reality* before the Jamaican parliament in 2009 to replace the Offences Against the Persons Act with a Termination of Pregnancy Act yielded no result, a case of what

Maxwell calls "Aborted Reform" (2012). This pioneering attempt echoes failed efforts of gay and lesbian activists to have relevant sections of the same act repealed through a parliamentary petition in 2001. *Jamaican Guidelines for Comprehensive Sexuality Education* emphasize that "People have the right to make personal decisions concerning sexuality and reproductive health matters" even though "abortion is illegal in Jamaica" and "there are laws in Jamaica that restrict some types of sexual behavior" (The Jamaica Task Force Committee for Comprehensive Sexuality Education 2008, 63). The National Policy for Gender Equality (NPGE) by the Bureau of Women's Affairs released by the Jamaican government parenthetically inserted "Gender" in its nomenclature as a promise to mainstream gender concerns largely based on the language of the CEDAW. The policy deliberately deploys the rhetoric of indirection that *Sistren* magazine used in the 1980s and 1990s: "The intention is to bring gender neutrality to the laws, regarding legal protection from sexual violence and exploitation, and to remove from the law the perpetuation of gender stereotypes and discrimination" (Bureau of Women's Affairs 2010, 14). It does not mention repealing anti-abortion and buggery laws.

In a typical postcolonial trajectory, social movements often (though not always) stake their rights claims through national frameworks and then seek transnational solidarities to "world" these claims. As indicated in Sistren's transnational affiliations with Caribbean and global South collectives CAFRA and DAWN, these claims can garner crucial support that may spur national bureaucracies into action. Unfortunately, this has not yet happened in Jamaica. The women's rights framework adopted by Jamaican civil society has operated within the 1984 CEDAW parameters signed by the Jamaican government, though the government has not opted to follow the optional protocol allowing a person or a group to appeal to the CEDAW at the UN if they feel their rights are not being protected at the national level. Since international appeal is foreclosed as an option, existing civil society coalitions working to advance a feminist-queer politics based on the broad strokes, ambivalent, and yes, sometimes blundering connections outlined in *Sistren* – health, safety, work, pleasure, and freedom – offer the best hope for imagined futures.

It seems appropriate to conclude this analysis with an account of the Tambourine Army, a feminist-queer group which protests sexual violence, celebrates survivors, and acknowledges Sistren's pioneering work in creating solidarities. A recent piece connects members of the Army to "counterideological groups such as gay rights and women's rights movements that function in direct contestation to the patriarchal and homophobic norms of heteropatriarchal recolonization" and states, "women's background in queer organizing is salient for their feminist vision, since members were already embroiled in struggles against gender violence as it is inflected by lesbophobia, transphobia, and homophobia." (Roper & Wint 2020, 40). In 2017 members of the Tambourine Army protested at the Nazareth Moravian Church against a pastor's assault of a teenage girl.[15] Joan French mentioned in a personal communication that "old guard" feminists who had been connected to Sistren in its hey-day – Jennifer Jones, Opal Palmer Adisa, Judy Wedderburn, Stephanie Martin, and herself – marched with the Tambourine Army on 11 March 2017, against the reservations of other sections of the old guard women's movement. French believes that clarity on the connections between feminist and queer struggles, especially on human rights concerns, is one of the lasting legacies of Sistren in Jamaica (2020). Bringing together feminist and queer activists, the Army marches onwards and ahead to world sexualities in inherently just ways, demolishing stigma, abuse, and violence in its path, and demanding concrete legislative reform as a future destination so that Jamaica is no longer a "problem" space in feminist and queer histories.

The next chapter moves my analysis of postcolonial sexualities to another context, charting feminist-lesbian convergence and divergence in the Indian women's journal *Manushi* from the 1980s to the late 1990s.

Notes

1 The title of this chapter invokes *Rights a di Plan, wid CEDAW in wi han': CEDAW for Jamaicans*, an informative booklet brought out by the Women's Resource and Outreach Center (WROC) and the United Nations Development fund for Women (UNIFEM) (2008).

2 This view is contrary to Karina Smith's opinion that "Sistren is unequivocally aligned with the Manley government, presumably because the group's initial funding came from government agencies" (2008, 236).

3 Since 2015, Joan French, formerly of Sistren, has been engaged in a voluntary collaborative initiative involving Sistren members, *Sistren* editors, and researchers, to preserve documents of the Caribbean feminist movement from the 1970s to the 1990s. I collected Sistren materials from 2008–2015 and shared some of these with French. Thanks to her time and labor-intensive efforts, three near-complete sets of WAND, CAFRA, and *Sistren* magazines have been digitally archived. These are available in the Making of Caribbean Feminisms WI Special Collection at the Alma Jordan Library of the University of the West Indies, St. Augustine. *Sistren* magazine can be accessed at: http://uwispace.sta.uwi.edu/dspace/handle/2139/45158

4 Other important publications included the Jamaica-based Women's Media Watch (WMW) newsletter, and those of the global South collective DAWN.

5 Mapping research on Caribbean sexuality, Kamala Kempadoo mentions that the way sexuality has been expressed or practiced in the region can be gleaned from "*grey* documents that include some mention of sexual praxis (reports, conference papers, theses and policy briefings) and the growing number of more accessible documents (published journal articles, electronic articles, chapters in books, media reports, and books)" (2009, 2).

6 My thanks to Honor Ford-Smith for this point and for her suggestion on clarity on internal differences within the group on LGBTQ+ rights; I am grateful for her insights on the reasons why Sistren could not advance a larger conversation on gender and sexuality in Jamaica.

7 This body of scholarship includes Carolyn Cooper's review of *Lionheart Gal* (1989), articles on Sistren's theatrical productions by Sharon Green (2004), Afreen Akhter (2008), Karina Smith (2008, 2013), and a chapter in my book-length study *Feminist Visions and Queer Futures in Postcolonial Drama* (Batra 2010).

8 Ford-Smith's three-part series was serialized over 1993–1994 (1993a, 1993b, 1994).

9 Grateful thanks to Joan French for emphasizing this point in a personal communication. French notes that such was the force of Sistren's interventions that even entities such as the Workers' Party of Jamaica issued a "rule" condemning sexual violence under pressure from its women's arm, the Committee of Women for Progress. French was among the women in Sistren associated with the WPJ.

10 These include articles by Imani Tafari Ama (1987, 1989) and Honor Ford-Smith (1991).

11 Sistren's play *QPH* represents women who were abandoned by their families, and spent their lives as domestic help, prostitutes, and beggars. Facing poverty and destitution in their old age, they live in a state supported almshouse. The play is based upon an incident when 144 inmates died in a fire at the Eventide Home for the Aged in Slipe Pen, Kingston in 1980.

12 Michelle Cave and Joan French's article "Sexual Choice as a Human Rights Issue," for the CAFRA newsletter discusses sexuality in the context of freedom of choice and freedom from violence, taking the Caribbean women's movement to task for failing to address the issue (1995, 17–19). The article is based on a paper first presented by French at a conference on "Critical Perspectives on Human Rights in the Caribbean" in Trinidad and Tobago in January 1995. The Conference was sponsored by CAFRA and the Caribbean Human Rights Network.

13 Staceyanne Chin's autobiographical persona is that of an angry lesbian growing up poor, parentless, and sexually vulnerable in Jamaica (2000). Chin connects her sexual orientation to the vexed question of reproduction by pointing to the lack of sexual education and reproductive choices in Jamaica. Chin carries forward Patricia Powell's discussion of rape, abuse, and pregnancy of a cross-dressing Chinese-Jamaica protagonist, who bears her captor a child in secret in the novel *Pagoda* (1998).

14 Here are the relevant sections of the Act:

Article 72: "Every woman, being with child, who with intent to procure her own miscarriage, shall unlawfully administer to herself any poison or other noxious thing, or shall unlawfully use any instrument or other means whatsoever with the like intent; and whosoever, with intent to procure the miscarriage of any woman, whether she be or be not with child, shall unlawfully administer to her, or cause to be taken by her, any poison or other noxious thing, or shall unlawfully use any instrument or other means whatsoever with the like intent, shall be guilty of felony, and, being convicted thereof, shall be liable to be imprisoned for life, with or without hard labour."

Article 73: "Whosoever shall unlawfully supply or procure any poison or other noxious thing, or any instrument or thing whatsoever, knowing that the same is intended to be unlawfully used or employed with intent to procure the miscarriage of any woman, whether she be or be not with child, shall be guilty of a misdemeanour, and, being convicted thereof, shall be liable to be imprisoned for a term not exceeding three years, with or without hard labour."

Article 76 (Unnatural Crime): "Whosoever shall be convicted of the abominable crime of buggery [anal intercourse] committed either with mankind or with any animal, shall be liable to be imprisoned and kept to hard labour for a term not exceeding ten years."

Article 77 (Attempt): "Whosoever shall attempt to commit the said abominable crime, or shall be guilty of any assault with intent to commit the same, or of any indecent assault upon any male person, shall be guilty of a misdemeanour, and being convicted thereof shall be liable to be imprisoned for a term not exceeding seven years, with or without hard labour."

Article 78 (Proof of Carnal Knowledge): "Whenever upon the trial of any offence punishable under this Act, it may be necessary to prove carnal knowledge, it shall not be necessary to prove the actual emission of seed in order to constitute a carnal knowledge, but the carnal knowledge shall be deemed complete upon proof of penetration only."

Article 79 (Outrages on Decency): "Any male person who, in public or private, commits, or is a party to the commission of, or procures or attempts to procure the commission by any male person of, any act of gross indecency with another male person, shall be guilty of a misdemeanor, and being convicted thereof shall be liable at the discretion of the court to be imprisoned for a term not exceeding 2 years, with or without hard labour."

15 The actions of the group received some notoriety when an "army" founder, Latoya Nugent (also a member of J-FLAG member and founder of WE-CHANGE), hit the leader of the church on the head with a tambourine for having abused her partner as a child (Lewis 2017). See also the Army's Facebook page for recent actions: www.facebook.com/tambourinearmy/

PART II
Azadi, emerging freedoms

4

CREATING A LOCATIONAL COUNTERPUBLIC

Manushi and the articulation of human rights and sexuality from Delhi, India

Overhearing a conversation about a new women's magazine in the early 1980s, I remember thinking that the word *manushi* (human/humane, gendered female), the counterpart of *manushya* (human) in Hindi rhymed with *khushi*, the word for happiness. On learning many years later that *khush* was adopted as a descriptor of South Asian gay and lesbian identity in the diaspora, *manushi* and *khushi* marked my growing vocabulary for connections between lesbian and straight women's voices. At a time when the movement for gay and lesbian rights in India was almost non-existent, independent journals such as *Manushi* articulated gender and sexuality through participatory modes such as fiction, poetry, letters, citizen-journalist reports, and articles to further the Indian Women's Movement (IWM).[1] This chapter shifts the gaze from Jamaica to India to examine *Manushi*'s coverage of sexual violence and a concomitant articulation of women's rights to bodily autonomy from the 1980s to the 1990s. The autonomous (versus political party based) IWM's sustained focus on sexual violence in the last decades of the twentieth century and its embattled relationship with the state is homologous to gay and lesbian rights activism, primarily on the grounds of a comparable violence, reclamation of geographic, institutional, typographic, judicial space, and a contradictory relationship with the state. I wish to emphasize that there is no causal link between the two, that is, sexual violence does not directly and always lead to an assertion of alternative sexual preferences. Here I argue that by placing women's sexuality at the forefront of national concerns through a rights discourse *Manushi* inadvertently furthered (though it did not initiate or continue) a discussion of non-normative sexual choices for women, despite a conscious steering away from such issues within the IWM and its publications in this period. In these ways *Manushi*'s status in the IWM is similar to *Sistren* magazine's place within the Jamaican and Caribbean women's movement.

Thinking of the autonomous IWM as a "counterpublic" or a "parallel discursive arena" allows an exploration of the strategic use of publications such as *Manushi* to

DOI: 10.4324/9781003170303-6

create national awareness of gender concerns from the 1970s onwards. The feminist print media was especially active from the late 1970s till the 1990s. Besides *Manushi* several other magazines such as *Sabla* in Hindi by Jagori, the *Saheli* newsletter, *Samya Shakti* by the Center for Women's Development Studies, and regular publications by political party women's organizations such as the All India Democratic Women's Association (AIDWA) appeared around this time. Other organizations such as the All India Women's Congress (AIWC) affiliated to the Congress Party had a longer history of publication from the 1930s, the period of the Indian independence movement. Feminist publishing houses such as Kali for Women in Delhi founded in 1984, Stree in Calcutta formed in 1990, and select university presses also created counterpublic spaces for women's concerns.

Nancy Fraser's important theorization of "alternative publics" constituted by members of subordinated social groups such as "women, workers, peoples of color, and gays and lesbians" as "subaltern counterpublics," demands qualification when applied to the Indian context. While Fraser's example of a late twentieth century "feminist subaltern counterpublic" with its "journals, bookstores, publishing companies, film and video distribution networks, lecture series, research centers, academic programs, conferences, conventions, festivals, and local meeting places" (1997) is on the surface directly applicable to the second and third "wave" of the IWM, any categorization of these networks as "subaltern," and even "feminist," requires several qualifications especially since upper caste middle class women's concerns diverge significantly from working class and lower caste women's lives. The political climate in the nation's capital and the social topography of the city determined the nature and scope of the Manushi collective's interventions through its public and journalistic activism. I begin by outlining social and political circumstances that facilitated the emergence of publications meant primarily for women, move on to consider the possible impact of these publications on changing conceptions of gender and sexuality, and modify Fraser's ideas to present print as a "locational counterpublic."

Although my discussion is limited to the northern Indian context and my archive is *Manushi*, an English language journal, where possible this is supplemented with an examination of autonomous publications in English and other Indian languages emerging from Delhi. The Delhi-based archive, though not representative of the nation in its entirety, gives a sense of the major shifts in the human rights narrative applied to women and sexual minorities. A crucial aspect of this narrative is the apparent disconnect between feminist and lesbian activism in organizations and publications where it is reasonable to assume that the focus on sexual rights would make space for both, though in all fairness, sections of the IWM made concerted attempts to address the concerns of women from the working classes, lower castes, and religious minorities. This narrative also helps contextualize the social, cultural, legislative, and mainstream media presentation of violence two decades into the twenty-first century: in 2012 there were swift changes in the Indian Penal Code dealing with rape and others forms of sexual violence, spurred by the "Nirbhaya" gang rape; in 2013 the Supreme Court of India reinstated article 377 criminalizing homosexuality, overturning the Delhi High Court's decision to read down the statute in 2009; then in 2018 the Supreme Court delivered a unanimous verdict scrapping article 377 as "irrational, indefensible, and manifestly arbitrary" to finally decriminalize homosexuality in India.[2]

Locating human rights and women's activism

Manushi, started by Madhu Kishwar and Ruth Vanita, Delhi-based academics, connected social thinking, activism, and the emerging autonomous women's movement in India from its inception. The journal was co-edited by Kishwar and Vanita from 1978 to 1991, although Vanita continued her association with it as an analyst, translator, and reviewer well into the 1990s and beyond. *Manushi* suspended print publication in 2006 but continues to exist as an online forum which also archives some of the print numbers. From the late 1990s its politics shifted right of center revealing the primary editor Kishwar's leanings towards the Hindu nationalist ideology of the political party currently in power, the Bharatiya Janata Party (BJP). Vanita's contributions to the journal have been sporadic since the late 1990s, even as her feminist queer politics is articulated in venues other than *Manushi*. Despite ideological shifts in recent times, for over two decades the journal consistently advocated and followed an intersectional approach. This approach is responsive to the complex terrain of women's issues in India which demand an engagement with the class, caste, religion, and geographical location of those it attempted to reach. In keeping with these aims, the collective and the journal involved itself in the rural and urban struggles of daily wage earners including agricultural, industrial, and construction workers, street vendors, and local service providers, as well as those faced by women professionals, students, and middle class homemakers. Though it is often not possible to make neat distinctions between mainstream and alternative publications, the contents of *Manushi* were also a response to sensational, hyperbolic, and stereotyped representations of women in mainstream print media and popular culture. As one of the earliest English language publications of the autonomous women's movement in the country, *Manushi* was a clear contrast to popular women's magazines such as *Femina* and *Women's Era* which enjoyed a national circulation based on a readership interested in fashion, food, romantic fiction, marital, romantic, and incidental career advice. (Srilata 1999, 61–72; Thapan 2004, 411–444; Joseph 2006, 204–231). Like many activist publications in the global South, *Manushi* was simultaneously published bilingually (in Hindi and English) to reach audiences all over the country, although the Hindi version was later discontinued.[3]

Since sections of the IWM adapted to local contexts in various parts of the country, spatial or locational accounts of specific struggles help contextualize its social and political goals. Among metropolitan locations in India, Delhi, Bombay, and Calcutta have been studied as rich sites for the emergence of party-based and autonomous women's groups. Besides the Manushi collective, which came up in the late 1970s, other women's groups in Delhi such as Saheli and Jagori came up in the early 1980s.[4] Speaking of Bombay and Calcutta as political fields, Raka Ray has examined the women's movement in India through a study of two organizations based in these cities to posit that "social movements that are oppositional to the state or the present government are embedded in a protest field, which in turn is embedded in a wider political field" (2000, 8). The "protest field" identified by Ray applies, though it is certainly not limited to, women's, gay, and lesbian activism in major metropolises in India – Delhi, Bombay, Calcutta, and Bangalore – including media collectives and journals.[5]

Feminist accounts assume the importance of Delhi as a political field giving rise to protest fields demanding freedom from sexual violence. More recently, the city has been prominent in queer analyses (Bacchetta 2002; Gupta 2005; Cohen 2011; Dave 2012). As Naisargi Dave mentions,

> the omnipresence and the absence of the state…has made Delhi a central site for Indian queer activism. Not only are national decisions made here, but the city's many sites of state power make for symbolically rich places of protest.
>
> (2012, 22)

Delhi's importance in women's activism following the IWM's focus on legislative change in the 1970s and 1980s depended, in large measure, on the political rallying, lobbying, visibility, and legal support available in the nation's capital.

The 1970s were an important decade for women's mobilization in India. The 1974 report *Towards Equality* by the Committee on the Status of Women in India reiterated that three decades into India's independence very little progress had been made towards achieving gender equality. Media reports of increased violence against women, including rape, sexual harassment, dowry deaths, and widow immolations led to a nationwide galvanization of which the Manushi collective was a small but significant part. During that period many autonomous feminist groups, including Manushi, focused on law reform as a conscious strategy to address violence against women, making Delhi a natural choice for their efforts. Furthermore, the political climate in the country following a declaration of Emergency by Prime Minister Indira Gandhi in 1975, the restoration of democracy two years later, the dynamic and varied women's movement in the country, and the social climate of the capital, where many institutions nurtured radical thinking, contributed to the emergence of publications like *Manushi* in the late 1970s. The effects of these efforts were present in my student days in the late 1980s when I felt surrounded with and supported by campus women activists who played a key role in specific urban activist trajectories of the movement. In those days, *Manushi* provided me and others of my generation with a succinct, sometimes controversial, but always brave account of the issues impacting women on campus, in the capital, the nation at large, and the world.

There were significant differences between the myriad women's groups in the capital. While *Manushi* eschewed the label "feminist," other Delhi based organizations embraced it; Manushi took up activism simultaneously in print and social spaces, while Saheli and Jagori emerged as women's collectives focused on activities that did not initially include a primary emphasis on print; finally, because of its founding members' literature and Delhi University backgrounds, Manushi was perceived as a forum for literate women in contrast to Saheli and Jagori which were seen as grassroots oriented. Following Fraser's categorization of print and publishing creating "feminist subaltern counterpublics," the applicability of subaltern and feminist as descriptive labels of these endeavors bears closer examination. Revisiting the category subaltern in relation to Marxism and feminism, Gayatri Spivak mentions that the "new *location* of subalternity also requires a revision of feminist theory." (2012, 327, emphasis added). Echoing Spivak's call, Ratna Kapur sees the task of postcolonial feminism as challenging "systems of knowledge that continue to inform feminist understandings of women and the subaltern subject" (2005/2012, 4). For Spivak, the United Nations construction of the commonality "woman" is a "discursive formation" which can generate oppositions since the subaltern can be located "outside of this commonality" (2012, 327, 328). Following these ideas, it is useful to consider journals such as *Manushi* as opposing the commonly understood discursive formation of "woman" or systems of knowledge that constitute this category in the UN Decade for Women (1975–1985) and beyond it in the era of International Conferences on Women in Mexico City (1975), Copenhagen (1980), Nairobi (1985), and Beijing (1995).

Though the word subaltern does not appear in the journal, language and nation are crucial aspects of the counterpublic that the journal sought to create. Revisiting her ideas on the Habermasian public sphere, Fraser has written about the imbrication of language and nationality in the imagination of publics, mentioning how English "favors global elites and Anglophone postcolonials at the expense of others" complicating "both the *legitimacy* and *efficacy* of public opinion in a post-Westphalian world" (2007). The "legitimacy" and "efficacy" of public opinion is evident when almost 12 years after the magazine's inception, Kishwar's piece. "Why I Do Not Call Myself a Feminist," provided a rationale for openly eschewing the label, stating: "We deliberately chose the subtitle 'a journal about women and society,' which, along with the word Manushi, with its emphasis on the word 'humane,' we felt would indicate that Manushi is concerned not just with women's equality, as the term "feminist" would imply, but with the *protection of the human rights of all the disadvantaged or discriminated groups in our society*, while having a special emphasis on women's rights" (Kishwar 1990, 2, emphasis added). Kishwar's reasons for rejecting the term are its Western origins, culturally imperialist connotations, separatist and anti-men stance in specific instances, a vocabulary of persecution adopted by some groups despite a generally supportive mainstream media, and a convenient shorthand labeling of the IWM: "those mesmerised by the rhetoric of other movements tried to force us to assume the existence at that time not only of a major women's movement here, but also of major divisions within it" (Kishwar 1990, 4). Countering the perception that the movement and the ideology focused on securely employed women's interests by ignoring social inequities of class, caste, education, and language, Kishwar places the organization and its journal's aims within a broader human rights umbrella than the IWM or even feminism could provide. This was an anticipatory umbrella, and one which positioned it at the cusp of the national and the transnational before 1995 when the slogan 'Women's Rights are Human Rights' acquired common currency.

Like feminism, the human rights framework can be easily critiqued as a culturally imperialist construct. In a succinct analysis of the various critiques of the human rights framework as it applies to civil and political versus social, economic, and cultural claims, eminent jurist and former Vice Chancellor of Delhi University Upendra Baxi writes that the "operative organizing principle" of the civil and political form of human rights is "the notion of impermissible *violation*, accompanied by duties of here-and-now implementation/redressal," marking a relation between the citizen and politically organized governance communities that include, but are not limited to, the state. In contrast, "forms of social, economic, and cultural rights stand addressed to these [politically organized] communities and networks only in terms of 'progressive implementation' of these rights, even when recast in terms of obligations of recognition, respect, promotion, and protection" (Baxi 2002/2008, 144). The logic of speedy implementation undergirds immediate mechanisms of redress following violations such as rape, especially when the incident emerges in the national limelight.[6] In contrast, social and cultural rights of gay and lesbian citizens to be free of violence, in particular the threat of criminalization and blackmail under outmoded colonial era legislation, were long in the making. Further, Kishwar's argument about decreasing the dependence on and interference of the state, stemming from a "mistrust of the State machinery and of attempts to arm the State with even more repressive powers than it already has" (1990, 8), sits somewhat uneasily with the IWM which looks to the state as the primary means of redress, while holding it accountable for human rights violations. The most recent instance is the police's horrific nighttime burial of the brutally mutilated body of the girl from Hathras, the victim of a caste-motivated rape, without the consent of her parents in 2020. As explicated in the sections that follow, *Manushi* consistently addressed civil and political rights without considering "subaltern women" and/or "subaltern men" as its special constituency or sphere of influence.

In the interests of conceptual clarity and because the category of the subaltern has been deployed specifically to refer to address caste and class marginalization in modern India, I propose a revision of Fraser's terms of analysis ("subaltern counterpublics") to think of efforts such as *Manushi* as "locational" rather than exclusively subaltern oriented. Even as the journal attempted to cover events happening in various parts of India through reports, interviews, letters, fiction, and poetry, its locally directed interventions pervade the printed pages. Baxi writes that "the local, not the global… remains the crucial site of struggle for the enunciation, implementation, and enjoyment and exercise of human rights." Feminists have emphasized how it is more empowering to narrate "stories of everyday violation and resistance which recognize the role of women as *authors* of human rights" than "weaving narratives of universal patriarchy or theorizing repression only as a discursive relation" (Baxi 2002/2008, 185). The Manushi collective wove these narratives by conducting fact finding missions to investigate incidents of sexual and domestic violence. By default, most of these were focused on Delhi and its environs making its efforts local. Such locationality also counters the implied critique of a Western notion of human rights being uncritically adapted to the Indian context without adequately considering intersecting geographical, cultural, social, religious identities. The next section details how location inflects counterpublic articulations of human rights in the journal.

Siting the local

Manushi's reports and articles were based on eyewitness accounts, investigative journalism, and detailed social and political contextualization. Its scrupulous siting/sighting of sexual violence in and around the national capital helped create a "locational counterpublic" as a primary means of resistance, particularly in times of widespread violence such as murders and rapes during the anti-Sikh riots after the assassination of Prime Minister Indira Gandhi in 1984. Following feminist analyses, including Shilpa Phadke and the Pukar collective's work in Mumbai, and Jagori's efforts in Delhi, we can see these feminist efforts, whether labeled as such or not, arriving at a shared assessment of constricted and endangered spaces marking women's sexual and social vulnerability (Jagori 2004; Phadke et al. 2011; Phadke 2013).[7] As part of their site/sight-clearing efforts, these organizations stake a claim to women's public safety and freedom from sexual harassment and violence. The most extreme forms of such violence were rapes of minors and poor women in and around Delhi. In addition to these, supposedly milder forms of harassment – euphemistically described as "eve-teasing" in Indian English – in public places were crucial areas of concern of the IWM in Delhi, Bombay, and other metropoles.

Mansuhi's coverage of sexual harassment and violence in public and private spaces for two decades from 1978 to 1998 marks an attempt to expose gender inequities towards a culture of gender parity and respect in India contemporaneous with similar efforts in Jamaica undertaken by the Sistren collective. My choice of these dates in the Indian context is not arbitrary since 1998 is now understood as a landmark year for the articulation of a lesbian feminist standpoint, following the national controversy over the release of Indo-Canadian Deepa Mehta's "lesbian" film *Fire* set in New Delhi. The city was one of the sites of Hindu nationalists' censorship campaign against the screening of the film.[8] The mythological framework of the film, in particular its evocation of the Hindu epic *Ramayana*, where the deity Ram tests the virtue of his wife Sita, enables an easy connection to Hindu patriarchy and forms of sexual expression. Recuperating mythology to theorize sexual oppression and liberation is a common strategy in Indian feminist analysis. Discussing the implications of the public disrobing of the mythological figure of polyandrous Draupadi in the Hindu epic *Mahabharata*, Rajeswari Sunder Rajan connects the incident to the myriad instances of "eve-teasing," public stripping, and rape that were the focus of feminist campaigns from the 1970s onwards. Placing these on a continuum of public misogyny and sexual violence, she mentions, "Delhi, the national capital, has the dubious distinction of being one of the least safe of Indian cities for women" (Sunder Rajan 2000/2002, 50).

Manushi's reports of sexual intimidation in its early numbers include a reader's letter about male hooliganism in two Delhi University colleges under the pretext of Holi celebrations. A festival of colors marking the onset of spring in northern India, Holi often serves as the occasion for behavior that borders on the verge of sexual harassment. The letter writer, president of the "Nari Adhikar Sangharsh Samiti" or Council for the Struggle of Women's Rights, mentions how such hooliganism has extended from enclosed spaces of educational institutions to public arenas:

> In 1982, a preplanned attack was made on the women students of Stephen's College. In 1983, a busload of boys drove to Lady Shri Ram College, molested the panic stricken girls and drove away. In buses, gangs of boys harass girls while the other passengers look out of the window.
>
> (Kulshreshtha 1983, 28)

As a teenager in the early 1990s, I felt anxious on seeing hordes of boys hanging out from buses with water pistols, colors, and water balloons waiting to "attack" the special buses for college going women provided by the Delhi Transport Corporation. As a public festival celebrated with friends and neighbors, Holi, which marks the change of season from winter to spring, became threatening for women in public spaces.

Readers' letters ensured that "eve-teasing" in public transportation was regularly discussed in the magazine. In another incident, a girl reports how she was verbally and physically harassed by a man who boarded the bus near a college and the manner in which she retaliated by asking the bus to be taken to the police station to file a complaint against the molester (Shewani 1985, 24). Amina Sherwani's letter elicited a congratulatory response from an anonymous reader who places this problem in the context of public and police apathy "Many fears and ideological bonds must go before other women in substantial numbers can act as Amina did" ("Name withheld" 1985, 25). Even in this relatively small sampling of the many incidents covered by *Manushi*, it is apparent that harassment in public spaces was meeting determined resistance both by individual women and men in addition to proposed collective action such as patrol squads, public awareness meetings, and media publicity (Kulshreshtha 1983, 28).

Another aspect of siting the local as the immediate sphere of violence involves the journal's focus on institutional and work locations. Deeptipriya's article "Challenging a Masculinist Culture" provides a history of male students at St. Stephen's College, an elite educational institution in Delhi, indulging in harassment of women including "the annual striptease and nude dancing in front of Miranda House and post graduate women's hostels, which continued up to as late as 1979" (1985, 32). Additionally, flimsy pretexts for not admitting women students into the college, absence of hostel accommodation, an all-male student's union, persecution during Holi, lack of a meeting space for female students, and "scandal sheets" glorifying sexist abuse are all mentioned as causes which led to a thousand students from various institutions protesting at St. Stephen's College in January 1985. The demonstration, according to the report, "diverged from the pattern of the average political…and was remarkable for its verve and visible emotion" and included slogans such as "We are neither pretty nor ugly, we're furious, We're neither chicks nor hens, we're furious" (Deeptipriya 1985, 34). A similar documentation is evident in Kishwar's opinion piece titled "Sex Harassment and Slander as Weapons of Subjugation" in which she assiduously chronicles the sexual misconduct of a professor at Delhi University (1992b, 2–15). The professor involved made sexual advances to women employees, exposed himself, and threatened women with sexual violence if they did not reciprocate his advances. Despite being brought to the attention of the university administration, the harassment was unchecked for years. Manushi's support of the protestations of a determined colleague brought the matter to light.

Kishwar suggests that women can counter such forms of exploitation by reclaiming publicness rather than retreating to the false protection of the private domain: "The larger the number of women entering the public realm the safer each woman is likely to be, just as currently our presence in small insignificant numbers renders the few who venture out far more vulnerable." In addition to numbers, the article emphasizes solidarity at the structural level on the premise that "women's safety is indivisible" and that "none of us is truly safe till each one is safe" (Kishwar 1992a, 14). Recuperating mythology and religion, Kishwar suggests women retaliate against acts of sexual intimidation by adopting the role of the angry goddesses *Chandi* or *Durga* since men are "conditioned to accept and fear this aspect of women" (1992a, 15). Such instances of locating and countering forms of sexual violence in metropolitan Delhi in the 1980s and 1990s attest to sustained feminist efforts to reclaim public areas through reportage and interventions. That these interventions were only partially successful is evident from the follow-up reports where the author describes the hostility she encountered while trying to ascertain what actions had been taken to redress complaints of sexual harassment (Kishwar 1992b, 19–20). The case was finally resolved many years later with the harasser being dismissed from the university in 1996 after a concerted effort by Manushi and a group of teachers. If "harassment" seems like an overly mild term in this context, it is useful to remember Sunder Rajan's observation that "the continuum on which eve-teasing, stripping and the rape of women exist" is as important as also the differences between them, "the first two are performed in open, public spaces, generally by a group of men, while rape is committed in some degree of privacy. Though not necessarily only by a single male" (2000/2002, 47). This continuum is clear in Kavita Charanji's report on the "stripping" of two first-year students at yet another Delhi University college as ritual hazing of incoming students. Charanji mentions that despite the prompt investigation ordered by the Vice Chancellor there was a considerable delay in locating and disciplining those involved in the incident (1992, 16). Manushi's action in these and other instances ensuring that culprits received due punishment were in locations in and around Delhi, though its diagnostic reportage extended beyond the metropolis, across the nation, and beyond it.[9]

Unsiting the sexual

Following widely publicized trials which had galvanized the IWM, *Manushi* adopted a pan-Indian perspective in its coverage of rape in the journal. Rape obviously attracts a greater sense of outrage that the supposedly mundane incidents of everyday sexual violence because it is often categorized as a human rights violation demanding immediate redress. Broader coverage in mainstream and autonomous media legitimized the IWM's position on amending rape laws to ensure humane treatment of victims and speedy delivery of justice. Widespread publicity on rape "cases" revealed collaboration between enforcers and violators of justice, especially considering the age, class, caste, and religion of the victims. What follows is an outline of how *Manushi* unsited sexual violence in the geographical breadth and analytical depth of its reports on rape. My use of the word unsiting indicates the paradoxical ways in which women's sexual vulnerability was both unmoored from its locational emphasis and displaced from the purview of the magazine. While an unsiting of violence beyond the environs of Delhi was commendable, the journal also accomplished another kind of unsiting by consciously steering away from any account of sexual choice and identity. This is a somewhat startling omission, particularly since Vanita, one of the founding editors, later conducted extensive research on same-sex love in Indian literature and culture within and outside the Manushi collective.

To consider the first and commendable unsiting, *Manushi*'s extensive coverage of incidents of rape included reports from states such as Karnataka, Bihar, Maharashtra, Delhi, Rajasthan, and Kashmir, among other places. Most of these reports identify police connivance in preventing justice even when the incident was promptly reported, and due procedure followed. Such connivance sometimes led to "custodial rape" as publicized by the IWM in the 1974 Mathura case when a young tribal girl was raped in police custody. According to reports in the magazine from the 1980s to the 1990s, there were many caste and class related sexual violations including the rape of women at Babubigha in Bihar (Braganza 1984, 13); 13 year old Gauri who was raped by her employer's son and gave birth to a boy (Dewan 1986, 26); and sexually vulnerable employees such as Deepa Murmu, a tribal girl from Bihar, who was impregnated by the Block Development Officer of the district and died in mysterious circumstances after childbirth (Varghese 1997, 17–19). *Manushi* covered these in meticulous detail especially in relation to the IWM's call for the amendment of rape laws to ensure speedy justice and to protect the survivor during the trial period. In almost every incident, rape survivors, their families, and/or activists supporting them attempted to secure justice, and some even adopted vigilante tactics to counter police apathy. These involved slogan-shouting by the Ahmedabad Women's Action Group and beating the rapist of a five year old girl, Farida, from Ahmedabad (Pathak & Amin 1990, 37–38). While the merits or demerits of these actions are debatable, they reflect rage against an ineffectual police and judiciary which allowed the perpetrators to go unpunished or deliberately delayed delivery of justice.

Despite the stigma accorded to rape, a clear picture of women's determination to fight back emerges in these decades. In an article titled "When a Poor Woman gets Raped," Rupande Panalal describes how a gang-raped woman from a Jogeshwari slum in Bombay coped with support from her community and a local youth organization but received little help from the authorities:

> Contrary to all established myths on rape, the incident does not seem to have shattered Narasamma or stigmatized her within the family. At least at the moment, the local organisation views it as an outrage on the community as a whole, and not as an issue concerning only Narasamma or even only the women.
>
> (Panalal 1990, 36)

Roma Debabrata faced a similar uphill battle with the police and judiciary when she got involved as a translator in the child prostitution and rape case of Hamida, a teenager trafficked from Bangladesh. *Manushi*'s articles over several years describe Ms. Debabrata's dedication to rehabilitating the child and her success in reuniting Hamida with her family in Bangladesh at the cost of a huge emotional and time commitment (Agarwal 1995a, 42; 1995b, 20–27; *Manushi* 1997, 33–34).

Unsiting sexual violence from local to national and transnational locations (as in the Hamida case), the reports and editorials also displayed a profound mistrust of

FIGURE 4.1 Photograph from *Manushi*'s report on Hamida's safe return to her family after a harrowing experience of child prostitution. Courtesy of Madhu Kishwar and *Manushi*.

the state machinery, especially its promises of new and improved legislation in rape trials. This mistrust has stood the test of time, where even improved legislation has not proved a deterrent to gruesome acts of sexual violence. The review of rape laws post-Mathura had involved *in camera* trials to protect the identity of the survivor and to prevent her from further harassment. As the Hamida case illustrated, this proved to be a handicap rather than a facilitator of the trial, particularly since Hamida did not speak Hindi and had to face her persecutors at close quarters, increasing rather than decreasing her anguish. Sunder Rajan's claim that "the ground and rationale for the existing laws are directed less towards ensuring women's rights to freedom of functioning in public than towards preserving an ideal of public morality and civic law and order" is proved by the fact that despite an extensive amendment of laws related to sexual violence in the 1980s, law enforcement agencies and the judicial machinery seemed as reluctant to convict the offenders as before (Sunder Rajan 2000/2002, 53).

On the second meaning of unsiting, the Manushi collective and its journal stands as a case in point for the IWM's faultlines on sexual choice and identity. As is typical of many Non-Governmental Organizations (NGOs) of this period, the focus on sexual violence within a human rights framework dictated the political and organizational strategies of the Manushi collective. In their account of NGOs and feminisms, Victoria Bernal and Inderpal Grewal observe how feminist activism "may be inspired by movements in other parts of the world, and new communication technologies may facilitate borrowings and commonalities, but also resistances" (2012, 13). Such resistance is evident in *Manushi* where apart from new stories, poems, readers' letters, and film reviews, women's sexuality in general and lesbianism are never really discussed. During the 1980s and 1990s, when a series of incidents led to an increased focus on sexuality outside the heteronormative framework, *Manushi* reported on all forms of sexual violence except the proscription of lesbian relationships.

Both the oversight and unsiting of sexuality is a surprising omission in a prominent journal about women and society, since accounts of the formation of a lesbian community in Delhi indicate its origins at least from the late 1980s onwards.[10] Careful in locating heterosexual violence as a writerly-readerly, real-imaginary, social-mythological concern, *Manushi* clearly made a decision to relegate its minimal references to homosexuality to the domains of readerly, the mythological, and the imaginary. Thus, there are references to alternative gender roles and sexual preferences in reader's responses and letters to the journal. Asha Chaturvedi's letter to *Manushi* mentions the marriage of two policewomen, Urmila and Leela, widely covered in mainstream media to pose the rhetorical question, "why cannot two people of the same sex spend their lives together?" (1988, 23). Discussing an article on reproductive health published in the journal, Abha Bhaiya, another reader and founding member of Jagori, mentions how subsuming women's health under reproduction excludes "women who are living outside heterosexual marital homes," including "single, deserted, and widowed women as well as lesbian women" (1992, 42). As these examples indicate, the onus of discussing sexuality is on the readers rather than those writing for *Manushi* in an editorial or journalistic capacity.

Similarly, the journal's discussion of Hindu mythology provides models for alternative gender and sexual roles. Over many years of co-editing the journal, Kishwar and Vanita presented revisionary accounts of Hindu epics, including folklore versions of the epics which contest the patriarchy of the more accepted Sanskrit versions. Among such revaluations are articles on the iconic figure, Sita, Ram's consort from the *Ramayana* (Cobrun 1995; Vanita 2005). Finally, the imaginary, including fiction and film, become a way in which the journal offers its readers a glimpse into alternative sexual preferences. Creative writing, especially stories, by Indian and diasporic authors such as Ismat Chughtai, Vijayadan Detha, and Suniti Namjoshi, whose works form the canon of South Asian lesbian writing, find a regular place in the pages of the journal from the 1980s onwards.

Manushi's editorial unsiting of sexuality from the social to the imaginary was not successful when the filmic representation of lesbianism provoked a major national controversy in 1998. Attacking Mehta's film in an article titled "Naïve Outpourings of a Self-Hating Indian," Kishwar denies dangers faced by gay, lesbian, and transgender people: "in the public sphere there are no campaigns or attacks against homosexuals in India, nor have they faced persecution in jobs, as has often happened in many western countries" (1998, 9). The denial sits oddly with the meticulous documentation of and interventions against heterosexual violence in the journal over the previous decades. Clearly the journal and the organization aimed for impact and change within a "national" space but did not take into consideration the national and transnational publics it was reaching. Some awareness of these is evident in the letters received from readers across South Asia and other parts of the world included in the sections "Letters to Manushi" and "Reader's Responses."

As indicated previously, Kishwar's rejoinder to critiques of her stand on *Fire* was to accuse elite readers of having a different set of priorities than her indigenous agenda. She writes, "most highly educated women respond to my articles only when they deal with issues like sex, marriage, dowry and relationships with men" in contrast to "a variety of other subjects that are important to both women and men such as India's farm policy, economic reforms, ethnic conflicts, sanitation, health and education" which have "hardly ever been subjects of animated debate within women's groups" (1999a, 6). The implicit charge of Westernization and hence disconnection from the "real" issues impacting Indian women gets added to other charges when Kishwar responds to letters from members of the diasporic feminist group South Asian Women's Network (SAWNET) (1999b, 38–44). In its dismissal of these opinions, Manushi's commitment to creating a locational counterpublic is disarticulated from national and transnational feminist solidarities. According to Fraser, "public opinion is legitimate if and only if it results from a communicative process in which all potentially affected can participate as peers, *regardless of political citizenship*" (2007, emphasis original). The promise of such a communicative process is crucial to any analysis of the journal despite its later invocation of an authentic "Indianness" as the only justifiable grounds for addressing women's concerns, and a dismissal of supposedly radical ideas about gender and sexuality, including the right to pleasure in heterosexual and homosexual relationships.[11]

FIGURE 4.2 Photograph of Hindu fundamentalists vandalizing Regal Cinema in New Delhi from Madhu Kishwar's article on the controversy surrounding Deepa Mehta's film *Fire*. Courtesy of Madhu Kishwar and *Manushi*.

Jyoti Puri has usefully commented on the disconnections between women's and queer activism in her discussion of Articles 375/366 of the Indian Penal code on the criminalization and punishment of rape, and Article 377 which criminalized homosexuality. Puri observes that mobilizations against these articles "seem to be split especially along the lines of women's issues versus queer issues" (2011, 205). Some awareness of both male and female sexual vulnerability led to a section of the IWM demanding that rape laws be gender neutral. The call was perceived in some circles as a positive move to punish sexual violence by broadening the definition of rape and persecuting child rapists under section 375, dealing with rape, rather than 377, which criminalized homosexuality but is often invoked to persecute child sexual abuse. Yet fears abounded of potential misuse of the amended rape law to persecute homosexuals, echoing M. Jacqui Alexander's claim in another context, that "the systematic conflation of perverted heterosexual violence, such as rape or incest, with same-sex desire" establishes

> a continuum of criminality in which same-sex desire is the apotheosis of a range of offenses including murder, robbery, dishonesty, lying, rape, domestic violence, adultery, fornication, and incest. Thus constructed, the psyche of criminality *is* the psyche of homosexuality.
>
> (2005, 41)

In the Indian context, this criminality was confirmed with the representation of homosexuals as threats to public morality and in the legal codification of "unnatural sex" that was punishable by law until just three years ago. Unlike Manushi, groups like Jagori addressed sexuality under euphemistic categories such as "single women" to avoid the social stigma attached to lesbian identities. The strategy was similar to gay male deployment of the clinical category "MSM" or Men who have Sex with Men to present their sexuality within a discourse of health and human rights.

State, human rights, counterpublics

Sections of the IWM have been antagonistic to discussions of sexual choice, and *Manushi* reveals some features of this antagonism despite queer activists' belief that since "women's movements were the first to articulate concern over the control over sexuality and the societal constructions of gender" they are "the closest link and support for the nascent 'queer' movements in the country" (Shah 2005, 153). Events which finally led to matters coming to the national forefront causing the IWM's contradictory stance include the following: controversy over the release of *Fire* in 1998; the nationalist government's pledge to introduce capital punishment for those convicted of rape in the same year; and the Law Commission of India's recommendation that rape law be made gender neutral in response to a 1997 writ petition filed by the Delhi-based NGO Sakshi on behalf of a sexually abused minor. In all three cases the IWM's response revealed divisions on the most effective way to address sexual violence within and outside the heteronormative framework.

The paradox of invoking a rights framework for women's rights and not including the rights of lesbian women within its ambit is explained by Alice Miller and Carole Vance's identification of three problem areas encountered by those working at the intersection of sexuality and human rights: hierarchies of respectability; the role of the state; and the presumption of "innocence" by those securing justice for victims of sexual violence (2004, 5–15). All three are evident in the IWM's reluctance to ally with the movement for sexual rights in the 1990s. In terms of hierarchies of respectability, rape as a form of sexual violence is assumed to bring "dishonor" not only on the victim but her family; in contrast, homosexual relations (rather than violence against homosexuals) are perceived as "dishonorable" in and of themselves. The same criterion underlies the presumption of innocence, where the rape victim (often, but not exclusively, female) is presented as an innocent victim of male lust (unless of course she is "provocatively" dressed, or outside the house at "unseemly" times) while a gay man or lesbian woman "invites" violence by his/her lifestyle and cannot be presumed innocent.

Miller and Vance's crucial point about the role of the state in addressing sexual violence as human rights violations requires an extended analysis since this connection is crucial to the work of gay and lesbian activists' publicization of sexuality as a human rights issue. Given the almost exclusive focus on (hetero)sexual violence, the human rights framework used to talk about Indian women in *Manushi* was not seen as applicable to sexual minorities. Indian gay and lesbian activists have strategically invoked human rights by making sexuality a health issue and pointing to discriminatory state legislation as severely impacting the quality of life of and gravely endangering an already at risk population. Almost since its inception, and perhaps rightly so, *Manushi* had demonstrated a mistrust of state machinery, especially its enactment of special provisos and laws to combat gendered and sexualized forms of violence. In this the collective and its journal reflects the autonomous IWM's contradictory stance, where, on the one hand, the state is called on to enact stringent legislation against sexual and domestic violence, but, on the other, the state's ineffectiveness and culpability is apparent in its emissaries such as the police and the judiciary doing little to combat (and sometimes even promoting) violence. In recent times, gay and lesbian activists have had a similar embattled relationship with the state.

The state machinery's response to women activists' concern about domestic and marital violence related to dowry demands in the 1980s was to set up an Anti-Dowry Cell of the Delhi Police in 1983. Some years later it was transformed into the Crimes Against Women Cell, with branches all over the city which examined complaints related to abuse, rape, and women's murders. The dangers in the enactment of state measures and laws for women's "protection" were brought to light in the consequences of the Indecent Representation of Women (Prohibition) Bill, 1986, which was discussed in *Manushi* as a repressive measure intended to control media and curtail free speech and expression. In addition, "certain urban women's groups" who took "their cue from similar campaigns in the West" were critiqued for demanding such legislation (Kishwar & Vanita 1987, 7). Comparing this legislation to the Suppression of Immoral Trafficking in Girls and Women Act (SITA), ostensibly meant to curtail sexual trafficking of minors, Kishwar and Vanita point out how this measure has been used to persecute sex workers with threats of arrest and to solicit bribes from them (1987, 4). Additional dangers of such inter-ference were evident in the forcible testing of Delhi prostitutes for HIV/AIDS transmission as well as police use of the law to register kidnapped or purchased minor girls as prostitutes in collaboration with pimps (Debabrata 1998, 28).

Based on an informative, interview-based study, Abha Thapalyal, Prabha Rani, and Ruth Vanita's article for *Manushi* questions the effectiveness of state machinery in curbing rampant violence: "The mentality of expecting government to solve all problems is fairly widespread in our society today, and is actively fostered by gov-ernment" (1987, 18). Nandita Haskar details problems in approaching civil liberties from a "liberal human rights" model in which legislative changes are demanded as an indication of a modern, progressive perspective on women's liberties. Haskar's opinion is that a movement should "resort to the law" only when it is "strong enough to carry the law reform forward" (2005, 149). Years of campaigning on violence against women by feminist collectives and associated publications like *Manushi* enabled more stringent rape, dowry, and anti-trafficking legislation to be enacted leading to mixed results. During the 1980s and 1990s the autonomous

IWN was never completely taken in by the promises of new legislation held up by the state as a panacea. Yet, in the absence of large-scale community mobilization, print remained a medium of communication and the state remained an entity whose mechanisms promised, even if they did not always deliver, redress.

Questioning the distinction between the private and the public especially in the domain of sexuality by bringing to light dowry related crimes, publicizing rape and sexual harassment cases, and asserting women's right to their bodies indirectly created a space for the sexual activism of this period. Bacchetta mentions the formation of a Delhi Group in the 1980s which met regularly to discuss sexual identities and choices (2002, 960). This informal discussion and social group morphed into Sakhi, the country's first lesbian focused organization, founded by Giti Thadani. The group had connections with the autonomous women's movement, though it did not use existing venues of publication such as *Manushi* or the Jagori newsletter, instead using *Bombay Dost*, a gay men's magazine, to publicize its existence (see Chapter 5). Outlining the contours of a queer politics, Michael Warner has written that a counterpublic can "do more than represent the interests of gendered or sexualized persons in a public sphere," since "it can mediate the most private and intimate meanings of gender and sexuality," and "work to elaborate new worlds of culture and social relations in which gender and sexuality can be lived, including forms of intimate association, vocabularies of affect, styles of embodiment, erotic practices, and relations of care and pedagogy" (Warner 2002, 57). Despite consciously steering away from lesbian and queer activism, the print-mediated counterpublic created by Manushi and other women's organizations introduced forms of intervention and pedagogy that altered the worlds of culture and social relations in which gender and sexuality were lived in Delhi. I have claimed that one way in which this was accomplished was through an unsiting of the sexual from the authorial to the readerly, from the real to the imaginary, and from the social to the mythological.

Dave's astute analysis of the reasons why the women's movement felt the need to distance itself from "the more radical, socially disruptive notions about gender, sexuality, and power emerging in lesbian politics" identifies how certain sections of the IWM had already been accused of being "Western" (2012, 123). On the IWM's dis/connection with lesbian activism, Dave further observes that those women activists who did engage in lesbian politics at all did so "through the rubric of human rights, ignoring critiques of the structure of the family or of feminist complicity with heteronormativity" (123). If the IWM has been reluctant to take sexuality on board, it is also because of a perceived disconnection between sexual violence and sexual liberation. Whereas violence is easily understood within a human rights vocabulary inasmuch as documents such as the UHDHR and the National Human Rights Council Act recognize claims to be free of danger, the human rights claim to sexual expression, identity, and choice is not easily translatable into this framework. Bernal and Grewal observe that within "the context in which women's rights is a long-standing language of NGO activism, the new frameworks of sexual rights change existing subjects and strategies of activism" (2014, 15). Although Manushi's strategies of activism changed over the decades of its existence, the refusal to take on board "new frameworks of sexual rights" perhaps because of growing Hindu nationalist influence made the journal less useful to women's activism in the early years of the new millennium. However, as this chapter has argued, the locational, selective, and necessarily incomplete counterpublic created by the autonomous IWM through publications like *Manushi* in the late twentieth century is of lasting historical as well as contemporary importance in the emerging narrative of sexuality and women's rights in India.

A murderous rape in Delhi in late 2012 galvanized women's groups to demand participatory inputs to the commission set up to reshape rape legislation, much as murderous attacks on gay men and lesbian suicides have provided the impetus for gay and lesbian legal activism since the late 1990s. The hastily implemented changes to article 376 on rape in the past years indicate that these counterpublic articulations are incomplete, ongoing, and in dialogue with the state and beyond the borders of its jurisdiction.[12] The next chapter describes how the emerging gay and lesbian movement in the country negotiated sexual rights claims.

Notes

1 Stuart Hall's definition of "articulation" is useful in this context: "An articulation is thus the form of the connection that *can* make a unity of two different elements, under certain conditions. It is a linkage which is not necessary, determined, absolute and essential for all time…The 'unity' which matters is a linkage between that articulated discourse and the social forces with which it can, under certain historical conditions, but need not necessarily, be connected." (1996, 141).

2 Article 377 of the Indian Penal Code. **Unnatural offences**: Whoever voluntarily has carnal intercourse against the order of nature with any man, woman or animal shall be punished with imprisonment for life, or with imprisonment of either description for a term which may extend to ten years and shall also be liable to fine. **Explanation**: Penetration is sufficient to constitute the carnal intercourse necessary to the offence described in this section.

3 Responding to various readers' letters to the magazine over the years, Kishwar mentioned that *Manushi*'s Hindi version was discontinued because of lack of subscribers and contributions. She addresses these concerns as part of her larger argument against the dominance of English in "Destroying Minds and Skills: The Dominance of *Angreziyat* in Our Education" (1997, 21–29).

4 *Jagori* emerged out of *Saheli* because of differences over sources of funding. However, many women remained members of these groups and a spirit of mutual respect and cooperation has marked their interaction. Both groups were named by Abha, one of the founding members. For more details, see the 25-year account of *Jagori* titled "Living Feminisms" available on their website: www.jagori.org/sites/default/files/publication/Living%20Feminisms.pdf.

5 In their introduction to *Because I Have a Voice: Queer Politics in India*, Arvind Narrain and Guatam Bhan mention the role of "community magazines" such as *Bombay Dost* from Mumbai, *Sangha Mitra* from Calcutta, *Darpan* in Delhi, and *Naya Pravartak* in Kolkata for their "attempts at articulating a worldview, an ethos and a shared sense of community forged under difficult times" (2005, 13).

6 The Mathura, Rameeza Bee, and Bhanwari Devi rape cases from the 1970s through to the 1990s indicate how mechanisms of redress from the state include quick and often hasty legislative changes. For a detailed account of these cases see Flavia Agnes' 1993 essay, "The Anti-Rape Campaign: The Struggle and the Setback." If listing these seems

like a "roll call of raped women" it is because I agree with Kalpana Kannabiran's assertion that "describing and naming the girls/women who suffer rape and the male perpetrators" helps "ground the narration of rape." Additionally, "placing the victims contiguously serves the added purpose of creating a collectivity and forging a collective identity for women in the discourse on rape" (2002, 106). In twenty-first century India, the names and the women disappear in the face of the brutality, to be replaced by attributes and places: Nirbhaya, Shopian, Kathua, Hathras.

7 With the nightly work schedules of the women's workforce in many metropolitan and non-metropolitan locations in India since the 1990s, feminists have focused on questions of transportation, access, and safety. Manushi's online articles since the 2000s address these concerns. Other analyses include Shilpa Phadke's essay, "Traversing the City: Some Gendered Questions of Access in Mumbai" (2013) and Kanika Batra's "Transporting Metropolitanism: Road-Mapping Feminist Solutions to Sexual Violence in Delhi" (2018).

8 Much has been written about this controversy and I will not spend time rehearsing the arguments. Seldom have these discussions focused on the question of sexual violence. See for instance essays by Brinda Bose (2000/2007), Jigna Desai (2002), Alison Donnell (2007), Gayatri Gopinath (2005b), and Namita Goswami (2008), which discuss respectively female pleasure as resistance, the identitarian exclusions of the film, its negotiation of globalization and postcoloniality, and its queer transnational trajectories. None of these refer to the domestic and public sites of bodily violence either directly or indirectly.

9 Kishwar candidly accepts limitations in covering events from all parts of the country: "We try hard to get reports of important struggles and happenings from different parts of the country, especially rural areas. But given that our resources are very limited, our coverage tends to be limited too. We invite our readers to take an even more active part in sending us reports from their respective areas" (1992c, 40).

10 See Naisargi Dave (2010) and Paola Bacchetta (2002). Bacchetta mentions that in the late 1970s and 1980s due to the coverage of lesbian suicides, lesbianism "began to appear in the national mediascape" (958). She identifies "single women" as one of the identity positions from which "lesbians" have made common cause with the IWM (Bacchetta 2002, 967–968). Dave notes that though there are clear connections between lesbian activism and the IWM in terms of strategies and language of rights, "women's groups have historically distanced themselves from lesbian politics…in order to defend a hard-fought image of being in step with national concerns" (2010, 598).

11 The promises of transnational feminist connections can sometimes result in colonial gestures. See for instance, Nivedita Menon, Vrinda Grover, Mary John and other feminists' critiques of Harvard University's Women's Studies Program's "Beyond Gender Equity" task force set up "to produce a working paper that advises on the implementation of the recommendations from the Verma Committee" (qtd. in Menon 2013b; see also Grover et al. 2013).

12 For a detailed account of feminists' disappointment with the 2012 legislation, see Nivedita Menon's blog post on Kafila titled "'The Impunity of Every Citadel Is Intact': The Taming of the Verma Committee Report, and Some Troubling Doubts" (2013).

5

OUTING INDIAN SEXUALITIES

Bombay Dost and the limits of queer intersectionality

New Delhi's downtown commercial area, Connaught Place, is home to the historic Regal Building where the legendary Regal Cinema and many small retail shops attract several thousand people daily. In 1998 Hindu fundamentalists successfully prevented a scheduled screening of Deepa Mehta's "lesbian" film *Fire* by ransacking the cinema and vandalizing the building. A couple of days later several hundred people showed up outside Regal to protest the vigilante tactics of the Hindu right, among them a contingent of brave lesbians who inaugurated the Campaign for Lesbian Rights in India (CALERI).

Months after that remarkable year when lesbian activism exploded on the streets of Delhi, I picked up my first copy of *Bombay Dost (BD)*, India's only regularly printed gay magazine, the CALERI report on lesbian emergence, and *Humjinsi*, a resource guide to LGBT activism in India from People Tree, a small shop in the Regal building. The shopfront displays handmade clothes, jewelry, and other bric-a-brac. Ignoring the goods and walking through a long, narrow space, the visitor arrives at a small bookstore at the back of the shop. Utilizing every inch of the premium space, the shelves are carefully curated with socialist, feminist, and queer books, newsletters, and magazines. In the early years of LGBTQ+ emergence in India, *Bombay Dost* other queer publications battled against limited financial support from advertisers and media outlets, looming threats of censorship, low circulation figures, and a mandate to protect the identity of their subscribers and readers. People Tree was one of three outlets in the country, and the only one in Delhi, which distributed *BD* in those times. LGBTQ+ activist literature (fiction, poetry, drama, scholarly studies, newsletters, magazines, reports) is now found in almost all major bookstores in the city.

Conceptualized by journalist and controversial gay rights activist Ashok Row Kavi with co-founders Suhail Abbasi and Sridhar Rangayan, *BD* first appeared as a bilingual Hindi and English newsletter. Within a year it was registered as an official publication with the Government of India. It helped its associated NGO Humsafar

DOI: 10.4324/9781003170303-7

Trust map desire, dreams, disease, death, and determination in the frenetic pace of globalization in a newly liberalized India. Three years in, the magazine decided to go the corporate route. It was then owned by Pride Publications and registered under the Indian Companies Act. As the only regular bilingual LGBTQ+ magazine in India at the time, *BD*'s stated aim was to serve as a means of information and socialization for gay men *and* lesbian and transgender persons all over India.

Moving from Delhi to Bombay, this chapter expands upon the claim that feminist magazines such as *Manushi* initiated conversations on gender and sexuality in India forwarded by *BD*. *BD*-Humsafar's focus on sexual identity, education, health, and community building emerged in newly opened spaces between the train rush to address sexual health concerns (primarily AIDS prevention) and the messy legislative reform and sexual rights platform supported by local, national, and transnational gay and lesbian organizations in South Asia. One sign of the uneven progression of sexual activism in the country is that though *BD* was first published in 1990, an Indian lesbian magazine did not emerge until 1998 after the lesbian

FIGURE 5.1 Cover page of first available number of *Bombay Dost* before it was officially registered as a magazine. Courtesy of Ashok Row Kavi and Humsafar Trust.

protests mentioned above.[1] Indian LGBTQ+ activist literature, including the magazines *Pravartak, BD, Scripts* and *Labia*, are scattered in personal collections and organizational holdings, partially explaining why they are only intermittently used as sources for cultural histories of sexuality in the region (Puri 2002; Katrak 2006). Unlike feminist sources, none of these foundational publications are available online. The move from print to digital forums in the twenty-first century makes these somewhat neglected archives of community formation amid new means of information and communication. Unlike the 1990s, a growing body of queer literature, including works by the publishing giants Harper-Collins, Penguin, and Seagull, and small, independent publishers such as Zubaan, Yoda, Stree, and Queer Ink, are available in print and electronic formats.

BD's aim of connecting sexual minorities was coterminous with those of other landmark South Asian gay newsletters/magazines in the US and UK including *Trikon/Trikone, Shakti Khabar, Anamika,* and *Shamakami. Anamika*, a short-lived lesbian newsletter published from Chicago – likely the earliest South Asian publication of its kind – preceded *BD* and *Trikon*. Correspondence and connections among activists involved in these publications illustrate the transnational-national itineraries of South Asian sexualities. These South-North-South LGBTQ+ trajectories mediated by diasporic and India-based interactions establish a recent history of worlding sexualities to effectively deny the charge that Indian gay and lesbian identities imitate Western lifestyles. *BD*-Humsafar not only helped counter facile charges of "imported" sexual identities, it paved the way for emerging legal, medical, and media forums to document and create the conditions for public emergence of sexual identity politics in India.

BD bridged the gap between already existing LGBTQ+ social networks in Bombay, neighboring cities such as Pune and Thane, and those within and outside major cities who did not have access to these networks, though they often developed other forms of socialization. Some scholars have analyzed the urban conglomeration of sexuality movements and the limited but crucial role of print in the formation of sexual communities in India (Vanita 2007; Shah 2015). *BD*'s representation of metropolitan gay and lesbian lives in Delhi and Bombay in the last decades of the twentieth century demonstrates how trajectories of socialization and activism developed via print. Networks of gay male affiliation in these cities were first formed through cross-class cruising spots (parks, beaches, public bathrooms, construction sites, historical monuments), work, and/or shared information about middle and upper class gay party circuits (clubs, bars, restaurants). Writing about place, marginality, and the creation of an archive, Gayatri Gopinath describes the "evocation of a queer regional imaginary" which allows "tracing lines of connection and commonality, a kind of South-South relationality, between seemingly discrete regional spaces that in fact bypass the nation" (2018, 5). We see this relationality in the way in which South Asia is imagined, represented, and traversed by *BD*'s anonymous circulation in the early years. With Bombay as the locus of its activities, *BD* radiated to other cities, regions, and locations in India, South Asia, and the South Asian diaspora.

SHAMAKAMI

Forum for South Asian feminist lesbians
June 1, 1990 Vol. I

"Identifying Ourselves"

FIGURE 5.2 Cover page of *Shamakami*, a diasporic South Asian lesbian magazine. Photograph by the author from the archives of the Deering Collection, Northwestern University Library.

Today, social media is the preferred mode of queer socialization, activism, and research. Print publications are, quite literally, relics of another century. Studies of largely gay male subcultures in Bombay and Delhi by Sandip Roy (2003), Pramesh Shahni (2008), Rohit Dasgupta (2017), and Akhil Katyal (2016) combine online and offline ethnographies to assess forms of sexual expression, identity construction, rights awareness, and political consciousness among gay men. Paola Bacchetta (2002), Radhika Gajjala (2004), and Naisargi Dave (2012) analyze online and onsite interactions among feminist and lesbian communities to emphasize the results of sustained ethnography. Many of these studies use organizational archives and make their claims about feminist, gay, and lesbian activism by testing them against the grain of online participant research as members and moderators of list-serves, web discussion forums, and social media platforms including Twitter, Reddit, and Instagram communities and Facebook groups. Following these methods but rejecting an exclusive focus on gay men, I read the early numbers of *Bombay Dost*, currently unavailable in digital format, for their representation of lesbian and transgender lives.

In this chapter, as in Chapter 2 on the *Jamaica Gaily News*, I assess the cultural reach of *BD* as an emergent counterpublic forum, its projected readership, and the limits of its coalitional politics. Crucial to *BD*'s cultural and geographical reach are its limited connections (and, sometimes, obvious disconnections) with lesbian women that replicate the pattern of gay publications like *Link/Skakel* and *Exit* from South Africa (Chapter 6). My analysis also focuses on *BD*'s minimal and stereo-typed attention to transgender populations in contrast to its offshoot organization Humsafar's extensive work on AIDS prevention that aimed to reach transgender people under the category Men who have Sex with Men (MSM). I conclude by examining the geographical and activist limits of sexual worldings attempted by *BD*-Humsafar.

Soliciting intimate readership

To address a broad constituency of readers *BD* first appeared as a bilingual magazine in Hindi and English. In the first numbers, the English and Hindi sections are almost equal in length, with the English editorial, the letters column, classified personal ads, and several articles translated into Hindi. The English articles represent a stratified gay social scene that is somewhat tempered by *BD*'s efforts to be inclusive of the interests and geographies of Hindi-speaking readers. In later years, these efforts are minimal, and the magazine is unabashed about the kind of readership it hoped to cultivate. An advertisement to potential advertisers in *BD* mentions that ads in the magazine reach "a very special target group comprising NGOs, influential individuals and gay persons who are mostly single men with high disposable incomes" (*BD* 1994a, 5). Here the closed circle of market imperatives and targeted readership led to a move away from the magazine's early goals of connecting gay men and lesbian women across the country. The implied language, income, and networked exclusiveness led to a gradual decline of the Hindi section and its eventual elimination.

As the title of the magazine reveals, *BD* projected itself in the "idiom" of sexuality as *dosti* or friendship to solicit readers from among the scattered gay and lesbian con-stituencies in the city and the nation (Katyal 2016).[2] *Dosti* is the preferred homosocial idiom of Bollywood. Hindi films often present a triangulation where two male friends desire the same woman and one of the men "sacrifices" heterosexual romance on the altar of friendship by helping the other woo the object of desire. The popular film song "Bombay se aaya mera dost" (my friend is from Bombay) often invoked by the editors is a nod to such instances of male-male friendship (Vanita 2002a; Katyal 2016). *BD* invokes cinematic and literary iterations of *dosti* to imagine Bombay as a city of extreme contradictions where wealth and poverty, make-believe and reality, sex and celibacy, crime and policing, exist in proximity. Literary and filmic representations offer a temporary respite from the rampant overcrowding, homelessness, and infrastructural collapse of the city. Indian English fiction by R. Raj Rao, Vikram Chandra, Suketu Mehta, Amrita Mahale, and Jeet Thayil taps into the desire for escape to offer a view of Bombay both as a city on the edge of collapse and offering a home to social and sexual outcasts. Following literary tradition *BD* published poetry, fiction, life-writing, and an advice column where readers wrote to "Papa Passion" seeking advice on love, life, and relationships. Many creative pieces in *BD* are about the search for an all-consuming passion leading to everlasting love. This idealized trajectory of relationships is belied by familial and social ostracism of gay, lesbian, and bisexual relationships. Much like the fiction in *JGN, BD* sought to provide its gay readers a respite from overwhelmingly heteropatriarchal social and cultural formations by creating a readership that immersed itself in make-believe literary representations of long-lasting gay and lesbian intimacy.

BD also sought to create intimate readership by regularly reviewing Bollywood films to connect readers in India, South Asia, and the diaspora where these films are avidly consumed. The earliest available number from Humsafar's archives in Vakola (Volume 1, Number 2), when the publication was still "unregistered" under the Indian Publications Act, contains a two-page review of the recently released Bollywood film *Veeru Dada*, featuring a homosexual character.[3] The review provides a vocabulary of gay and lesbian life in India: vernacular idioms of sexuality as "*shauk* or interest/hobby/passion" and "*nawabi* or royal passion"; local terms for sexual alterity including "chakka" or number six as describing "eunuch, transvestite, transsexual, and homosexual," and "gur" or jaggery as a Hindi label for gay; and class divisions differentiating between the "intellectual elite," "rich elite," "economically weaker section" (*BD* 1990b, 19–20). Embodying "queer cinephilia" – characterized by an explosion of queer representations in Bollywood over the past two decades – the reviews lead to the emergence of a "queer-identified spectator" in *BD* (Ghosh 2010, 18)

BD's next number reviewed another Bollywood film, *Mast Kalandar*, portraying Pinku, a feminized queen, and Sher Singh (fierce warrior), an alpha-male policeman. The reviewer is unimpressed by Sher Singh's self-castigations when he falls head over heels for Pinku; he questions the filmmaker's motives by asking: "Who interpolated this scene? The writer or the director? Is it okay for a 'pansy' to be homosexual and not for a 'normal' man?" (*BD* 1991a, 15). A review of the blockbuster *Main Khiladi, Tu Anari* (I am the Player, You are Ignorant) lauds attraction between the lead characters played by Bollywood superstars Saif Ali Khan and Akshay Kumar even as the writer ironically observes, "neither the directors nor the actors have shown any awareness of the fact that homosexuality underlies the theme" (Ashok 1995, 8). These reviews encourage *BD*'s readers to think about their representations of same-sex desire and participate in the ongoing conversation about sexualities in India.

Bollywood actors are the equivalent of dancehall and reggae artists in Jamaica. Not only are Indians avid filmgoers, robust circulation of film magazines in the country suggests eager consumption of information about the lifestyles and opinions of film stars. *BD* solicited Bollywood actors' opinions to democratize and popularize discussion of sexualities. The magazine interviewed Bollywood superstar Akshay Kumar and the model and actor Milind Sonam, (*BD* 1996a, 11). While lamenting "nasty film gossip in filmy mags," an early editorial commends actors who have gone on record to state their views on homosexuality (*BD* 1991b, 3). In an especially innovative design, the December 1992 back cover was a collage of short snippets of Bollywood luminaries' views on safe sex. Engaging readers through the appeal and reach of popular culture was one of the magazine's most successful strategies. Not only did this increase readership, it provided the basis for a cross-class, relatable, homegrown discussion of sexualities in its early years.

Despite the democratizing appeal of Bollywood, when the magazine became an exclusively English language publication, its primary readers were affluent gay men. *BD*'s class focus is clear from articles on the gay party scene in Bombay. Sridhar edited a special number on Gay Parties where Row Kavi describes partying as the primary means of socialization in a satirical piece titled "Bombay Parties: Then and Now." He reminds readers of how he started the first "pay party" in Bombay in 1985 in the suburbs: "Everybody was equal in the eyes of the organizer because each person had paid the equivalent amount." With no hint of irony in his defense of cash-mediated equality, he laments the predation and fragmentation of the community:

> The Malabar Hill crowd is busy with its own scene and seems to depend only on predatory sex where gorgeous members of the working class get entry for their physical endowments. The middle-class queens have their own thing going on the Walls after the quick shindig at Voodoo and its sweat, Palestinians and all.
>
> (Row Kavi 1998a, 13)

Other contributions echo Row Kavi's blatant snobbishness and ethnocentrism. Sridhar describes in detail the dress codes and "seduction theme" expected at social events such as a special dinner, a birthday party, and a huge public party. In an apt rejoinder, another writer mentions the lack of community feeling and asks

> would you rather put in your two-bit to help educate the ignorant or spend your energies cruising, partying, and looking for opportunities to have sex?… This is no moral bullshit, it's to commit ourselves to what the word gay, community, and equality stand for.
>
> (Karani 1998a, 14)

These contentious exchanges between various members of the gay scene in Bombay echo the socialization-activism dilemma faced by the GFM-*JGN* members in Jamaica.

Some of the assumptions of the party scene came to the forefront when a "white party" in Bombay went horribly wrong. Vikram reports on how the party was infiltrated by plainclothes policemen and policewomen who came prepared to attack the organizers, the attendees, and the drag performers. Singling out attendees and demanding their names and addresses, the police humiliated the performers and the hosts, took their photographs, and held them overnight in the police station as an intimidation strategy. After the raid, the police released reports to various newspapers leading to a lot of negative publicity for the organizers and performers. In "White Out," the writer deliberates on the conspicuous consumption and publicity leading to the series of events: "Everything about the party – the scale, the fancy flyers printed with a nude man, and freely distributed, the lavish decorations, stage, top quality music, fireworks, drinks, and of course, the strippers – was setting it up as a target" (Vikram 1999, 18). Since homosexuality was criminalized in India under Article 377 at the time, the incident served as a reminder that gay complacency about large disposable incomes and social status was misplaced, as these afforded no guarantees against intimidation and harassment.

Another controversial instance of the deleterious and exclusionary party syndrome is reflected in the column "Mumbai Masala" by "Poison Pudi" (Marathi for "a packet of poison"). Like the gossip pages in a newspaper or Mampala Morgan's "Sussuration" in the *Jamaica Gaily News*, Mumbai Masala was a campy, irreverent take on gay events in Bombay and the surrounding areas. These poisonous packets were penned by Row Kavi, identified as "Mata Kavi" in one of the columns. Row Kavi's campy comments on the food, fashion, and social activities of gay people, imitating social gossip on Page 3 in mainstream Indian newspapers, catered to readers who moved in the same circles, were likely familiar with the people and events mocked, or were otherwise in the know. The writer assumes the persona of a "queen," a brazen, bitchy, bad-mouthing, rumor-mongering, hand-clapping *chinaal* (similar to but not the same as a transgender person of the *hijra* community) with access to high and low brow social activities. Poison Pudi soon changed their mode of address to include people outside familiar social circles. Targeting those who (in their opinion) were neither classy nor generous, the columnist aims to shame the hosts out of their wannabe socialite status by stereotyping upper class hospitality and lower class thrift (Poison Pudi 1997, 1998a). References to Hindi films and descriptions of real or imaginary queens caught stealing cutlery and linen from hotels play into the stereotype of the affluent gay male community's disdain for impoverished *lamdis* or "old tarts" (Poison Pudi 1997, 19). In one of the last columns to appear in 1998 titled "Purr…Fect Parties" Poison Pudi's spectacularly salacious mixture of Hindi and English lambasts the lack of spaces available to transgender people and expresses admiration for how they stake a claim to a city which shuns them as social and sexual outcasts. Pudi describes how a group of queens dressing in a women's restroom shock the real ladies, while another queen decides to pursue and attack a person who threatens them after a casual sexual encounter (Poison Pudi 1998b, 4). Semi-fictional, short-lived, snide, snobby, and very salacious, the transgender persona of the eponymous Poison Pudi introduced feminized subjectivities as a critical component of gay socialization. The column was discontinued when readers called for an end to the "gossiping" they felt was at odds with the seriousness they expected from *BD*.

The inextricability of sexuality and class in *BD*'s editorial and reporting practices and the magazine's implied readership does not merely reflect differential locations of gay male socialization but, in effect, reinforces such differences. Even as *BD* moved to an English readership, colloquialisms, idioms, phrases, and words from Hindi, Urdu, and Marathi in the English articles indicate that its elite readers avidly consumed "other" class and caste subjectivities and vocabularies. In sum, *BD* solicited intimate readership by publishing simultaneously in English and Hindi, providing a space for LGBTQ+ literary expression, establishing a close connection with Bollywood films and actors, covering the gay social scene in and around Bombay, and including a mixture of fact and fiction in the short-lived gossip column. The limited success of these approaches was revealed in *BD*-Humsafar's lesbian and transgender alliances.

Lesbian and trans dosts

While *BD* aimed to foster LGBTQ+ communication and community in India, it also sought alliances outside the country. Its closest connections were with *Trikone*, a US based magazine for gay and lesbian South Asians. *Trikone*'s founding editors, Arvind Kumar and Suvir Das, were in communication with Row Kavi since the inception of *BD*. The interaction between two South Asian diasporic publications – *Anamika*, a short-lived lesbian newsletter, and the longer-running *Trikone* – presents a model of intersectionality that *BD* tried to emulate. Here is a brief account of *Anamika* and *Trikone* framing my analysis of limited lesbian and transgender presence in and collaboration with *BD*.

Published in the United States, *Anamika* emerged when Utsa and Khayal, diasporic South Asian women who had dreamed of starting a lesbian magazine, received some financial support from the Asian Lesbians of the East Coast (ALOEC) in 1985. To my knowledge, *Anamika* is the earliest South Asian lesbian newsletter. The life-narratives, poetry, articles, and personal advertisements in available numbers of *Anamika* allow a glimpse of how South Asian women in the diaspora imagined themselves as a community through creative self-expression, conversation, and organization. The editors state: "We are both Indian lesbians currently living in New York. Khayal has been in the US for four years and Utsa has been here for one. We are students and were lesbians before we came here." Acknowledging that launching a newsletter in the US might lead to accusations of "foreign" influence, they assert that being unable "to work on this issue within our own country at this time" they "cannot afford to wait" for an indefinite future to talk about lesbian lives (Khayal & Utsa 1985, 1). While this claim can support the charge leveled by sections of the Indian women's movement that lesbianism is a characteristically Western phenomenon, Khayal and Utsa counter the metronormative diasporic lesbian narrative which maps a story of migration onto the coming-out narrative (Halberstam 2005, 37). Lesbian life narratives in the three available newsletters of

Anamika map migration onto the coming out narrative but do not map sexual preference or identity onto migration. In fact, their focus is on the difficulties of charting South Asian cultural traditions of family, religion, food, fashion, films, and music onto a sexual identity which is perceived as inauthentic and un-Indian.

Anamika informs its readers early on of "another S. Asian gay and lesbian newsletter...Trikon – brought out by two gay Indian men" (*Anamika* 1986, 2). During

FIGURE 5.3 Cover page of *Anamika*, a diasporic South Asian lesbian magazine. Photograph by the author from the archives of the Deering Collection, Northwestern University Library.

these years when *Trikon* (later renamed *Trikone*) was the only South Asian magazine for gay men, readers from the US, Europe, and South Asia, including big cities and small towns in India, sent in letters to seek connections with gay men within and outside the country. *Trikone*'s important role in cultivating a South Asian (rather than specifically Indian diasporic) identity and readership is like the goals of its short-lived lesbian predecessor *Anamika*. The third and final number of *Anamika* reflects the ephemerality and circulatory reflexivity of gay and lesbian counterpublics in a letter sent by the editors of *Trikone*:

> here we were, thinking we (trikon and libindia) were the only gay south asian groups in the universe, but you have proved us wrong…we were unaware of your work because we had gotten so discouraged with searching the gay media for signs of others like us and turning up nothing, we had stopped looking!…yes, we were very much aware that there was a gay male bias in the first issue of trikon. the only reason for it was that we didn't know any gay south asian women then and we wanted to be honest, even when it came to our ignorance and lack of experience…we very much want women's participation in trikon, their input, their ideas and criticism. We do not want to create an exclusive club for men.
>
> (Kumar 1987, 3)

Although *Anamika* ceased publication soon after the number in which the letter appeared, *Trikone*'s acknowledgment of gaps reflected its LGBTQ+ inclusivity. Over the next years, *Trikone* revised its mission statement to include gay and lesbian solidarity, and assiduously covered lesbian lives, social networks, and activism in its reports, articles, and features. If "the notion of a public enables a reflexivity in the circulation of texts among strangers who become, by virtue of their reflexively circulating discourse, a social entity" (Warner 2002, 11–12), then the "stranger" relationship between scarcely remembered lesbian publications such as *Anamika* (and later *Shamakami*) and the intimate relationship between their famous gay counterparts *Trikone* and *BD* allows us to chart the discourse which consolidated South Asian LGBTQ+ social identities and activist trajectories. *Trikone* emerged as a model of organizational structures premised on gender parity (Puri 2002, 192–193), committed to rigorously documenting lesbian presence in South Asia and the diaspora as seen in its regular updates about *Anamika*, *Shamakami*, and the Indian feminist journal *Manushi* (see Chapter 4).

BD was in regular contact with *Trikone* as a source of news about gay and lesbian rights in the US. Like *Trikone*, *BD*-Humsafar also envisaged gay and lesbian solidarity as a sound activist strategy. However, lesbian, bisexual, and transgender presence in *BD* is limited to personal ads in the Khush Khat (Gay Letters) section primarily used by gay men seeking love, companions, and sex. Though lesbian and trans letter writers in *BD* were never deliberately excluded, the magazine revealed clear discrepancies between lesbian and gay social and sexual connections. As in most narratives of gay male emergence, *BD* readers used the Pen Pal section to look for sex and companionship in India and abroad. In contrast, only two lesbians sought pen pals in the first decade of *BD*.

There were some letters by gay men and lesbian women seeking marriages of convenience to fend off pressures from their families. To include lesbians within the ambit of *BD*-Humsafar, there was "Chhokri" (Girl), a column for lesbian and bisexuals by Bombay-based activists, Lesley Esteves and Ashwini Sukthankar, who invited women to the space to share their poetry, life-experiences, and fantasies (1996). The column was accompanied by an inset expressing the need for unity among the community which comprised "isolated women" including "married gay women," and was hopeful that "there could be a space for such debate on the pages of *Chhokri*, on the issues that threaten to fragment the community" (Esteves & Sukthankar 1996, 33). The column did not become a regular feature and was soon discontinued. *BD* then introduced "Khush Chhokris" (Gay Girls) where women could seek other women, though this too was discontinued without any reason or explanation. Though *BD* published articles on lesbian mobilization and sought lesbian connections, absence of a regular forum and lack of shared lesbian-gay editorship meant that the magazine was unsuccessful in its goal of connecting lesbians with each other and with gay men towards a more inclusive LGBTQ+ community.

BD's limited lesbian news falls into three broad categories: reports on various seminars and events by emerging activists and groups; reprints of mainstream newspaper articles on the growing number of lesbian suicides in India; and reviews of important books and anthologies. Among the most prominent lesbian groups of the time were Sakhi from Delhi and Stree Sangam from Bombay. Giti Thadani,

EXPLODING MYTHS

TO
BOMBAY DOST

We are writing to you because of the persistent and suffocating lesbophobia in the denial of open lesbian space by Indian feminist groups. We have been in existence for three years but have not received one letter of acknowledgment or support from any Indian feminist orgnisation. Various myths are mentioned by feminist groups for not taking up lesbian issues or challenging heterosexism.

We urge the lesbian, gay and international feminist communities to be critically responsible in their support of feminists and feminist groups. We ask you to condemn lesbophobia and pressurise feminists to take up lesbian issues and challenge the myths mentioned below. We ask for letters of solidarity and support. We also urge you to publish this document and disseminate this information.

SAKHI COLLECTIVE
(Lesbian Resource Centre and
Research & Networking Institute)

Myth 2: Historically, Indians are tolerant by nature and there is no need for either a lesbian identity or debate.

Indians are by no means tolerant by nature. There have been known incidents of lesbians being killed, beaten, drugged, given electric shocks, exorcised, rejected, punished in various forms. Further, the old British law on sexuality has been used as an instrument of coercion, often by fathers to break up lesbian relationships.

languages in India. It is O.K. for feminists to use terms like marxism, socialism and communalism which have either originated outside India or are English words. Whereas these have been adapted and contextualised to the different Indian situations, the word lesbian is singled out as only being western property. No attempt is made at looking at the reason for the construction of lesbian invisibility or researching into lesbian histories and languages.

This is what Sakhi is doing and in the process has uncovered some very rich histories, visual, written and oral languages.

Myth 7: Women must be victims to receive any kind of support and they cannot aspire to be autonomous, free, visibly sexual and erotically affirmed, particularly if they are lesbians. The victim space is taken over by arrogance by heterosexual women but any acknowledgment of self determination and affirmation, particularly of sexual identity, is seen as dangerous, selfish and elitist. Thus the only terminology used for women outside marriage is that of a single woman.

FIGURE 5.4 A letter and sections of an article by Sakhi, a lesbian group in Delhi, addressed to the editors and readers of *Bombay Dost*. Courtesy of Ashok Row Kavi and Humsafar Trust.

co-founder of Sakhi, wrote for *BD* in its initial years of publication. Her seminars and workshops on gender construction and alternative sexualities were regularly covered by *BD* columnists.

BD also reported on the Bombay-based Stree Sangam's gatherings of "women who love women." Parvez Sharma's "Emerging from the Shadow" marks a belated, begrudging recognition of lesbian activism when he commends Thadani and Aparna for founding Sakhi with the somewhat backhanded compliment that the "cult of positivism is creeping into the yet nascent Indian lesbian movement" (1994, 15). *BD* included news of lesbian suicides and articles on lesbian life experiences. For instance, "Violence in our Lesbian Lives" covers transphobia to describe how a young lesbian dressed as a man was beaten up in the women's compartment of a local Bombay train. The author urges women to use *BD* and other local publications to publicize violence against sexual minorities (Sakshi 1995, 17). Finally, largely appreciative reviews of landmark books such as Rakesh Ratti's *A Lotus of Another Color* (1993), Ashwini Sukthankar's *Facing the Mirror: Lesbian Writing in India* (1997) and, later, Ruth Vanita and Saleem Kidwai's landmark anthology *Same Sex Love in India* (2001) indicate that *BD* was attentive to gay and lesbian literary representations.

To learn more about *BD*'s origins and editorial policies, especially its efforts at lesbian inclusiveness, I spoke to Row Kavi in New Delhi (2008).[4] This was not a formal interview as he was nervous at my suggestion of recording the conversation, and, in deference to his wishes, I took copious notes rather than use a recording device. Looking over these notes from our meeting, our conversation focused on Humsafar's plans to revive *BD* (published intermittently since 2000), organizing Pride on Independence Day to mark queer azadi (freedom), decoding Bollywood's gay idioms, and a certain defensiveness about the lesbian presence in the community *BD* hoped to foster. Despite evidence to the contrary in *BD* and in assessments of the gay movement, Row Kavi is of the opinion that there was less diversification of LGBTQ+ social and political spaces in India unlike the diversity of queer social spaces in the global North (2008). Responding to my question about lesbian involvement, he said that lesbian activists had been part of the formation of *BD* (he did not provide any names) and that the magazine had facilitated delivery of letters addressed to women. Although he did not specify the addressee, I am almost certain these letters were delivered to Sakhi, the Delhi-based lesbian organization, since there was no lesbian group in Bombay in *BD*'s early years. *BD* thus served as a conduit for connecting lesbians not *in* the magazine but "through the magazine" leading to "a flood of letters – friendly, desperate, romantic, lustful. Letters from teenagers, middle aged married women, women in love, lonely women; letters coming from Ludhiana, Meerut, Gauhati, and predominantly from Hyderabad (the reason has not been discovered yet)" (Rege 1999, 93). The claim is borne out by Naisargi Dave's research on Sakhi's archive of lesbian correspondence from the early 1990s, including letters by women based in small towns across the country. Sakhi maintained a list of women who wished to correspond with other women. The group shared addresses of those expressing a desire to connect with each other (Dave 2012, 39).[5]

During our meeting, Row Kavi described a letter from a woman who was perplexed at not receiving replies from those she wrote to at the addresses in *BD*'s personal advertisements. He recollected discovering that most lesbians were not responding to "poor women." His acerbic critique of divisions among the emerging lesbian community rests upon the claim that "cross-class coupling is not common among lesbians" (Row Kavi 2008). If I had a chance to respond beyond my role as an interlocutor, I would ask him: why is it surprising that class demarcations evident in gay male socialization and communication were equally prominent among lesbian women? After all, alternative forms of sexual expression are not necessarily more egalitarian than heteronormative forms. In societies as structured on language, geographical, income, and caste distinctions as India, it is not surprising that gay and lesbian interactions emulate the hierarchies in which they are embedded. Recent research into the emergence of lesbian subcultures in India confirms the elitism of English-speaking, metropolitan, and political-activist women in the Delhi group Sakhi, and later the Bombay-based organization Women to Women, explaining it as "exclusions based on political competence and practical freedoms in lesbian community" (Dave 2012, 55). These explanations are not acceptable to dalit queer activists who are clear that the LGBTQ+ community in the country is not "casteless" and that lower castes consistently face discrimination within queer spaces (Team Culture Lab 2019).

Despite relatively scant lesbian voices in the magazine, *BD*-Humsafar and Row Kavi's foundational influence on gay and lesbian sexual activism in India is undeniable. His public stand as an openly gay man encouraged Delhi-based Geeti Thadani and Bombay-based Lesley Esteves to emerge as lesbian activists. Writing on differences between urban sites of queer activism in India, Dave mentions that queer alliances in Bombay are formed largely in relation to a personality "cult" associated with Ashok Row Kavi, "the 'father' of India's gay movement.... [who] has shown disdain for lesbians, believes kothis are false constructions, and has been repeatedly linked to pro-Hindu, anti-Muslim communal positions" (2012, 28). Thadani's interview for Humsafar's Project Bolo documenting LGBT lives presents a somewhat different opinion. She states Row Kavi initially sought lesbian participation in *BD* by approaching her to write for the magazine; she also dismisses the charges of Hindu fundamentalism leveled against him (Thadani 2011). During our conversation, I noticed a distinct anti-Muslim and anti-Christian bias in Row Kavi that he made no attempt to conceal. Many of his comments were directed at Muslim and Christian gay academics, filmmakers, and activists, who, he felt, had "hijacked" the agenda of gay liberation (2008).

Unlike loud declarations of solidarity and mutual respect for lesbians, *BD*'s coverage of transgender lives is quite ambivalent. *BD*'s perspective on transgenderism, transvestism, drag, and cross-dressing demands a clearer explication than can be gleaned from the pages of the magazine, not only in the interests of queer solidarity but also because Humsafar was actively involved in outreach work with some of these communities. An early column "The Transvestite" was later folded into the personal ads in the Khush Khat section. *BD* carried short articles on local transvestite celebrities such as Sylvie and Bobby Darling who were successful fashion and cinema icons. The number of transgender people seeking companionship among the classifieds is marginally more than lesbians. Many offer culturally specific details on the particularity of and differences among trans lives in India. In one classified ad, a person describes themselves as "an Ardhnareshwari male with breasts looking for transvestites" (BD 1996b, 22). Another's self-description includes "transvestite drag queen" who "loves the feminine life and is still a virgin" (BD 1998, 21). The Ardhnareshwari (half-man and half-woman, a representation of the Hindu god Shiva) figure represents indeterminate gender. Similarly, the cultural importance of virginity reminds us how indigenous queer formations imitate heteropatriarchy, an unfortunate trope used by BD in its work among transgender populations, as explicated later in this chapter.

BD-Humsafar's political moves towards a coalitional queer politics can be tested against its interactions with trans people and its articles on religious rituals involving trans subjectivities. The magazine often represented trans people in anthropological ways, as embodying an early stage in the evolution of modern gay male subjects. Sultan's "Hijra or High Camp?" is an account (mediated by an outreach worker who speaks Tamil) of the writer's encounter with Usha, a castrated hijra. As a trans sex-worker and native Tamil speaker, Usha's status in the LGBTQ+ community is largely outside the ambit of BD's readership. Usha describes some of the medical and economic struggles she encountered while transitioning. The title of the piece deploys indigenous and Western vocabularies to present Usha as an attractive young woman knowledgeable about sexual safety and disease transmission (Sultan 1992, 16). Another article places trans subjectivity in a religious framework by reporting the wedding of Yellamma/Renuka, the goddess of hijras, prostitutes, and other sexual minorities. The author informs gay men that this "heritage" is being "suppressed by modern-day Brahminism and secular industrial culture." Children dedicated to Yellamma are either sold into prostitution or mysteriously disappear. This is not objective reporting; rather the piece glorifies a ritual where "there is no stigma or shame attached to the hijras who renew their 'contracts of love' with the men." The tradition of breaking coconuts and "smearing the followers of Renuka with kum-kum/gulal powder" to mark their union with the goddess affirms the quasi-marital relationship in fundamentally heterosexist terms (BD 1995a, 16). Other transgender traditions described in the magazine include ritualistic weddings of men who seek hijra blessings and an account of Musa, a cross-dressing saint (BD 1995b, 8–9; Sikand 1995, 11). In themselves these anthropological and religious-ritualistic perspectives do little to further trans recognition and respect. Instead, the veneer of celebration in these rituals masks the violence, stigma, and shame experienced by trans people in their families and mainstream upper caste society. Further, the heteronormativity in indigenous gender transformations and sexual expressions tests queer solidarity.

BD's attempts to clarify its position on trans populations in an article titled "To Drag or Not to Drag" deconstructs representations of homosexuals as effeminate queens through a survey-based approach. Responses describe the gay community's varying opinions on drag; the reporting team concludes that the "gay community must realise that just as we need protection from the hostility of the straight world, the drag queen has an equal right to exist as a special segment of our own gay community" (Dost Team 1995, 7). As campy forms of self-fashioning, the *chinaal, hijra,* or drag queen, are easily recognizable and more stigmatized than the cis gay man who can usually pass as straight. While *BD*'s HIV-AIDS outreach especially targeted trans populations, its limited and confused attention to trans subjectivities, primarily in the anthropological mode, tested its stated goal of inclusiveness.

Desire and disease

BD's homegrown AIDS activism emerged at a crucial period in the spread of the disease in India. Though Euro-American nations were developing experimental drugs and treatments to manage the pandemic, Jamaican, Indian, and South African trajectories indicate that these were not readily available to postcolonial nations facing rapid transmission of the virus in the early 1990s (Dube 2000; Cameron 2005). Since 1998, AIDS Bhedbhav Virodhi Andolan (ABVA), an activist group based in Delhi, was involved in AIDS outreach, specifically medical testing, condom distribution, and rehabilitation of women in prostitution, professional blood donors, and intravenous drug users, gay men and lesbians living with the disease. In 1991 ABVA published *Less Than Gay: A Citizens' Report on the Status of Homosexuality in India,* a groundbreaking account of discrimination against gay people in India arguing against presumed connections between gay sexuality and AIDS transmission.

Despite these efforts and the recently formed National Aids Control Organization (NACO), AIDS awareness in India was in its early stages when *BD* appeared on the scene. Before the formation of NACO in 1992, the work of prevention and medical testing was largely shouldered by NGOs such as ABVA. As national and international funding for HIV/AIDS became available, *BD*-Humsafar was in a unique position to receive these funds. During this period AIDS was often a code for homosexuality in donor discourse. *BD*-Humsafar is thus also a case study in the distinction "between political practice that is self-consciously counter-hegemonic, and the increasingly acceptable discourse about homosexuality that is restricted to AIDS-prevention." (Menon 2012, 99–100). Lesbians in particular, and women more generally, were largely excluded from South Asian AIDS organizing that consumed the energies of *BD*-Humsafar's gay male founders.[6] Heterosexual modes of transmission among married gay men were largely ignored in an early focus on male sexual practices. I describe here *BD*-Humsafar's multipronged efforts to combat the incidence and spread of AIDS in India, the medical and social ramifications of equating AIDS with homosexuality, and the attenuated potential of queer solidarity due to contentious understandings of gender normativity and sexual identity.

For the most part *BD*-Humsafar's activities demonstrate realistic goals with an eye towards competing identities within LGBTQ+ constituencies. *BD* directed sexual minorities to available medical resources, though the actual work of sexual health and HIV prevention was increasingly accomplished in Humsafar offices, first by volunteers and later by trained counsellors. Supplementing *BD*'s limited coverage of AIDS outreach, Humsafar's reports reveal its volunteers and colla-borators encountered diverse gender identities, sexual behaviors, and varying levels of sexual risk. These included: *kothis* or mainly anal receptive men; double-deckers or both anal insertive and receptive men; *panthis* who are typically anal insertive; and trans men. To better address the needs of these varying constituencies, Hum-safar's Drop-in Center offered sexual education, counselling, and condom dis-tribution. *BD* describes how these goals were accomplished through the goodwill and influence of local Mumbai Municipal Corporation officials, though "so bur-dened is the civic health service with the burgeoning population that, marginalized segments of the population have nowhere to turn to." To advance its reach Humsafar set up a Helpline in 1996 publicized through informational insets in *BD*. Twenty percent of the callers sought medical advice, and some went on to become resource persons for the Trust (Ramesh & Prakash 1996, 16).

With the emergence of other gay groups in Bombay such as *Udaan*, serving *kothi* and MSM constituencies, differences in the health, sexuality, and rights platforms within and between these organizations emerged. While reporting on a workshop to advance gay, lesbian, and bisexual rights in Bombay, Nitin Karani calls for the need of a coali-tion between various constituencies (1998b, 34). Later with the input of a member of the Larkins Street Drop-In Center in San Francisco, a "code of conduct" was drafted for services provided at the center. In describing the facilities, Row Kavi mentioned that efforts to include lesbian members in the functioning of the center had been unsuccessful (Row Kavi 1996, 15). Over the years the center served as a venue for conducting community discussions or "Mahacharchas," one of which I attended at Humsafar's Vakola offices (Jojdand 2008). These activities indicate that local, national, and international support was crucial to the growth and work of the organization.

Early AIDS prevention efforts encountered virulent opposition from the state as is clear from the controversy surrounding the Delhi government's measures to distribute condoms to prisoners in Tihar Jail, the largest prison in the country. Tihar houses thousands of convicted and under-trial prisoners, and there were legitimate concerns among AIDS activists that unprotected sex among the inmate population would lead to unchecked HIV transmission. Among others, Kiran Bedi, then Inspector General of Delhi Police, a staunch butch feminist and human rights advocate, was opposed to the measure since it meant admitting the high incidence of (homo)sexual activity among inmates. Amid the controversy, Farzana Varsey's article in the Bombay newspaper *The Sunday Observer* offered a homophobic rationale for opposing condom distribution. *BD* reproduced Versey's article "A Gay Life, Indeed" on the back cover in 1994. The placement cleverly and humorously indicated that Versey's piece represented a backward, asinine (puns intended!) view of sexuality and AIDS prevention efforts in the country.

Versey's article raised several red herrings that distracted from AIDS prevention efforts: prisoners were unaccustomed to using condoms; the move would encou-rage "unnatural" sexuality; and the far-fetched suggestion that it would lead to rampant child abuse in prisons. Using Row Kavi's words against him, Versey stated in spectacularly vulgar language:

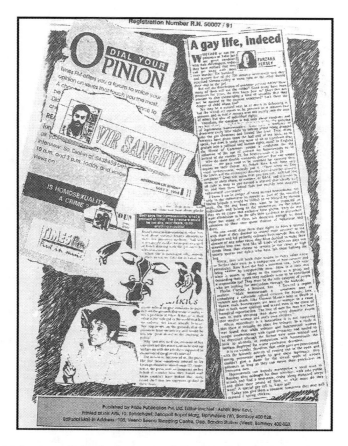

FIGURE 5.5 Section of the back cover of *Bombay Dost* reprinting Farzana Versey's homophobic article. Courtesy of Ashok Row Kavi and Humsafar Trust.

In a comparison of homosexuals versus prostitutes, Row Kavi did find a common link, "both were being ★★★★★★ by irresponsible men." How is it then that when it comes to taking the streets as a group and demanding their rights they suddenly want to be considered a responsible lot? They must be the only category of people who are looking for martyrdom through the backside.

(1994)

Row Kavi responded to the piece in the mainstream newspaper *The Sunday Observer*; Sultan Khan also sent in a response to the same newspaper expressing outrage. Both responses reappeared in *BD* with Sultan advising Varsey to "leave her misplaced sense of moral outrage aside while the effort is on to prevent the spread of HIV" (1992, 8). In these early years of gay and sexual health activism, Humsafar-*BD* inadvertently reinforced misconceptions of AIDS as a gay male disease even as they combated this link. Ironically, Humsafar-*BD*'s prevention efforts were understood as a covert promotion of homosexuality eliciting opposition from women's groups affiliated with major political parties in the country.

BD-Humsafar is also susceptible to charges of tailoring its work to match funding priorities in AIDS outreach. These critiques invite an assessment of the discrepancy between the organization's stated aims and actual deliverables. *BD*'s Charter lists the publication's mandate as "counselling, information, and advice in all such areas which are of interest to expressing alternate sexuality and its safe practice." The first two numbers included informative articles on AIDS and a report on the first national conference on AIDS. The second newsletter editorial announced counselling services and asks for volunteers including trained psychologists, social workers, pathologists, and blood bank technicians. It clearly states its order of priorities: "Psychiatric counselling, career and personal problems will come in that order" (*BD* 1990a, 3). A short report describes how Row Kavi attended the first national conference on AIDS where he had spoken about *BD* (*BD* 1992a, 11) and included his article on pan-Asian efforts to deal with the AIDS crisis (Row Kavi 1992a, 13–14). In keeping with the sustained attention on AIDS, the newsletter began carrying full page public health advertisements to educate its readers about modes of HIV transmission. When *BD* was folded into the activities of the Humsafar Trust four years after its launch, it became the only regularly circulated publication serving the dual purposes of sexuality rights and health awareness in India. *BD* was also then the only Indian organization with membership in the International Lesbian and Gay Association (Row Kavi 1992b). Relations with ILGA were cemented through conferences and meetings including ILGA's first South Asia conference in Bombay in 1994. *BD* and Humsafar's other collaborations with organizations such as the UK-based Naz foundation arose out of connections between founders Shivananda Khan and Row Kavi.

Much of the AIDS related work in India was and remains donor funded; it also invokes medical and social categories derived from epidemiology in the global North. Scholars and activists involved in AIDS prevention in India agree that MSM constitute a high-risk, though not the only, category in HIV transmission. As the ABVA activists in Delhi and *BD*-Humsafar recognized, heterosexual populations such as internal migrant labor, those involved in the transportation industry, intravenous drug users, and female and transgender prostitutes are additional high-risk categories. Bombay is considered one of the epicenters of the epidemic largely because of the migratory patterns of the inhabitants of the city (Chandrasekaran et al. 2008; Verma et al. 2010; Mishra et al. 2012). MSM are crucial vectors of transmission in India where the trajectory of infection is male to male to female. The MSM category is both diverse and fragmented on sexual identity choice and sexual politics and replicates religion and caste hierarchies in India. *BD*-Humsafar's focus on the MSM population and its various subcategories was consistent with the statistics released by NACO in its first stage of programming. *BD*-Humsafar's AIDS education efforts – including surveys on sexual habits sent to its readers on behalf of the Mumbai District AIDS Control Society – were initially focused on local constituencies. Later the organization publicized this work on the national level by participating in conferences and symposia. Most of the initial support and funding came from the Mumbai Municipal Corporation, the Director of Health Services of

Maharashtra State, and the Mumbai District AIDS Control Society. Humsafar targeted the complexity and diversity of at-risk groups, and the local scale of its activities provided an accurate account of incidence among the general population at a time when support for such projects was limited. Concurrently, it also sought South Asian and global connections.[7]

BD-Humsafar's health awareness platform necessitated specific aims parsed out in terms of its target populations' gender identification, marital status, class-caste-religion, and sexual preferences. Unlike its failed efforts to create a cross-class, cross-gender community, *BD*-Humsafar's attention to sexuality and health as a rights issue involved trans constituencies more than lesbian women. The material reality of AIDS in India demanded that activists "speaking" about nonnormative sex depart from conversations on violence against women, forms of population control, or matters of sexual morality (Dube 2000, 41; Menon 2012, 99). Nowhere is this more evident than in differing perspectives on the role of *kothis* in the larger struggle to secure gay rights. Speaking of the dynamics within LGBTQ+ populations, Alok Gupta, who came out during Humsafar's Friday gatherings at the Vakola Center, describes meetings held by organizations like Humsafar, Humraahi, and Counsel Club in Bombay, Delhi, and Calcutta. Gupta writes that these were all "frequented by the urban, middle-class, gay- and bisexual-identified crowd," were conducted primarily in English, and slowly began to include an HIV-focused discourse "at the level of safe-sex awareness *with little discussion on kothis, hijras and lesbians or even bisexuals*" (2005, 126, emphasis added). He cites *kothi* (effeminate men, usually assuming the role of the penetrated in MSM relationships) and *hijra* refusal to be bracketed within a gay, bisexual, and transgender framework as causing "the first official rifts in the larger queer community" (Gupta 2005, 126). Humsafar's Charter and code of conduct meant that it was obligated to welcome these communities and that its discussion sessions, including the one I attended, were conducted in the local languages (Hindi and Marathi) rather than English, somewhat qualifying Gupta's claims. The moderator of the session, Nikhil Jojdand, did not gloss over differences between transgender and MSM identifications though he emphasized that despite differences *kothis, panthis, hijras*, and MSM are all part of the same community (2008).

Subsequently, *BD*-Humsafar's attention to preventive measures and HIV management meant that it targeted high-risk groups. Because *hijras*, especially castrated or *nirvan hijras*, constitute one of the highest risk groups as sex workers (usually without the bargaining power of condom use), some of the organization's resources were directed to them. Homosexual transmission of HIV was traced to *hijras* and other male sex workers such as massage, gym, hotel, and dance bar employees. A report discussing Humsafar as a case study on HIV prevention mentions that "disconnection between identity and behavior among MSM appears to be a global dynamic that manifests itself in different ways, depending on the country or culture," a view shared by scholars analyzing disconnections between MSM gender normativity and same-sex practices (Robertson 2010, 3; Rao 2017, 25). Row Kavi implicates *kothis* for diverting the route of successful interventions by putting forward "a new identity politics which borrowed a construct conflating gender and sexual orientation from older hijra cultures (genderized males in ethnoreligious cults) and started talking of a 'genuine' Indian gay identity called *kothis*" (2011, 394). In his opinion, *kothis* are "empowered" MSM populations who rushed to occupy "the vacant victim space" even when there was very little evidence that they were most at risk. In this way they brought a "heterosexual paradigm" into a "subjugated MSM framework" by taking advantage of their passivity and effeminacy (Row Kavi 2011, 395). Ironically, in forwarding this opinion, Row Kavi echoes critics of Humsafar who argue that *kothi* rapidly became an identity in the late 1990s and early 2000s largely due to NGOs supported by international donor agencies (Tellis 2012, 146).

These harsh assessments of foreign funds influencing the direction of medical and social interventions in indigenous queer formations are contested by fieldwork (Dave 2012). Consolidation of identity-based groups such as *hijras* and *kothis* who stake a claim to national and international funding, employment, and electoral opportunities, describes the expanded terms of the intersectional alliances that *BD*-Humsafar sought to cultivate despite the obvious hostility of some members to *kothis*. The proliferation of competing identity claims eventually disconnected *BD*'s gay male leadership from making common cause with larger queer formations including lesbian, trans, and MSM groups and allies.

Worlding South Asian sexualities

Though *BD*-Humsafar's trajectory illustrates differences in political and activist goals based on gender identities, sexual behaviors, and target constituencies, its assiduously cultivated transnational connections ensured that it was and continues to be a well-respected NGO in the area of health and sexuality even as other actors stepped into the field. *BD*'s "The World" section informed its readership of wider developments on sexuality and health rights and its own place in transnational conversations. Its contents reveal two distinct forms of networking: maintaining and sustaining global South connections while reporting on happenings in the global North; and providing models of community and communication to emerging Southern local, national, and South Asian networks.

Maintaining its South Asian and Southern connections, *BD* usually relied on the information provided by *Trikone*, the Naz foundation, UN publications, and the ILGA to include short reports on emerging coalitions in Asia, Africa, and Latin America. Searching for connections between postcolonial feminist and queer activism, it was deeply moving to see *BD*'s short report on the Organization of Lesbian and Gay Activists (OLGA) in Cape Town endorsing the recommendation that the African National Congress include sexual orientation in the Draft Bill of Rights for the newly emerging South African Constitution. (*BD* 1991c, 9). To create awareness of South Asian and Asian initiatives *BD* regularly printed letters and informative pieces from various organizations including the lesbian group Anjaree from Thailand, August 4 from Bangladesh, the Indonesian Gay Society, the Reach Out Gay Foundation in Philippines, advertisements on South Asian diasporic networks, and gay and lesbian groups in India.

The clearest statement of such a worlding is in an editorial announcing "HOMASIA, an umbrella organisation of gay organisations from South and South-East Asia" and an open invitation to all sexualities to participate in the Asian conference on AIDS planned later that year in Delhi. The editorial also mentions the creation of gay and lesbian Arab and Iranian unions and *BD*'s increasing contact with gay groups in China and the USSR (*BD* 1992b, 3). Over the years it included informational insets about groups such as the South Asian Lesbian and Gay Association (SALGA) in New York, Khush Khayal in Toronto, Shakti Khabar in London, and informative articles on diasporic lesbian and gay activists including Shakti's founder Shivananda Khan and Urvashi Vaid, Director of the National Gay and Lesbian Task force in New York.

Regional conferences were another way *BD*-Humsafar sought to world its important work. Row Kavi participated in the first national conference on AIDS held in New Delhi where there was very little discussion of homosexuality, and any meaningful discussion on HIV prevention was foreclosed because of the presence of "homophobic doctors" (*BD* 1992a, 11). At a regional meeting of AIDS service organizations in Singapore later that year, the "biggest contingent" was a group of homosexual and transvestite organizations from the Asia/South-East Asia region. Here there was a collective decision to follow existing political structures such as SAARC and ASEAN for organizational purposes to "facilitate networking through existing orthodox linkages like inter-government bonds" (Row Kavi 1992a, 13). Asian solidarity and organizational goals at the Second International Congress on AIDS in Delhi led to a three point program: recognizing sexual minorities in Asia as "legitimate sub-cultures"; dispelling the premise that Asia is the epicenter of hetero-sexual transmission of AIDS; and building and sustaining connections among gay and lesbian subcultures in Asia to support mainstreaming (*BD* 1993b, 5).

As the largest and economically dominant nation in South Asia, India has often assumed a leadership role in these events. Humsafar's prominence as one of the first Indian NGOs involved in sexuality and health education ensured its place in these deliberations. While these were important connections, fault lines in *BD*'s gay world-ing of South Asia were clear from 1994 when plans were announced for a "South Asian Gay Conference" to be held in Bombay. Led by the London-based Naz Project under the leadership of Shivananda Khan, the "closed" conference involved local groups such as Dost, Khush Club, and Udaan; it "restricted" participation to "gay men who are involved in community issues." From the announcement it is unclear whe-ther lesbian participants were allowed, though the suggested range of topics included

> the role of the unmarried gay in the South Asian family, Section 377 of the Indian Penal Code, sexism within the gay community, feminist and lesbian issues, gay men who are married, problems of HIV-positive gays and care for them, gay literature, etc.
>
> (*BD* 1994b, 18)

A few years later, NGO representatives from South Asia were invited to the US by the Rockefeller-backed Asia Society. Without any specific health or rights agenda, this gathering of NGOs, to use Row Kavi's words, satisfied the "curiosity" of the American gay and lesbian community about Indian homosexual traditions (1998b, 27). There were serious local repercussions of BD-Humsafar's participation in such closed door and/or apolitical activities. One effect was the organization's noticeable exclusion from a national workshop on rights organized by feminist and gay groups from Bombay, Calcutta, and Bangalore in 1998. BD's article on the event made heroic attempts to connect it to the exclusionary 1994 South Asian Gay workshop by asserting solidarities and shared goals. Additionally, the reporter makes excuses for the 1994 conference while lauding the organizers of the 1998 gathering:

> Looking at it optimistically, the seeds of an organised gay movement are being planted. One can't say though because the idea of one such coalition was also mooted at the '94 gay men's conference but apart from some networking no follow-up has been done. Gay men's groups tend to get bogged down with the work of peer counselling for men who are just coming out to themselves. Another important area of work which takes upon their energies is sexual health and STDs/HIV prevention strategies.
>
> (Karani 1998b, 34)

While emphasizing solidarity, Karani observes differences between current LGBTQ+ efforts to change the legal status of homosexuality and BD-Humsafar's attention to sexual health. He churlishly comments that BD's participation in the workshop could have streamlined the discussions (1998b, 35). Evidently, in its focus on making connections across the world, with long-term partners ILGA, SALGA, and the Naz foundation, BD-Humsafar had lost ground in local and national efforts.

BD-Humsafar's status as an NGO with a declared interest in public health provides a clue as to possible reasons why the publication became somewhat irrelevant in the last years of the twentieth century. One of the central contradictions was that the magazine and the trust were working in collaboration with local or national level state agencies such as the Mumbai District AIDS Control Society and the NACO to promote safer sexual practices among populations who were under constant threat from another set of state agencies, the police and the judicial system, for their "unnatural" sexual practices. These competing ideas of "legal illegality" buttressed by local political support enabled the organization to survive relatively free of persecution for some years in the communally charged Hindu right-wing environment (Hindutva) in the country. As home to the militant Rashtriya Swayamsevak Sangh, a political organization opposed to any challenges to the Hindu way of life, including alternative expressions of sexuality, Bombay was the epicenter of religious and caste turbulence sweeping across the country in the late 1990s when Hindutva emerged with renewed force. This was also the period when a coalition of organizations (including Humsafar) legally challenged Article 377 criminalizing homosexuality. The struggles and successes of the legal challenge made gay and lesbian organizations more public and vulnerable than during the peak of the Hindutva wave in 1992. Moreover, following Humsafar's lead, NGOs took up the challenge of AIDS awareness in Bombay, Delhi, Calcutta, Bangalore, and other metropolitan centers in the country. The magazine lost its competitive edge in gay male publication in the newly liberalized media environment as other organizations became more visible. The prominence of digital communication in India at the end of the twentieth century was one reason *BD* ceased regular publication after 1999. In 2001, when I stopped by People Tree hoping to pick up the most recent number of the magazine, the young woman in the bookstore said *BD* had temporarily ceased publication fearing attacks by the Hindutva moral police.

This chapter has narrated *BD*-Humsafar's efforts to create intimate readership with an incipient LGBTQ+ community. Its key contribution was initiating AIDS awareness in the country. Lack of sustained lesbian and transgender participation meant that *BD*-Humsafar remained primarily a gay male organization that failed to learn crucial lessons of social movements and political projects. One of these is that existing organizations remain relevant by revisioning their current practices. Another is that the emergence of new activist priorities (as in the shift from AIDS activism to decriminalization of homosexuality) leads to the creation of new solidarities. And finally, a coalitional politics involves many organizations working together to achieve the common goals of securing the safety, dignity, and health of sexually vulnerable populations. Had it re-examined its strategies and policies *BD*-Humsafar might have been able to honestly assess its hierarchical and inadvertently exclusionary practices, its (a)political direction, and somewhat formulaic pronouncements on sexual difference and gender binaries. Constant self-assessment and revisioning are central to the aims of social transformation (Sangtin Writers & Nagar 2006; Bernal &Grewal 2014), and such efforts might have minimized the homonormativity assumed in *BD*'s implied readership and competing identity claims in its work with MSM populations.

Nevertheless, *BD*-Humsafar's worlding of sexualities is an important phase in the changing direction of the LGBTQ+ movement in India. The trajectory of law reform to repeal Article 377 of the Indian Penal Code criminalizing "unnatural sexuality," a central focus of activist energies for the past two decades, was different from the organization's focus on community formation and AIDS prevention. Curiously, both projects sidelined lesbian women who were not considered an AIDS risk group or a visible target of police extortion and blackmail under 377. Today, while *BD* is no longer published, Humsafar continues to cultivate intimate communities through conversations on LGBTQ+ rights including health and legal provisions. With homosexuality no longer criminalized, the conversation on postcolonial sexualities in India has moved beyond law reform and sexual health. Sexual activism has subsequently developed new counterpublics including print and online queer zines; crowdsourced queer literature; demonstrations of queer lives through Pride Parades in big and small cities throughout the country; annual queer film festivals; and transgender mainstreaming in public and private domains.

The third and concluding part of the book moves from India to South Africa. It describes how South African LGBTQ+ and feminist activism and activist literature secured legislative and constitutional gains as yet unsecured in Jamaica and only recently achieved in India. South Africa also presents a model of feminist–queer alliances that are of value in other postcolonial contexts.

Notes

1 As in the chapters on Jamaica, it is difficult to chart trajectories of the gay and lesbian movements in India based exclusively on publications, though print does give us insights into key concerns of the period. My account would undoubtedly be richer for having looked at the early print runs of the Indian lesbian magazine *Scripts* in the wake of the Campaign for Lesbian Rights in India in 1998–1999. Its early numbers are not archived online or onsite in any library. The Library of Congress and other university libraries catalogue *Scripts* from 2007. My attempts to contact the Labia collective (previously known as *Stree Sangam*) have thus far not yielded any responses.

2 I was unable to locate *Bombay Dost* Volume 1, Number 1 (1990). Humsafar offices have preserved all numbers except the first one. According to founder-editor Row Kavi, *BD*'s first number (with a run of 650 copies) contains "a charter, pieces on Section 377 and HIV, personal classifieds and an advice column" and was circulated "largely underground, passed hand to hand like the dissident samizdat publications in the old Soviet Union" (qtd. in Lalwani 2014).

3 There is some confusion in the numbering of the magazine's issues since its first two news-letters were published for private circulation before the magazine went "legitimate." The editorial explains that this means that the publishers could "use the Indian postal system" and "legally accept advertisements from anyone willing to give them" (*BD* 1990a, 3). In keeping with its newly acquired legitimacy the magazine begins anew with the 1991 numbers label-led Volume 1, Numbers 1, 2, 3–4 and so on. This explanation is relevant at least till the digital archive is created and the volume and numbering explained.

4 Ashok helpfully connected me to contacts in Bombay including Vivek Anand, then CEO of Humsafar.

5 Dave writes, "Between 1991 and 1994, most of Sakhi's letter writers claimed to have learned of Sakhi from one of these newsletters or from *Bombay Dost*. It is important to keep in mind here that the form in which information about a lesbian world was initially circulating in India – in specialized magazines that required subscription, public purchase, or semipublic, furtive reading – would radically limit most women's access to this world, even if they did initially learn about these magazines through the more neutral medium of a widely read daily newspaper" (2012, 44).

6 Humsafar's stand is in direct contrast to ABVA which consciously tried to "broad base its work" by involving "voluntary groups and community people including people with leprosy, women in prostitution, women from slums around Delhi, and gay people." Furthermore, ABVA displays self-reflexivity and assessment of its own position missing in the Humsafar documents examined in this chapter. ABVA acknowledges that its members worked to bring to the surface their "discomfort, myths and queries about sexuality in general and homosexuality in particular" (ABVA 1991, 4).

7 Humsafar's funders and partners have included: the United States Agency for International Development (USAID), the National AIDS Control Organization, (NACO), the Mumbai District AIDS Control Society (MDACS), the Bill and Melinda Gates Foundation, The Elizabeth Taylor Foundation, the United Kingdom (UK) Department of International Development (DFID), The Bombay Municipal Corporation, the Global Fund for TB, Malaria and AIDS (GFTAM), the Johns Hopkins University, Brown University, and Harvard University and Medical School.

PART III
Amandla, embodying power

6

WORLDING SEXUALITIES UNDER APARTHEID

From gay liberation to a queer Afropolitanism[1]

In 1982 when the Gay Association of South Africa established its offices in Hillbrow, the area was bustling with activity. A host of businesses, residential complexes, bars, and restaurants made Hillbrow the locus of an emerging gay and lesbian presence in the country. On a 2012 visit to Gay and Lesbian Memory in Action (formerly the Gay and Lesbian Archives of South Africa) in Johannesburg, archivist Gabriel Hoosain accompanied me on a Queer Walking Tour of Hillbrow, a cultural historical experience translated in this chapter. The area is no longer the gayborhood it was in the 1980s and 1990s. There are some buildings and spots which stand out as legendary: Connections, which began as a gay bar about three decades ago, but soon became a popular venue for lesbians; Skyline bar, where the first pride parade was planned; and the corner of Twist and Pretoria streets named after the black gay activist Simon Nkoli. Today, though there are identifiable gay areas in Johannesburg, the venues for socializing and activism are found in various locations in and around the city.[2] There are many ways of accessing this period when inner-city Johannesburg areas such as Hillbrow, Berea, Joubert Park, and surrounding locations emerged as a hub of gay socializing and activism. Examining gay liberation publications, this chapter shifts the focus from India to South Africa with the goal of providing a postcolonial history informed by comparative urban, feminist, and queer studies. My main claim is that South Africa's first apartheid era gay liberation publication with a national circulation lags behind important shifts in sexual activism; and my larger aim is to extend the valences of postcolonial queer studies towards a historical examination of North-South interactions in theorizing sexual activism.[3] Gay liberation literature here refers to texts which contributed to the emergence of gay and lesbian sexualities in South Africa, including works of fiction, poetry, drama, and anthologies as well as newsletters, newspapers, and newsletters.[4] The primary archive is *Link/Skakel*, the official newsletter of the Gay Association of South Africa (GASA), which later became a mainstream gay newspaper called *Exit*.

DOI: 10.4324/9781003170303-9

The analysis offered here extends into the domain of sexuality what Aihwa Ong has theorized as "worlding projects" of emergent global formations which "seem to form a critical mass in urban centers, making cities both critical sites in which to inquire into worlding projects, as well as the ongoing result and target of specific worldings" (2011, 12). Achille Mbembe's elaboration of Taiye Selasie's term "Afropolitanism" to the realm of urban studies is also useful to my analysis of worlding sexualities under apartheid. Mbembe posits Johannesburg as the center of Afropolitanism, based on its "multiple racial legacies, a vibrant economy, a liberal democracy, a culture of consumerism that partakes directly of the flows of globalization" (2004, 26–29). Mbembe's and Sarah Nuttall's discussion of Johannesburg as an Afropolis extends the theoretical valence of Afropolitanism to a cityscape marked by change and reinvention (2008).

An overly celebratory view of Afropolitanism has been countered by discussions highlighting easy access to mobility across borders, consumerist and elitist connotations of the term, and its exclusions. Simon Gikandi's foreword to *Negotiating Afropolitanism* strikes a cautionary note by mentioning how the term which can be "read as the description of a new phenomenology of Africanness – of being African in the world" – also invites a consideration of "the negative consequences of transnationalism, the displacement of Africans abroad, the difficulties they face as they try to overcome their alterity in alien landscapes, the deep cultural anxieties that often make diasporas sites of cultural fundamentalism and ethnic chauvinism" (2011, 9, 11). Among others, Binyavanga Wainaina and Yewande Omotoso have taken issue with Afropolitanism as a descriptor of a literary or social condition. Wainana's memoir of his closeted childhood and adulthood, *One Day I Will Write About This Place* (2011), can be read as a gloss on Afropolitanism. Here multiple linguistic influences, an anglicized education, the experience of intra-African migration, awareness of sexual difference, and international literary acclaim prefigure the emergence of a sexual identity. Wainaina critiques the term Afropolitan in favor of "pan-African" in his 2012 address to the UK African Studies Association. Similarly, in a conversation with Rebecca Fasselt, the South African novelist Yewande Omotoso comments on the term as "useful for the West as it gives the West an opportunity to understand and even 'consume' Africa" (Omotoso & Fasselt 2015, 235). There are different ways of being Afropolitan: migratory, consumerist, and Western-oriented; localized, anti-consumerist, and Africa-oriented.

Acknowledging various aspects and uses of Afropolitanism and its important critiques, my focus is on specific forms of worlding to analyze the transformation of a predominantly white male gay activism in Johannesburg from the 1980s to the 1990s. Mbembe and Nuttall describe Johannesburg as "a thoroughly polyglot urban formation whose influence, connections, and identifications extend beyond its locality and well beyond South Africa" (2008, 25). Explicating "African Cosmopolitanism," Neville Hoad notes the contradiction in this formulation since the word African "designates a geographic, if not racial, specificity" in contrast to cosmopolitanism, which "aspires to a worldliness unbound by either geography or race and suggests that multiple specificities exist" (2007, 113). I am arguing that from the 1980s to the 1990s we see the worlding of sexualities as evidenced in the changing nature of LGBTQ+ activism. Afropolitanism, which is both invoked and placed under erasure, when prefixed with queer, helps me think of connections between the movement for sexual rights and the anti-apartheid movement arising within a specific urban metropolitan context, but extending beyond it to national and transnational spaces and arenas. My purpose is to further discussion around the term through the juxtaposition of "queer Afropolitanism," and to present its generative potential for debates on literary, national, and sexual identity.

A key concept connecting the anti-apartheid and sexual activism is "visibility." Ashley Currier writes that social movements desire both visibility and invisibility at different times, and this was certainly true of the gay liberation movement in Johannesburg. GASA's "cultivated apolitical visibility," dictated in part by concerns of safety in the early 1980s, was followed by pressure by black and lesbian GASA members to abandon the apolitical stance in favor of alliance with the anti-apartheid movement in the mid-1980s and 1990s (Currier 2012, 10–15). In the early 1980s gay activists demanded legal change and political representation but did not pursue a broad conception of rights inclusive of racial and sexual equality. In a retrospective look at GASA and in response to the question "Where were you in the eighties?" Ann Smith, one of the founding members of the organization, mentions that rather than see "oppression as a continuum," the creation of a "safe space in which gay men and women could meet and interact without fear of being condemned, brutalized, shamed, humiliated or arrested" constituted a "gay liberation movement" for the organization (2005, 58–63). Early 1980s gay efforts were often directed towards claiming urban and national spaces without challenging segregation, reflecting a distinctly narrow conception of rights based on consumerist sexual identities. Indeed, the earliest essay on *Exit* and gay publishing in South Africa, by Gerry Davidson and Ron Nerio, describes how despite the state of Emergency in 1986 and 1987, the newspaper "focused almost totally on parochial affairs" and continued to "reflect the white gay establishment's attitudes by steering clear of politics" (1994, 225–231). A genuine desire for inclusivity was expressed by some GASA members, among them lesbians in the organization. Often these efforts were hampered by GASA's apolitical cautionary reformist orientation. It was only in the late 1980s that the gay and lesbian collectivity engendered in Hillbrow and sustained through print came to be identified as "queer." Brenna Munro (2012) and Chantal Zabus (2013) take up the valences of queer in African contexts by strategically using the label and challenging its Euro-American connotations. A similar reclamation of the relevance of queer to Africa is evident in Jack Halberstam's contribution to *Reclaiming Afrikan* where the term is deployed "to think about the queer critique of racism" and to point the way "to radically new articulations of sexuality, race and postcolonial political futures" (2014, 15). While it is accurate to note the use of queer in the African context as a "shorthand for practices that cannot be fully subsumed into identitarian labels of lesbian, gay, transgender, bisexual, or those that cannot be adequately translated into European languages," my call is for a specificity in the deployment of the term based on historical, national, and activist contexts (Osinubi 2016, xv). To this end, my suggestion is that in the South African context queer marks the emergence of a politics that connected the anti-apartheid and gay and lesbian rights movements. I take my cue from important feminist work which has extended the notion of intersectionality in ways that allow me to speak of the exclusions within social movements while recognizing the work they accomplish (Swarr &Nagar 2004; Nash 2013).

Recognition of and respect for racial, cultural, geographical, and gender differences within the gay movement, building connections between multiple forms of oppression, and a conscious effort at international connections best describes the worlding of sexualities in the changing political climate of apartheid South Africa.[5] As revealed in the pages of *Exit*, the emergence of a sexual subculture in Johannesburg was initially influenced by models of gay consumerism and activism in the North with a disregard for inequities created by racial, gender, and class privilege. However, the direction of comparison from North-South and the exclusivist racial and gendered assumptions were challenged first by lesbians in GASA and later black activists from the Gays and Lesbians of Witwatersrand (GLOW). These groups urged for attention to racialized, gendered, and non-metropolitan articulations of sexuality, a process which has continued in ongoing interrogations of South Africa's historic enshrinement of gay and lesbian rights co-existing with increasing levels of homophobia in cities and townships, still tarred with sexualized violence.

Profit and pleasure in the Afropolis

Many studies of Johannesburg focus on the dissolution of spatial segregation from the 1980s onwards, which led to some areas becoming more racially diverse than had been the case in the previous decades (Mandy 1984; Morris 1999). In this respect, Johannesburg can be compared with other African cities which have been analyzed as sites of discursive, economic, cultural, and social transactions and as gendered, raced, and sexualized spaces.[6] Loren Kruger's description of Johannesburg as an "edgy city" describes the "pervasive nervousness expressed by blacks and whites in the face of crime and grime in the 1990s" (2013, 3). The story of the passage of time in Johannesburg and its difficult transition from racial exclusivity to a mixed-race, gray space in the 1980s and 1990s establishes a direct connection between desegregation and the flight of white people from the inner city to the suburbs.[7]

This section describes patterns of gay life and consumption in Johannesburg represented by *Link/Skakel* as directly linked to the processes Ong labels "urban modeling" and "inter-referencing" where the initial trajectory of influence from the North to the South acquires an African worldliness following the dissolution of spatial segregation. According to Ong, this trajectory has shifted in the late twentieth and early twenty-first century, such that the modeling and inter-referencing is now between cities in the global South (2011). One of the earliest studies to discuss the slow process of desegregation in the context of economic growth, urban architectural needs, and housing scarcity for black and colored people, Nigel Mandy's work is also important for describing how the North American city model was adopted by Johannesburg planners (1984).[8] This model arguably influenced white gay subculture from the 1960s onward, though Mandy does not directly address this. Noting this connection, Hoad observes the "superficial sameness to commercial gay life (representationally white) in the major South African metropolises that is recognizably North American urban" (2007, 72). The historical evolution of this sexual subculture therefore needs to be examined in ways that are local, national, and transnational. In a commonly repeated explanation Mandy mentions that the Group Areas Act of 1950 ensured that "voluntary" ethnic residential separation, a natural feature of all cities, became a formalized and involuntary process (1984, 89). Mandy recounts in detail the long struggle for desegregation of inner-city restaurants from the 1970s onwards by using those in the Carlton Center as an example. Kruger's description of the Carlton Center as a "site of apartheid absurdity" where the restaurant was open to "international" blacks including Bantustan bureaucrats but not to black township residents further explains the spatial inequalities of the era (2013, 22). The free-market rationale used to justify such desegregation echoes the propaganda of the Association of Chambers of Commerce of South Africa (Assocom) that the growing city economy demanded a desegregated city space where blacks were free to secure gainful employment and to avail services offered in the city as consumers (Mandy 1984, 160).

These two contexts – that of the city as modeled on North American urban development; and the growing presence of black, colored, and Indians as workers and consumers following the relaxation of "petty" apartheid principles – characterize Hillbrow's emergence as a gay area in the 1980s and its apparent "degeneration" in the 1990s. Increased international attention on South African racial policies in print and other media, combined with an acute housing shortage for black and colored people in Johannesburg, led to the slow integration of the city, explaining the change in Hillbrow from an upscale white to a reluctantly integrated neighborhood. Building on Alan Mabin's important work, Beall, Crankshaw, and Parnell observe that during "the 1970s and 1980s, inner-city residential areas continued to enjoy a bohemian reputation, a flourishing urbanism unknown anywhere else in South Africa" (2002, 112). In a sense then, the flourishing Afropolitanism of the 1980s and 1990s was as much due to established non-African models of commercial and residential planning as it was due to the sexual, racial, cultural, economic, and national diversity of the inhabitants.

This then was the urban context for the emergence of *Link/Skakel* (hereafter *L/S*), the official newsletter of the Gay Association of South Africa (GASA), published simultaneously in English and Afrikaans, creating a homonationalist 'imagined community' in Johannesburg through the medium of print. Edited by Henk Botha, who had previously made a name for himself as a journalist and publisher, the newsletter's regular publication and high production quality invites comparisons with similar publications in the South: the *Jamaica Gaily News* emerged out of a similar need to connect gay men and lesbian women but was not professionally published; the slickly produced *Bombay Dost* reached gay men (and some lesbian women) all over India, but it was not regular, especially after 1998. The inaugural *L/S* published in May 1982 mentions that at its first meeting, GASA, an amalgam of three organizations, Lambda, Unite, and Amo, discussed "subjects as diverse as the need for community service, welfare, law reform, the improvement of the gay image, the establishment of a gay identity, entertainment, and subjects of a more organisational nature" (*L/S* 1982a, 1–2). The publication's activist-informational-consumerist purpose was evident from the beginning. Mark Gevisser's comprehensive review of the South African gay and lesbian movement from the 1960s to the 1990s in *Defiant Desire* mentions there was never a clear demarcation between the social and organizational needs of GASA (1994, 14–86). This is reflected in the contents of the first newsletter which contains an announcement to compile a Pink Pages Telephone Directory where "business concerns can advertise under appropriate headings" as well as information about membership dues to the organization (*L/S* 1982b, 2).

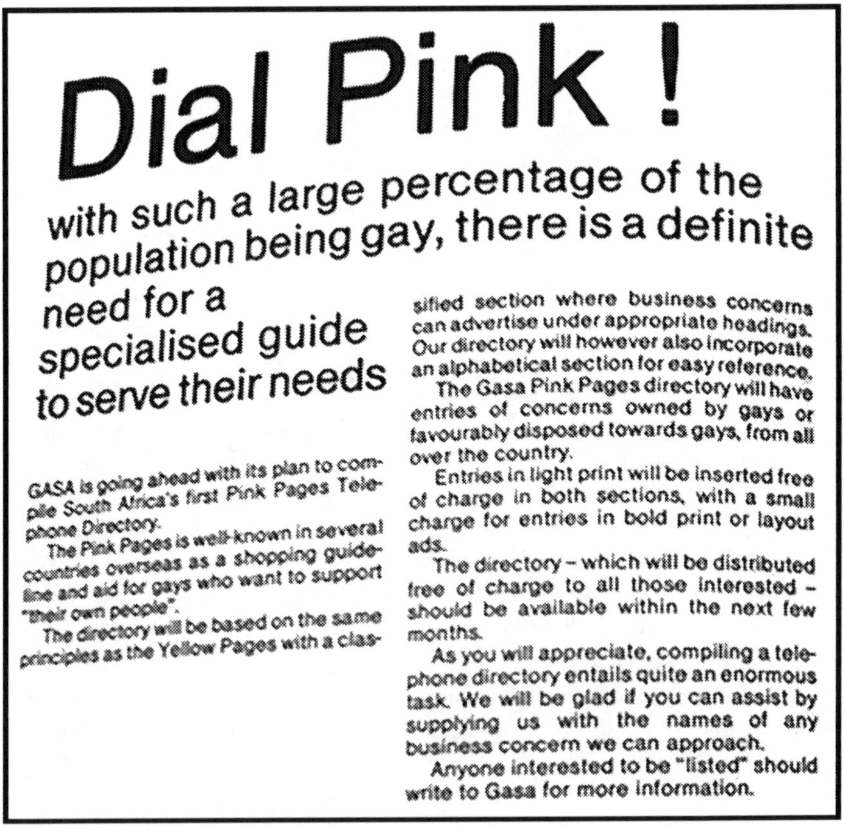

Dial Pink !

with such a large percentage of the population being gay, there is a definite need for a specialised guide to serve their needs

GASA is going ahead with its plan to compile South Africa's first Pink Pages Telephone Directory.

The Pink Pages is well-known in several countries overseas as a shopping guide-line and aid for gays who want to support "their own people".

The directory will be based on the same principles as the Yellow Pages with a clas-sified section where business concerns can advertise under appropriate headings. Our directory will however also incorporate an alphabetical section for easy reference.

The Gasa Pink Pages directory will have entries of concerns owned by gays or favourably disposed towards gays, from all over the country.

Entries in light print will be inserted free of charge in both sections, with a small charge for entries in bold print or layout ads.

The directory – which will be distributed free of charge to all those interested – should be available within the next few months.

As you will appreciate, compiling a tele-phone directory entails quite an enormous task. We will be glad if you can assist by supplying us with the names of any business concern we can approach.

Anyone interested to be "listed" should write to Gasa for more information.

FIGURE 6.1 Section of an announcement to compile a Pink Pages Telephone Directory in *Link/Skakel*. Courtesy of Henk Botha and Gay and Lesbian Memory in Action.

Initially the newsletters are a dazzling display of conspicuous consumption, with advertisements from gay friendly businesses offering luxury commodities including cosmetics, flowers, jewelry, clothes, furnishings, and international travel services. In addition, there are several "news" reports on various gay friendly restaurants. The circulation of capital and services to world these emerging sexualities are a key feature of gay and (to a lesser extent) lesbian lives in the Afropolis in the 1980s.

John D' Emilio's argument about capitalism and the emergence of modern gay identity through changes in family structures and urban migration in postindustrial America is often accepted as explaining the evolution of gay urban spaces (1998). In Johannesburg, capitalism and industrialization thrived in an African setting on African labor with the discovery of gold mines in the late nineteenth and early twentieth century, followed by American style urbanization from the 1950s onwards. Before assessing the applicability of D'Emilio's ideas to gay urbanisms in South Africa, it is useful to see how they have been challenged by recent studies. Robert Bailey claims that the location of "gay and lesbian safe spaces" in American cities "was not an expression of economic change effected by the emergence of the postindustrial urban complex or the new social movements of postmaterial politics" but rather "predated the economic restructuring of postindustrial cities and took root in spaces previously identified as bohemian, minority, or some other identification not associated with middle class values" (1998, 53). Similarly, Marc Stein's study of gay and lesbian presence in Philadelphia comments on the collective efforts of lesbian women and gay men in the creation and gentrification of urban gay spaces. Stein's study proves that separation of gay and lesbian spaces and communities cannot always be assumed, although this has sometimes been an assumption in Euro-American ethno-histories (2004). The relation between capitalism, migration to urban areas, gay and lesbian identity is applicable to Hillbrow, which was already recognized as a bohemian inner-city area before it became the center of gay socialization and activism in Johannesburg in the 1980s.

Available scholarship on gay men's relationship to urban spaces fails to indicate significant differences between lesbian women and gay men's expression of sexual identity in the consumption and utilization of space. Work on gay identities in "small-town" South Africa demonstrates that consumption of "fashion, style, and glamour" remain a key feature of gay lives in the post-apartheid scenario even away from the center of the Afropolis, a queer Afropolitanism that is refigured in peri-urban locations (Reid 2013). Zethu Matebeni reminds us that while gay men "dominate" spaces such as clubs, bars, and cafes, "lesbians rarely have territorial aspirations" (2011, 121). There was an instance of an area in Bloemfontein, a small city several hundred miles from Johannesburg, which developed as a leisure space for white lesbians in the late 1980s. Formerly known as Orange Grove, and later renamed Buzerant, the development of this space was initiated and partly supported by GASA, "which recognized that there were no dedicated gay venues in Blomfontein, unlike other cities in South Africa" (Visser 2010). In Bloemfontein, gay men tended to frequent the Central Business District; Orange Grove was, therefore, a venue where a lesbian subculture could develop, though not as a "commercial venture" since favored avenues for socialization were largely privately organized parties. In the mid-1990s when attempts were made to develop Buzerant as a commercial gay space with nightclubs and bars, lesbians largely eschewed the overt sexualization of the gay male scene. The only exception was Roxy's, a lesbian-owned bar, which became a meeting spot for lesbians before they made their way to other social venues in Buzerant (Visser 2010).

The visibility and activism of lesbians in Johannesburg can be documented in relation to (and not distinct and separate from) dominant gay male activism in GASA and later in queer politics in South Africa in the 1980s and 1990s, as in Karen Lotter and Ann Smith's participation in GASA and regular contributions to its official newsletter. With the publication of an anonymous article titled "Notes from a Token Sister" in June 1982, lesbian voices in the movement began to be heard. The article earned a reply from Ann Smith, stating that women should certainly be involved in GASA. Lotter and GASA Rand's chairperson Smith's articles on social lesbianism, lesbian identity, role playing, and radical lesbian opposition to gay liberation ensured that women had a voice in GASA and its print publications. However, L/S as a publication had a misogynist slant that was clear from its early numbers. An article by Hans van der Laagen titled "Fag hags and sex" singled out lesbian and heterosexual women frequenting clubs and bars in Hillbrow, lauding the decision of a popular club called Zipps, which had recently "closed its doors to women and non-gays on Fridays." Blatantly embracing the charge of prejudice against women within the "gay community," the writer describes sexism as "a psychological trick to help bolster a strictly gay identity or somehow to counter guilt about sleeping with other men – a mentality with which one should have little sympathy" (van der Laagen 1983, 3). The stereotypes in the article did not go unchallenged. In the next number, Jimmy Backwash (likely a pseudonym) challenges the "presumption and self-contradiction" in the previous article and labels the writer's attitude as "egoistical," "an excuse to flaunt his bisexuality." Backwash firmly denies the charge that women who are friends with gay men are confused about their sexuality and/or bisexual (1983, 3). Lesbian and feminist gay voices thus challenged misogynist perspectives expressed in L/S.

Still, black lesbian voices were conspicuously missing from the pages of the newsletter. One recent study observes that the role or even the existence of black lesbian activists in the early lesbian and gay organizations, including GASA, was unclear (Nkambule 2018, 11). Some lesbian women obtained access to restaurants and bars, indicating a trajectory of socialization and activism that spatially converges with but ideologically diverges from that of white and Afrikaner gay men. For example, venues such as Buddies on Twist Street, which first advertised itself as an "all male bar/disco," continued to remain gender segregated for a while before revisiting its strategy and marketing itself anew as a "private club" open to "men and women" (Buddies 1983, 3). Other establishments, upon realizing that there was money to be obtained from a lesbian clientele, soon abandoned the policy of all male bars and clubs.

While participating in the worldliness of metropolitan gay life offered by Johannesburg, black gay men and lesbians of all colors often found themselves sidelined from the movement and its patterns of consumption. Next I examine some of the legal challenges to governmental jurisdictions on sexuality and race and differing ideologies among the activists that inhibited an egalitarian worlding of sexualities.

Law, politics, and "community"

While I use the term "community" in the analysis offered here, any notion of the gay community invoked by *L/S* and *Exit* must consider the exclusions already mentioned: white lesbians; black and colored gays and lesbians; bisexuals; transgendered people of all races; those living in townships surrounding Johannesburg; and those who could not access the club and café culture thriving in Hillbrow and its environs because of limited purchasing power. Similarly, there were significant divisions about effective strategies to decriminalize and mainstream gay and lesbian lives in South Africa in the face of draconian laws.

Of the laws on record, the Immorality Act of 1957, later renamed the Sexual Offences Act, banned sexual relations between all whites and non-whites. Until the ban was lifted in 1985, homo or heterosexual relations between people of different races were proscribed under this act. The history of law reform by gay and lesbian activists can be charted to the 1960s when the apartheid government introduced amendments to existing legislation that sought to include homosexuality under its purview. The gay community came together to form the Law Reform Movement in 1968 to prevent draconian applications of the Immorality Act against homosexuals. Gevisser observes that the movement was "successful" as only three amendments to the current law were proposed: raising the age of consent from 16 to 19; outlawing dildos; and the prohibition of sexual activity between men at a "party," where party was defined as the presence of more than two people (Gevisser 1995). Besides these restrictions applicable to all, black people were not permitted to move into the city through the provisos of the Group Areas Act of 1950 which was amended several times in the 1960s and 1970s to exclude them from living in well-developed urban areas. The act was untenable in Johannesburg from the 1970s onwards when a shortage of housing and the emerging service economy led to increasing, though technically illegal, migration to the city.

Identity-based movements in the South, especially women's and LGBTQ+ movements, are sometimes analyzed in terms of victimhood since social and legislative discrimination are often the basis of sexual rights activism. This tendency is pronounced in Euro-American analyses of African social movements, marked by what Ashley Currier and Thérèse Migraine-George call "Afro-pessimism" which includes lamentations about political corruption, violent conflict, pervasive indigence, and worsening health outcomes experienced by Africans. For Currier and Migraine-George, the "'victimage' produced by discourses of 'African homophobia' stems from an intersection of area and sexuality studies: cynicism about

African sociopolitical conditions and confining portrayals of lived gender and sexual diversity" (2016, 281, 282). Despite discriminatory laws on record during apartheid, gay men and lesbian women combatted the description and ascription of victimhood by focusing on law reform in the 1960s, community education during the 1980s, and political involvement in the 1990s, as documented in *L/S/Exit*. Mbembe identifies a refusal of victim status as one of the key attributes of Afropolitanism, yet gay activists' struggle against victimhood was sometimes marked by a suspect racial and gender politics that prefigured the demise of GASA and a move away from the original aim of its publications. In this GASA's stand was no different from that of similar organizations in North America, for instance, the Gay Activists Alliance, which followed a "single issue politics" in the 1980s that, according to Urvashi Vaid, operated "under the assumption that gay rights are related to but disconnected from other kinds of civil freedom" (1995, 60). Reformist rather than radical in its orientation, GASA followed a controversial trajectory of selective legal reform as evident from its coverage in the newsletter.

During the first two years of its publication, *L/S* took its role of educating the gay men in the city about their rights seriously. A column by Michael titled "You and the Law," published regularly from 1982 onwards, addressed several persistent problems faced by gay men including their status within Common Law, and information on statutory offences, on being accosted by the police, and on procedures of criminal cases.[9] Since lesbian sexuality was not under the purview of the Immorality Act Amendment, and black movement in the inner city came under the Group Areas Act, the primary and implied readership of these articles were urban, gay men who risked persecution by cruising in public spaces. Identified only as the GASA lawyer, Michael attempted to address the rights of couples from different races in June 1983 in response to several queries about the "question of occupation of residential premises," particularly if the "association is between people of different colour." His final advice to people of different races cohabiting in an urban area is "You need a sympathetic area, a sympathetic landlord, and nerves of steel to be able to feel at all comfortable about it" (1983c, 11). Other legal advice offered in the newsletter was about violation of privacy, intimidation, employment rights of sexual minorities, wills, the rights of partners in gay relationships, and of gay parents after divorce from a heterosexual partner. In summary, this column offered comprehensive legal advice in non-specialist, accessible language for a largely white, gay male readership.

Gay liberation literature faced other challenges including censorship. In early 1984 the April and May numbers of *L/S* were sent to the Directorate of Publications in Cape Town as samples after its registration as a newspaper for public sale. However, since the Publications Act applied only to commercial publications, in August 1984 the leadership decided to cancel the registration of *L/S* as a newspaper and to distribute it free of cost to members of GASA. The movement's awareness of gay people's right to the city which was apparent in the advertisements and columns of the newsletter, and the threat of persecution under the Publications Act, led to strategic changes in both the group's activism and its official publication. From July 1985 onwards *L/S* was converted to *Exit*, described as "totally independent and not connected to any gay organisation or group" (*L/S* 1985, 1). A specific instance of this independence is the discontinuation of "You and the Law," perhaps because of GASA's increasing focus on a broader campaign for law reform.

Taking inspiration from the Law Reform Movement in the 1960s when the gay community had come together to fund a legal campaign, GASA planned a similar move in the 1980s. Law reform became a nationwide effort in 1986, partially in response to incidents such as the Vice Squad raid on the GASA convention in Johannesburg that year. In October 1985 *Exit* announced with much fanfare GASA's Legal Reform Fund planned in early 1986 and a fundraising effort called Benefit to collect R 100,000 for legal costs (5). Gevisser, a distinguished journalist, gay rights advocate, and supporter of the campaign, has written about the discrepancy between the grandiose aims and disappointing consequences of the campaign, using 1968 as a point of comparison with 1986:

> Unlike 1968, however, there was not the same government focus: PW Botha's campaign to smash anti-apartheid resistance overtook all else and the gay issue was forgotten. The NLRF [National Legal Reform Fund] had raised R 59,000 by January 1987, but had nothing to spend it on: it was thus transformed into the National Law Reform Charitable Trust. Three trustees were appointed, and *it was decided that this money would be used in future to "market gay lifestyles"* and to intervene, in any possible way, in the gay law reform struggle in South Africa. Of the 59,000 raised, however, only R 10,000 was spent, and there was much dissatisfaction within the gay community: talk abounded of misappropriation of funds.
>
> (Gevisser 1995, 61, emphasis mine)

Not only was the national fund used for purposes other than those for which it was originally intended, but its largesse was restricted to metropolitan urban locations where gay lifestyles were already being marketed through venues such as *Exit*. The damning charges of corruption and misuse of funds by key GASA members in 1986 were followed by debate over the organization's support of the National Party candidate Leon de Beer from Hillbrow in the 1987 elections. By proclaiming in the headlines that "Election was Gay Victory" the publishers of *Exit* were clearly defining white gay interests in electoral and spatial terms. This announcement of the gay "community's" role in swinging politics was followed by a declaration that the "community will get a far better deal from the Johannesburg City Council in the future" and that this is "directly attributable to the election result in Hillbrow and the coming by-election determining who will rule Johannesburg" (*Exit* 1987a, 1). Gay voters questioned the candidates belonging to various parties, expressed their concerns about obtaining space for the Gay Advice Bureau and accessing other city amenities. However, as before, a myopic advocacy of gay rights to the city did not include awareness of restrictions on black and colored populations (*Exit* 1987b, 1). Such blindness was publicly challenged by the Wits Gay Movement (WGM), which made it clear that the newspaper and its current editor David Moolman's support of de Beer and his "arrogance" in claiming to speak for the entire gay community equated gay rights with *white* gay rights. WGM's letter points out that when 25 million people in South Africa are denied the right to vote, the correct stand should be "against racism, sexism, and all forms of discrimination" (1987, 2).

Besides limited voting rights, the National Party's stand on maintaining apartheid brought the Group Areas Act into the limelight at a time when gay voters were deciding which candidates would best represent their interests. Despite the awareness that the Group Areas Act privileged white people's use of the city, *Exit* made no attempt to address the matter in its list of questions to the party nominees. Calling out this tunnel vision as a sign that the community was distinctly limited in its outlook, one reader asked: "Are we voting for a 'Gay Group Area?' If so, please count me out" (Lorentz 1987, 2). The Cape Town based Lesbians and Gays against Oppression or the LAGO collective publicly repudiated Leon de Beer's election as Nationalist MP in *Exit*. LAGO pointed out the contradictions in the National Party's ideology and in the political awareness of gay voters in Hillbrow:

> How can anyone committed to democracy support a candidate whose party has been responsible, inter alia, for the forced removals of thousands of families to enclaves of rural deprivation, the arbitrary incarceration of hundreds of children and the systematic abuse of police powers with the concomitant abrogation of the rule of law.
>
> (Lago Collective 1987, 2)

While the Group Areas Act was finally repealed in 1990, GASA and the urban gay community's avoidance of the race question exposed the divisions in the movement. These incidents reveal the failing fortunes and ineffectiveness of GASA in the late 1980s, an ineffectiveness which was brought to national and international attention in the movement's and its associated publications' handling of the Treason Trial involving Simon Nkoli.

Queer Afropolitanism

With the official repeal of the Immorality Act in 1985, a new generation of activists committed to worlding sexualities through an intersectional anti-apartheid queer politics sought to use popular publication avenues such as *Exit*. One of the leading figures in this move was Simon Nkoli who had been an active member of GASA from the early 1980s. Establishing *L/S* and *Exit*'s presentation of race is the key to understanding the political divergences within the organization.

Even at its inception, *L/S* could not afford to be perceived as overtly racially biased. The early *L/S* numbers contain articles which purport to understand black gay identities and cultures. The newsletter also carried some racially inclusive advertisements from gay friendly businesses such as Ebony casual and designer clothing housed in Melville and Browser's picture framing in Hillbrow. Ebony's ad shows a stylized black and white shaded male torso. Browsers advertised their picture framing business in August 1984 by depicting figures shaded black and white in a sexually suggestive pose, perhaps indicating that interracial relations were allowable in private if not public contexts, for after all the picture would be framed and kept at home. Another version of the Browsers ad in September 1984 depicts the sexualized figure of a woman to indicate that women customers were welcome.

Through the 1980s advertisements represented potential clients in varying ways. Minimally inclusive ads included those by Stud Barn restaurant (racially coded towards a mixed-race clientele) and by Jameson's bar on Commissioner Street which had applied for an "international" license allowing it to serve black customers. Those for Stud Barn in April and June/July 1984 show an ambiguously shaded man in a mining hat indicating the restaurant was willing to serve non-white customers; additionally, it is described as "The Butch Bar Where You Can Still Hear Yourself Think" possibly to encourage lesbian women, who often preferred quieter venues for socialization (Stud Barn 1984, 10)

Many other businesses were unambiguous in their preference for white customers, and often did not welcome women. Lourenco Marques Restaurant mentions in its July 1983 advertisement that the place allows "strictly members only," and emphasizes white membership through the image of two white men (Lourenco Marques Restaurant 1983, 9). Suggestive and unabashedly pretentious names – Connections, Chittendales, Saddle, Parzival, Heaven, Butterfly, and Cranks etc. – targeted white gay men with disposable incomes as consumers.

Not only the services advertised in its newsletter but also the social activities organized by GASA were often racially exclusive. In one instance, an outing organized by the GASA Rand hiking group towards the end of 1983 was critiqued for being a white only excursion. In response to this criticism, the editor defends the exclusivity by stating, "The fact that there are no multiracial venues in Pretoria is something that cannot be blamed on Gasa. Even in the Johannesburg area the number of venues open to all races can be counted on one hand" (*L/S* 1983, 10). These incidents exposed GASA's hypocritical claims of welcoming all races and rendered suspect *L/S*'s goals of serving gay liberation. Such a stand led to GASA's internal disagreements with its lesbian and more progressive members and an embattled relationship with the International Gay Association (later the International Lesbian and Gay Association or ILGA). In a chronological review of this relationship from the later 1980s to the end of the decade, Jens Rydström observes that when GASA had applied for membership to the IGA in 1983, the application had been opposed by the Scottish Human Rights Groups (SHRG) on the grounds that the organization's politics was not inclusive (2005, 34–49). GASA's representative Pieter Bosman managed to convince IGA to ignore SHRG's recommendations. Ironically, since the majority of IGA members voted in favor of GASA, this was reported as a victory in *Exit* in the August 1987 headline "International Body Welcomes SA Gays" (*Exit* 1984, 1). Rather than take international

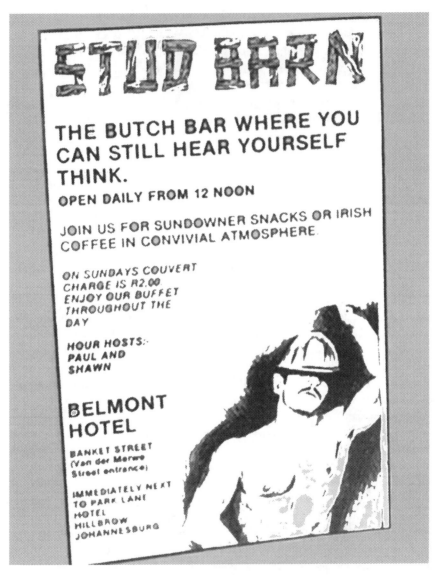

FIGURE 6.2 Ambiguous advertisement soliciting clientele for a gay bar printed in *Link/Skakel*. Courtesy of Henk Botha and Gay and Lesbian Memory in Action.

opposition to GASA as a moment for self-reflection and scrutiny, the organization and the newspaper applauded Bosman and Smith's lobbying efforts. In 1986, at the insistence of SHRG and some other anti-apartheid groups in ILGA, GASA's racial politics again came under scrutiny. This time the opposition came from Swedish and Scottish groups, and GASA sent Kevan Botha as a representative to prevent its expulsion from the organization. Botha's apparently candid account of GASA's multiracial work helped avoid the organization's expulsion, an account he later admitted had been insincere in its representation of the organization's political stance on race and apartheid era exclusions.

Behind the scenes others had been working to avoid this expulsion. While in detention as a co-conspirator in the Delmas Treason Trial, Nkoli had written to the ILGA pleading with them not to expel GASA from its fold. Later this connection helped the international community become aware of the mutual imbrications of racial and sexual justice, particularly when African LGBTQ+ organizers, including Nkoli and Sheila Lapinsky, attended the annual ILGA conferences. Black lesbian activist Phumi Mtetwa, who served with Nkoli on the National Coalition for Gay and Lesbian Equality, was elected as Secretary of ILGA from 1999–2001. Hence the impact of a black South African perspective on ILGA which had a predominantly European and North American focus till the mid-1980s cannot be overstated.

Nkoli's involvement with GASA and *Exit* lasted through his detention from 1985 to 1988 in one of the longest running and most widely publicized political trials in South Africa documented in gay as well as mainstream South African history. Nkoli and 21 others associated with the United Democratic Front, a broad coalition of anti-apartheid groups, were accused of attempting to overthrow the state by violent means. These men were attending the funeral of 20 people shot dead by the police during a protest march against rent increases when they were arrested. The trial brought to national and international attention GASA's unwillingness to take a stand on the struggle for gay rights as connected to racial equality in South Africa. When the organization did comment on the incident, many months after Nkoli's arrest, it was in a short piece appearing in *Exit* which justified not taking an "official stance" since Simon "is not detained because of his gay activities" (*Exit* 1986a, 1). Ann Smith, Chairperson of GASA Rand and International Secretary of the organization for many years, pointed out the contradictions in the organization's stance. Smith also made her own position and the differences with the official position clear: "Personally I believe we should be fighting discrimination in all its manifestation, but Gasa's members think otherwise. As Rand chairperson I must observe this and thus find myself, in terms of my own conscience, in an untenable position" (1986, 5). Many lesbians in the movement did not share the official GASA position reflected in the newspaper, despite the claims of the publication being an independent entity. In the late 1980s *Exit* was edited jointly by Karen Lotter and Henk Botha before their disagreements over GASA's racial politics led to the latter giving up his second stint at editorship.

In this context, Nkoli's founding of the Saturday Group within GASA in 1984 signals an emerging queer Afropolitanism that expands the racial and geographical reach of gay liberation, a worlding of sexualities that was first, simultaneously local, national, and international and next, openly political and community oriented. From 1984 GASA had taken some note of worlds other than the one in Hillbrow by supplementing the local gay news column "Link Up" with one called "World Link" containing snippets of gay and lesbian news from international sources, indicating an awareness of its role in the circulation of gay liberation literature.

In this worldly context where white gay activism was increasingly becoming untenable, a small inconspicuous notice placed by "Simon and Roy" in *L/S* announced: "Gays of all races, sexes, ages and creeds are welcome" (*L/S* 1984, 3) Under the leadership of Simon and Roy, his white partner at that time, the Saturday Group soon acquired its own offices to plan a series of activities which involved not just people living in Johannesburg but also township and homeland areas. The group's practices of socialization were markedly different from that of the white gay community, sometimes leading to hostility between more established GASA members and those belonging to the Saturday Club. After Nkoli's acquittal in the Treason Trial, the Saturday Group resumed its activities. There is little coverage of this in *Exit* except through very brief letters sent by readers.[10]

Nkoli formed the Johannesburg and Soweto Working Group, precursor of the Gays and Lesbians of Witwatersrand (GLOW), on his release and acquittal. The new organization was founded on principles of fulfilling the educational, cultural, and social needs of the black lesbian and gay community. Responding to a letter in *Exit* he says, "Our general non-negotiable principles are: non-racism, non-sexism and non-heterosexism" (Nkoli 1988, 2). One of the crucial aspects of queer politics in this period is a realization that city spaces cannot exclusively encompass gay and lesbian activism and that worlding sexualities involves work beyond the Afropolis. The reclamation of a black queer identity from a predominantly white GASA meant reaching out to people of all races living in the city and outside it, in townships such as Soweto and Kwa-Thema. To this end GLOW's 1988 celebration of Gay Pride included a meeting in support of Ivan Toms, a gay activist, at the University of Witwatersrand, a drag show, a braai, dance, and poetry reading at a private house (*Exit* 1988, 9). Later in the year, there was a Gay and Lesbian Contact Rally that included presentations by various South African gay and lesbian organizations (*Exit* 1988, 1989).

The definitional correlates of queer embraced by GLOW derived as much from African social realities as they did from the emerging models of activism by North American groups such as the AIDS Coalition to Unleash Power (ACT UP) in the late 1980s and Queer Nation in the 1990s. Both groups were characterized by their public actions and often confrontational tactics including theatrical protests and a boycott of businesses following homophobic practices. Karen Lotter mentions Nkoli's 1989 trip to London, from where he went to Vienna to attend the ILGA meeting, and then to Canada and the US to raise money for the Township AIDS Project (Lotter 1989, 7). This history of exchange and influence is part of GLOW's international connections maintained by visits abroad and exchange of information about LGBTQ+ movements that were taking on a different face in the wake of the AIDS crisis. GLOW's efforts to address the crisis reflected queer activism in North America but also a recognition that the situation in South Africa demanded a different response. In these ways it differed from GASA's reaction to the crisis.

Mandisa Mbali notes in her account of South African AIDS activism that GASA circulated information about AIDS through its publications and at its meetings but did not address the issue politically, and that there was some disagreement amongst its members regarding the urgency of the crisis. Additionally, GASA opted to collaborate with the apartheid regime's ministry of health as a representative gay organization at a time when other organizations refused collaborations with the state (Mbali 2013, 55–56). Mbali's view is corroborated by GASA's sporadic attention to the AIDS crisis in the pages of *L/S*. Some of the group's efforts were directed towards conveying information to the gay community about modes of transmission and medical testing, but more energy was spent on collecting funds, whether to aid medical research or to support education groups. Much like the controversy over the Law Reform Campaign, a series of disagreements and accusations marred these efforts. In May 1986 *Exit* reported that the Johannesburg branch of GASA had taken the first place in collecting donations for the Law Reform Fund at Benefit functions, whose next priority was collecting money for the "Aids fund, followed by other deserving causes" (*Exit* 1986b, 1). Connecting the two issues led to conflict over the collection and disbursement of monies by Benefit, a conflict that GASA tried to cover up by short articles outlining the goals of the fund drive: "apart from the constantly rising cost of the law reform issue, which will necessitate additional funds, Benefit will also address the Aids issue…Aids also impacts on the law reform issue" (*Exit* 1986c, 8). In these forced connections and false claims to unity amid serious disagreements, we see the community's fragmented, apolitical, donor, and fund-driven approach to the AIDS crisis rather than serious attention to the medical emergency it posed to the community. Specious racist connections between over a hundred black heterosexual miners discovered to be infected with the virus and the situation of homosexuals were further proof of GASA's racially blinkered approach to the situation (*Exit* 1986d, 1).

In contrast to GASA's model of gay liberation, Nkoli and GLOW's queer Afropolitanism involved an effort to connect races, genders, and classes within and beyond the nation when the apartheid regime was beginning to unravel. Because of its work with non-urban, underprivileged gay, lesbian, and transgender people living under threat of isolation, violence, and disease, this politics also came to be called the gay Left in South Africa. One of the reasons for this focus was GLOW members' non-metropolitan backgrounds. The varied worldly geography of GLOW's activities (by 1991 it had branches in Kwa-Thema, Tembisa, Soweto, and Johannesburg) is reflected in Nkoli's "Open Letter to Nelson Mandela" for the *Village Voice*, reprinted by *Exit*. He attempts to make the leader understand "what it means to be a gay or lesbian person in the townships" and establishes a direct link to the situation under apartheid where people, feeling unsafe in their home communities, "are moving into the so-called 'grey areas' of the white cities, which also happen to be gay areas." In a savvy move that connects the local to the global or South Africa to the world, Nkoli reminds Mandela of his promises to secure "the rights of all people" on a visit to the Township AIDS Project in Soweto, of his support for gay rights in a meeting in Stockholm, and of the promises made by Mandela's close colleagues, Thabo Mbeki and Frene Ginwala, who had publicly declared outside of South Africa that gay rights would be secured by the ANC (Nkoli 1990, 16).

Finally, the emergence of local, national, and international queer Afropolitanism of the kind articulated by lesbian women in GASA, Nkoli, Beverley Ditsie, and GLOW in Johannesburg and the surrounding areas, was also a response to a lack of credible gay and lesbian leadership in the wake of GASA-era politics. Beverley Ditsie's film *Simon and I* points to some of the exclusions from GLOW's politics that, ironically, replicated GASA's sidelining of women and black members. GLOW published its own newsletter from 1990 onwards. Often it was a record of meetings, activities, and important organizational briefs, rather than a primary vehicle of gay liberation that was the stated aim of *L/S*. As reported in *Exit*, Alfred Machela, a black activist, had started the Rand Gay Organization (RGO) when Nkoli was in prison. But the RGO was ineffective, practically invisible, and deemed suspect by the late 1980s. GLOW emerged as the natural leader for organizing the first ever Gay Pride Parade in October 1990. The route charted for the parade from Bloemfontein to Hillbrow symbolized the educational, commercial, and social needs of the gay and lesbian community in Johannesburg and asserted that people of all races and beliefs had a claim to this vibrant Afropolis.

News coverage in mainstream and gay media of this period belies the assumption that visibility of the annual Pride in Johannesburg in the 1990s made the city and its surroundings safer for gays and lesbians. *Exit* reported many incidents of homophobic violence when a national collation of gay and lesbian groups was being planned to place sexual equality in the draft South African constitution. Reid and Dersuweit mention that the visibility of gay men and lesbian women may have contributed to the rise in gay bashing. This is borne out by their citation of Beverley Ditsie's memory of the first Pride Parade which made her a public figure, and hence subject to homophobic threats in her Soweto neighborhood (Reid & Dirsuweit 2002, 103–106). Similarly, Amanda Lock Swarr analyses lesbian masculinities and sexual violence in South Africa (Swarr 2012a). In 1996 South Africa became the first nation in the world to constitutionally guarantee non-discrimination to its gay and lesbian citizens through what came to be called the Equality Clause, the result of a complex process of negotiations between gay and lesbian activists and the ANC, with support from the legal community. Studies conducted on the incidence of homophobic violence in Johannesburg and its environs in the post-apartheid era after this constitutional mandate conclude that the city remains a "homophobic landscape" and that further "investigations need to be embedded in discussions of the complexity and suppleness of gay urban politics in Johannesburg" (Reid & Dirsuweit 2002, 124). Xavier Livermon's account of black queer bodies' estrangement from freedoms enabled by the constitution, though it does not explicitly deal with urban geography, mentions that this estrangement "cannot be resolved at the state level but must occur in communities that ultimately can provide safety and security to black queers and thus make the rights of the constitution meaningful" (2012, 297–323). Resonating with the call of a "queer South African sexual politics" that offers an "alternative to the current global and national status quo, speaking back to a postapartheid social order that might prefer gays and lesbians to remain mutely happy emblems of the new nation" (Munro 2012, xxvi), my suggestion is that the exceptionality of constitutional and legislative successes and the unexceptionality of sexual violence in South Africa are both crucial projects for a postcolonial feminist and queer historical enquiry. The next chapter on the Durban- and Johannesburg-based women's newsletter *Speak* and the feminist magazine *Agenda* addresses heterosexual and lesbian women's sexual precarity, sexually transmitted diseases (including AIDS), and lack of availability of reproductive choices during the decade preceding the end of apartheid.

In conclusion, sidestepping GASA-era politics, gay liberation moved toward a queer Afropolitanism in the late 1980s and early 1990s. However, rather than transitioning from gay liberation to queer liberation literature, *Exit* lapsed into an infomercial tabloid still in circulation. During our conversations in 2012 and 2013, GALA's previous director, Anthony Manion, was clear about *Exit*'s lack of relevance to the queer movement in the country. Despite this disappointing trajectory, the historical importance of Johannesburg-based gay journalism of the 1980s is in the connections that complicate a one-way North-South comparison. Many of these comparisons present LGBTQ+ mobilizing in the North as emulated in the South with little or no legislative gains.[11] Within South African gay social formations there was and remains modeling and inter-referencing of Northern gay urbanisms and modes of protest, but there is also localized Southern consciousness addressing exclusions through legal reform, and modes of racial, class, and gender inclusivity that extended sexual rights awareness beyond the gay world of Johannesburg. GASA lesbians and GLOW's invocation of and departure from Northern and international queer activism stands out as exceptional not only in the gains secured at the turn of the twentieth century but also in its ability to inflect international sexual rights with racial and geographical specificities. Engendered in Hillbrow, but spreading beyond it to embrace the racially, geographically, culturally diverse worlding of spatiality and sexuality in print, this queer Afropolitanism emerged in the face of obstacles encountered, overcome, and still faced by those tirelessly working to secure justice and rights for sexual minorities in the South.

Notes

1 An earlier version of this article appeared in the journal *Postcolonial Studies* in 2016.
2 Some organizations supporting sexual rights activism are located a little off inner-city Johannesburg in Braamfontein and Yeoville. These include GALA, Forum for the Empowerment of Women (FEW) in Braamfontein, the Gay Boxing Group, and the Gay and Lesbian Legal Advice Centre in Yeoville. Additionally, there are several health-based organizations with centers or branches in Soweto such as SOHACA (Soweto HIV/AIDS Health Counsellors Association) and Health4Men with clinics in and around Johannesburg. The exhibition, *Joburg Tracks: Sexuality in the City*, developed by GALA in 2008, is permanently housed at Museum Africa in Newtown, Johannesburg.
3 There is a wealth of scholarship on North-South interactions in studies of sexuality. Many of these works are categorized as queer diasporic analyses. See edited collections by Cindy Patton and Beningo Sanchez-Eppler (2000), Arnaldo Cruz-Malawe and Martin F. Manalansan (2002), and John Hawley (2001). See also works by Martin Manalansan (2003) and Gayatri Gopinath (2005a).

4 See the landmark anthology of lesbian and gay writing edited by Matthew Krouse (1993).
5 Ivan Vladislavic offers a fascinating account of the changing racial composition of Johannesburg where the narrator's growing discomfort in his favorite haunt Café Europa is explicitly linked to sexual and racial unease in *The Restless Supermarket* (2001/2014). Vladislavic also meditates on the city in an aphoristic style reminiscent of Walter Benjamin in *The Arcades Project* in *Portrait with Keys* (2006).
6 For an exploration of such exchanges in Johannesburg, see Loren Landau (2006) and Abdoumaliq Simone (2004). Urban and cultural studies analysis of other African cities such as Kinshasa, Lagos, and Accra include those by Filip de Boeck (2002), Jonathan Haynes (2007), and Ato Quayson (2010). Accounts of the visibility and safety of gay men and lesbian women in urban South Africa often focus on the post-apartheid city with minimal reference to the situation in the 1980s and early 1990s. This trend is evident in the work of Graeme Reid and Teresa Dirsuweit (2002), Xavier Livermon (2012), and Andrew Tucker (2009). Gay newsletters and newspapers, such as *Link/Skakel* and *Exit*, are therefore valuable sources for analyzing the situation during apartheid.
7 In chronological order, these include works by Nigel Mandy (1984), Jo Beall, Owen Crankshaw, and Susan Parnell (2002), Ivan Vladislavic (2001/2014, 2006), Keith Beavon (2005).
8 The system of rigid racial classification was introduced by the Populations Registration Act of 1950. The South African population was divided into three racial groups: "White," "Black" ("African," "Native," and/or "Bantu") and "Coloured"; further subcategorized into "Cape Malay," "Griqua," "Indian," "Chinese," and "Cape Coloured." These classifications were repealed by the Parliament in 1991. Petty apartheid meant the day-to-day restrictions on various racial groups, such as separate facilities and restrictions in travel, entertainment, and other social spaces. In contrast, Grand apartheid was the policy to keep the different races as separated as possible, for example by ensuring that they lived in different areas.
9 Michael (1982a, 1982b, 1982c, 1983a, 1983b).
10 Nkoli's life and career has been the subject of much academic discussion over the past two decades yielding many nuanced interpretations in writings by Munro (2012), Chernis (2016), Imma (2017), and Martin (2020), a play, and a documentary film. The tradition of letter writing as an immediate and forceful medium of expression is carried forward by Nkoli's close associate, Beverley Ditsie, whose address, "A Love Letter to my Queer Family" (2019) describes the continued imprisonment of South African LGBTQ+ activism in the cells of racial and class privilege evident in the devolution of the Johannesburg Pride March into the Pride Parade and the takeover of the celebration by white organizers.
11 To a certain extent this is true of many countries in the global South: in Uganda, homosexuality is punishable by life imprisonment; in Nigeria, it is punishable by imprisonment; in Jamaica homosexual acts are illegal under the "buggery" and "indecency" laws; in India, after decades of activism, the Supreme Court of India legalized homosexuality in 2018. Even in the face of mixed gains and losses, it is unproductive to see LGBTQ+ activism in the South as merely imitative of the North without taking into consideration local histories of resistance.

7

MEDIATED SEXUALITIES

Civic feminism and development critique in
South Africa

In contrast to the struggle for gay liberation in South Africa which initially distanced itself from anti-apartheid politics, resistance against apartheid galvanized the South African women's movement. This chapter describes how two influential magazines, *Speak* and *Agenda*, contributed to the ongoing discussion of gender and sexuality initiated by black South African lesbian and gay organizations such as the Gays and Lesbians of Witwatersrand (GLOW) and the Organization of Lesbians and Gays Activists (OLGA) founded during this period.[1] Examining these non-mainstream publications to learn about the cultural history of postcolonial gender and sexuality in South Africa reveals not the expected tensions between feminist and LGBTQ+ activism (as in India) but rather an initially hesitant and then a more confident conversation about sexual autonomy during politically turbulent times. As in the previous chapters of the book, here too my aim is to examine and describe the social, political, and historical significance of activist literature. Thus far my analysis of Jamaican and Indian print media addressed reproductive choices and campaigns against sexual violence as either combating or complementing the emergence of gay, lesbian, and queer struggles in these nations. Following this trajectory, I examine the representation of sexuality in two South African women's magazines to demonstrate how they worked towards participatory democracy for heterosexual and lesbian South African women by simultaneously invoking and questioning the paradigm "development." My primary sources are articles, reports, news briefs, case histories, and narratives from the women's magazines *Speak* (1982 to 1994) and select numbers of *Agenda* (1987–1996).[2] This analysis also draws on South African media history, histories of women's movements, and feminist urban studies.

Shamim Meer, co-founder of *Speak*, a newsletter published from Johannesburg and Durban, mentions that alternative media "carried very little about women [...] and it was more often the voices of men that were heard in their articles" (1998, 9). South African women's alternative media brought supposedly private concerns of

DOI: 10.4324/9781003170303-10

reproduction, sexual violence, and sexual choice into the public sphere in ways that were in dialogue with party-based women's groups, operating under the broad coalition of the African National Congress (ANC)-led United Democratic Front (UDF) towards nuanced conversations on race, class, gender, and sexuality. Beginning in the 1950s, ANC-leaning publications such as *Liberation* and *Fighting Talk* and those by feminist organizations such as *Black Sash* analyzed interlinked concerns of political disenfranchisement, unequal conditions of employment, education, housing, and healthcare for women and non-white populations. In the 1960s as even influential newspapers such as the *Guardian*, aimed at a black and white liberal readership, only survived for a short while, newsletters for black readers, among them *Inyaniso, Africanist*, and *Isizwe*, discontinued publication. In the 1970s worker's newsletters *Abasebenzi* and *Umanyano* were launched, and in the 1980s community newspapers such as *Grassroots* emerged as "struggle" publications.[3] From the 1980s magazines such as *Speak* and *Agenda* focused on South African women's concerns during a period when the struggle against apartheid and the achievement of independence from colonial rule was center stage. Not only are these important documents of South African women's activism, scholars use them as historical sources to correct erasure of women in mainstream and party-based publications. Feminist historian Shireen Hassim extensively cites *Speak* and *Agenda* in her landmark account of women's organizations and democracy (2006); sociologist Zethu Matebeni references *Agenda* in her doctoral dissertation on black lesbian sexualities in Johannesburg (2011); and anthropologist Mandisa Mbali draws on them to document contemporary AIDS activism (2013).

Glenn Adler and Jonny Steinberg define South African civic movements as a "family of locally-based residents' organizations" that emerged in South Africa in the early 1980s. They note the "dualism" animating civic activity marked by "a certain distance from the sphere of the political in their capacity as non-aligned civic representatives" and "a deep immersion in the political as a fundamental arm of the Charterist liberation movement" (Adler & Steinberg 2000, 1–5). The major characteristics of civics from the 1970s to the late 1980s were: an oppositional stance towards local authorities; direct involvement in public concerns such as housing, electricity, water, sanitation, transport, education, wages, and conditions of work under the broad category of rights and development; and, at least initially, a local focus on urban communities, although the efforts of the ANC-led United Democratic Front "facilitated a rapid and successful scaling up of the movement" (Heller & Ntlokonkulu 2001, 11). Even as women were already participating in civic activities by questioning traditional economies of rent, housing, work, and taxation, *Speak* and *Agenda* foreground the rights of women to choose their modes of participation in traditional production-consumption and sexual-reproductive economies. As instances of locational counterpublics, initially focusing their work in and around Durban and Johannesburg, these publications intervene in redistribution, recognition, and representational claims, and expand the analysis of women, rights, and development to a more inclusive understanding of gender and development.

As mediums of expression and empowerment for urban township women during a time of turbulent political transition, *Speak* and *Agenda* reflect multiple influences of local civic organization and national and international development discourse. Though concerns like reproductive rights, bodily autonomy, and sexual choice were "deemed apolitical by nationalists," *Speak* and *Agenda* introduced a political urgency and legitimacy to discussing these (Hassim 2006, 77). These private concerns, apparently outside the purview of traditional domains of civic activism, influence women's active participation in public life. Women's direct or indirect relationship to civic activism led them to address traditional gender roles and to perceive a connection between sexual choices and sexual health. This chapter claims that some of these questions can be better understood with the descriptor *civic feminism* that evolved into women staking a claim to reproductive/ sexual health and choice as fundamental human rights even as various postcolonial *development critiques* emerged during this period.

Speak began as a biannual, bilingual newsletter in English and Zulu, before it became a monthly publication in the early 1990s. It was started by members of the Durban Women's Group, involved in community work over high rents, employment conditions for women workers, and provision of educational and childcare facilities. Meer, a founding member of the group, and co-editor of the newsletter with Karen Hurt, mentions that the collective took a decision to separate its publication from the activities of the Women's Group as a tactical move since the latter was already under police scrutiny (1998, 14). Funded by an overseas church organization and sales, the collective published the magazine and later began Speak Radio to communicate with and among women involved in civic struggles. *Speak* addressed race and class disparities as fundamental but also saw gender parity and sexual equality as crucial to establishing a new South Africa. Its early numbers directly reflect the influence of civic activism and anti-apartheid movements on women's lives. Articles in its early numbers are typically reports on women's civic efforts in the Lamontville, Phoenix, and Claremont areas around Durban. Among the matters addressed were: setting up street level pre-schools and handwork groups; collective childcare by women of different neighborhoods; a women's action group to lobby for a burial ground near their community; and establishment of a community health clinic run by a nurse from the yard of her own house. While attentive to the local, the newsletter also kept a keen eye on national level organizational efforts.[4] *Speak* newsletter – later a magazine with a circulation of about 6,000 copies in South Africa and abroad – was in conversation with the place and structure of women's organization in the UDF, a coalition of several hundred religious bodies, civic associations, student groups, and worker organizations formed in 1983 to protest against the exclusion of black populations from the South African Constitution.

Agenda came into existence in the late 1980s through the efforts of a group of women academics at the University of Natal in Durban, among them Meer from *Speak*. It was established as an explicitly feminist "journal." While it too scrupulously reported on local community matters, it established a theoretical, scholarly

FIGURE 7.1 Hand-drawn illustrations in the second number of *Speak* depicting women's domestic and waged labor. Image courtesy of Shamim Meer and the magazine archive of Digital Imaging South Africa.

framework to analyze structural conditions impacting South African women. Though the goals of the two publications overlapped and they shared concerns about accurate representation, *Agenda*'s connection to the university meant its constituency was largely academic. Testimonies, stories, poems, anecdotal pieces, and women's life-writing were as essential to *Speak* and *Agenda* as their reports on community activities.[5] The first number of *Agenda* emphasizes these connections between the two ventures by advertising *Speak*:

> Have you heard of SPEAK? It's a women's magazine with stories from women in South Africa and everywhere. Writing about all kinds of things that concern women – battles with bosses, sexual harassment, men and the way they treat women – and how women are organising to change these things!

Also a regular women's health feature from a critical perspective.

> Poems, drawings, photographs, stories, letters and features all make SPEAK colourful and exciting!
>
> (*Agenda* 1987b, 24)

Speak likewise included advertisements for *Agenda* during the years 1987–1994 when the two publications overlapped. These advertisements further clarify differences between their constituencies and the readership. Like *Speak, Agenda* emphasized women's consciousness-raising but presented this effort in a sophisticated, analytical, urban developmental, and explicitly feminist vocabulary, as in an article titled "What is Feminism?" in its very first number. Meer is of the opinion that *Agenda* carried forward the strategies of the broader struggle for women within the political movements of the times (2012). Early *Agenda* numbers carried articles on the history of male and female domestic workers in Johannesburg, gender politics of the Inkatha party's women's brigade, the social and economic impact of the commuter labor workforce in the cities etc. The format of both magazines changed in the 1980s as new technologies for printing and publishing became available. From the mimeographed sheets arranged by volunteers of *Speak* to the professional desktop-published contents of *Agenda*, the mediated types of women's print had indeed come a long way.

From civic feminism to development critique

The Speak and Agenda collectives' feminist focus was at once in dialogue with and significantly different from the anti-apartheid movement in its attention to women's concerns. Hassim describes a "polarization" in the 1980s where anti-apartheid activists labeled analysis of sexual and reproductive rights as "feminist issues" in opposition to "community-based issues" such as women's access to services, support for displaced populations, and an end to political violence which they saw as "grassroots" demands (2006, 29). The artificiality of polarization is evident from *Speak*'s reports on women's neighborhood initiatives in African, Indian, and colored townships, involving grassroots participation and locally negotiated approaches to spatial and structural inequities under apartheid (Hassim 2006, 48).

A mushrooming of local civic movements in the country led to the South African National Civic Movement (SANCO), an umbrella organization formed in 1992 at the cusp of the transition to a democratic South Africa. Tracing development of civic consciousness in the 1980s to urban associations during the inter-war years in South Africa, one commentator notes that these became a "political vehicle for issues affecting African women" particularly around employment matters such as brewing and selling beer (Bundy 2000, 43). In Jeremy Seekings' opinion, resurgent civic efforts in the 1970s and 1980s were initially marked by a lack of direct engagement or confrontation with the state (2000, 54). Seekings is one of the few scholars to track the role of alternative media in the civics movement, especially the political education of local activists through the newspapers *Ukusa* from Durban, *Grassroots* from Capetown, and *The Eye* from Pretoria (2000, 64).

These useful historical and media-centric accounts by and large lack a focus on women's direct involvement in and reimagining of the anti-apartheid movement through civics. Hassim strives to provide a "gender corrective" to literature about the UDF which, in her opinion (she notes Ineke van Kessel's work is an exception) has paid "no attention to women's roles in the civics movement or to women's organizations in alliance with the civics movement" (2006, 49). Meer's role in the

Phoenix Women's Circle is an example of women's complicated involvement in localized movements. Unlike the broader non-political aims of women in civics who were hopeful of immediate solutions to local problems in the townships, Meer and some others made connections between "struggling for basic needs and larger political struggles...to expose the structural roots of inequalities" (Hassim 2006, 57). Ineke van Kessel observes that "women's issues were frequently marginal to the civic's central concerns" (2000, 179).[6] Disagreeing with Seekings' views on violence among communities as a possible reason for low level of women's involvement, van Kessel suggests that since many civics were actively involved in public safety, violence was not necessarily a reason for women's low participation, rather traditional gender ideologies about the distribution of domestic responsibilities and a suspicion of politics in general and feminism in particular may be some of the reasons (2000, 180–183). In his *Agenda* article, "Gender Ideology and Township Politics in the 1980s" surveying the role of women in civics, Seekings writes: "women seem to have protested over specifically women's grievances," but then fails to follow up specific aspects of such "grievances" (1991, 84). Later, he describes the 1989–1990 "moment" in civic strategy as focused on "struggles over development" (2000, 56), a view that is consistent with the emergence of women's health and sexuality as civics and development concerns during this period.

Extending the purview of traditionally defined civics, one of *Speak*'s aims was to create a constituency of sexually educated women who could exercise choices about their role in the reproductive economy just as those previously involved in civic efforts were participating in and/or withholding their participation from traditional economies of rent, housing, basic services, work, and taxation. *Agenda* embraced some of these aspects of *Speak* though its vision of development was of an equal partnership between political and civil society. There is thus feminist continuity as well as transition from *Speak* to *Agenda*, with the former characterized by feminist associationism, and the latter marked by feminist critique of developmental concerns.[7] If women's print in this period provided counterpublic articulations that may be called *Speak*'s *civic feminism* and these cleared the ground for *Agenda*'s *development critique*, it is absolutely crucial to assess the role of sexuality in these moves. Looking at continuities, overlaps, and transitions between feminist print counterpublics helps avoid dichotomization since both magazines presented private-public dimensions of women's lives, especially reproductive and sexual autonomy, albeit in different ways.

To clarify, I do not claim that publications such as *Speak* and *Agenda* existed in a pure space free of national politics (that would mean denying the impact of oppositional and apartheid nationalist politics in the 1980s and 1990s) but rather suggest that they highlight matters which did not easily find a place in the nationalist challenge to the apartheid regime or civic efforts to mitigate horrendous inequalities between black, white, and colored populations under that regime. Sexuality was one such concern.

Sex and gender in the South African city

Speak and *Agenda* began as Durban-based publications that soon achieved South African circulation, and in the case of *Speak*, sales in Johannesburg surpassed those in Durban. What follows is an overview of the emergence of women's activism and content analysis of the magazines to indicate how they conceptualize women's structural positions in urban and peri-urban constituencies and communities.

Urban scholars have analyzed the spatiality of Durban within and beyond apartheid for over half a century. Early accounts of the city focus on the role of the local state by highlighting how transportation and infrastructure impacted Durban's development from the nineteenth to the twentieth century. Shortage of housing for whites is seen as one of the primary causes of the "control and regulation of black labor" and scholars argue that the demand for segregation in Durban came from "white urban property owners" (Maharaj 1996, 592; Maylam 1995, 25). Some of these opinions engage directly with issues of capital accumulation and black workers' resistance to unfair and undercompensated work, claiming that residential segregation arose out of a need to "ensure a stable labour supply with fixed wages." They also call for a perspective which dissociates the local state in Durban from the central state apparatus such that the local state "in many respects pioneered measures of reproduction, repression, and segregation" (Maharaj 1996, 593, 598). Brij Maharaj is one of the leading voices in (D)urban analysis, and his ideas have been central to the ways in which the city's spatial politics have been studied. Building on Maharaj's ideas, though not directly invoking them, Paul Maylam cursorily includes gender concerns by pointing to connections between urban, economic, political, and women's histories. Listing various causes of segregated accommodation including employer control, class differentiation, and ethnic zoning, he warns against viewing urban control in "teleological, monolithic, functionalist terms" because the "apparatus of urban segregation and apartheid has been riddled with contradiction and dysfunctionality" (Maylam 1995, 34). Maylam suggests a way of centering gender in urban contexts when he states that apartheid-era contradictions invite an examination of urban policy in the context of the central-local state relationships.

In an essay published concurrently with Maylam's 1995 study, architecture and planning scholar Alison Todes (a frequent contributor to *Agenda*), examines gender in development planning using Durban as a case study. Todes emphasizes that much urban analysis has focused on local and national levels thereby leading to a neglect of "gender at a metropolitan or regional scale" (1995, 328). Implicitly critiquing dominant perspectives such as those offered by Maharaj and Maylam, Todes is of the opinion that "metropolitan development strategies contain considerable opportunities to influence the direction and prioritization of development in more gender-aware ways" (1995, 328). These views on the lack of organizations articulating gender-specific demands therefore seek to extend the mandate of the civics movements in the 1980s. They are presented in *Speak* from a civic feminist perspective; as development critique they are crucial to *Agenda*. Todes' idea about some of these efforts containing "considerable opportunities to influence the direction and prioritization of development in more gender-aware ways" merits further analysis.

A retrospective account of the Durban-based women's movement's "failure to ask the pertinent questions about social relationships of gender" (Beall et al. 2011, 99) provides a lens to examine *Agenda* and *Speak*'s coverage of gender and sexuality. Bill Freund describes the "liberal moment" in city management from the late 1970s to the 1990s when Durban's Progressive Party challenged segregation, there were attempts to directly engage businesses on social issues, many key urban developments were initiated, and city administration was reorganized (2002, 11–41). South African scholars agree that this liberal moment dissipated in the 1990s with the National Party councilors negotiating with the Inkatha Freedom Party and the newly unbanned ANC. Civic organizations' involvement in the desegregation of Durban during the 1970s has been well documented, and women's organizations undoubtedly played a role in these efforts. At the same time deep-seated racial and economic divisions within the city marked access to its public services and facilities before, within, and beyond the liberal moment and women's mobilization. Filling in the gaps of civic organization, collectives such as Speak scrupulously analyzed employment conditions, lack of healthcare, patriarchal structures, and biased legislation as factors contributing to women's vulnerability to violence in the city as common problems faced by women of all races. These analyses also emphasized inadequate urban and suburban infrastructure (the subject of much civic activism in these decades) as contributing to these conditions.

Speak included reports on city and township infrastructure related to schools, day care centers, water supplies, provision of lighting, transportation, and home construction; it occasionally connected these conditions to the daily threat of sexual violence faced by women and children due to the lack of some of these amenities. In the late 1980s a short article titled "We are not Toys!" concludes by asking its readers:

> Why do young girls have to be afraid to go out, even in the very streets where they live and grow up? Why do we have to defend ourselves from men we work with, who are our comrades at meetings and rallies?
>
> (*Speak* 1987b, 5)

Epitomizing what Pumla Gqola calls the "female fear factory, and the fear of gendered violence in public spaces" (2015, 52), the series of questions situates the rampant threat of violence in all areas of urban life – housing, community, and labor organization – that were the focus of women's civics in this period. In December 1991 *Speak* closed its Durban offices and moved its base of operations to Johannesburg. Over the years its focus on working class lives meant that concerns such as women's participation in trade unions as equals of their male comrades, maternity benefits and childcare provisions, or harassment of women workers on assembly lines and shop floors were regularly covered. Reports from

Johannesburg brought out systemic attacks against women more than the Durban numbers. Libby Lloyd's article on the rape and murder of Stella Mabale while she was returning from her night shift in a fast food restaurant addresses the structural constraints of safe transportation and its direct connection with sexualized violence (1991, 20–22). Extending the scope of its coverage, *Speak* also reported on employment in traditionally male sectors. A very informative piece on women bus drivers in Johannesburg and another on a woman ambulance driver adds to this analysis (*Speak* 1992g, 24–25; 1993a, 22–23).

Interspersing these grim reports with humor, in 1992 *Speak* introduced a section called "Taxi Talk." Here, reversing the trope of men sexualizing women, the contributor compares men to Putco Buses:

> With all this stopping and starting, picking up different women, they end up looking like the scraps of PUTCO buses packed up at New Canada. They are all for sale, but nobody wants to buy them. You'll keep yours in your home, even though its scrap, because it's yours.
>
> (Mkhuma 1992, 32)

When the magazine was sold in Johannesburg, matters taken up by the column included daily problems faced by commuters routinely harassed by male bus and taxi drivers on the streets of the city. Replicating the bantering tone and tenor of conversations between women as they share taxi rides across the city, the column analyzed concerns that were unaddressed in other publications of the era: gendered privilege during social events such as birthday parties or Christmas celebrations where the men sit around drinking instead of joining in the celebration or organization; the decision not to have children and be unduly burdened with childcare responsibilities; the impact of parents' divorce on children; the price of essential commodities. Behaviors imitating sexual objectification such as women's commodification of belly dance performers in the city were also stridently, though humorously, critiqued.

Speak's civic feminism emerges most clearly in its attention to rampant sexual violence in private and public spaces. Letters from readers, reports on the significance of take back the night marches around the world, and information about the setting up of Rape Crisis Centers in Durban and Capetown initiate discussions of sexuality other than as a reproductive or health issue in the magazine. *Speak* occasionally carried detailed features by Rape Crisis. An article printed in 1986 described rape as a form of power, suggested what can be done following an attack, described the judgment of the death penalty for a man who assaulted and murdered a woman, and directed survivors to the Rape Crisis Center in Overport (Rape Crisis 1986). Zaidi Harneker's piece "She Still Wanted to Scream" relates the rape of a 15 year old girl whose parents reported the incident to the police but did not know how to help her through the trauma she had experienced (1986). The January 1987 number covers Port Alfred Women's Organization's "stayaway" from work to protest the rape of a 59 year old woman by a man who had "raped other women in the past," he was first arrested, and later released by the police. The Port Alfred women invited white sisters to see the problems in the townships and talk to those who lived there. The protest and a seven-day stayaway from work resulted in the police charging the rapist with "assault" (though not rape), who then moved away from the township to live elsewhere. The article's conclusion reiterates the group's commitment to supporting survivors of sexual violence: "Our men and women do not blame a woman for a rape. We do not say the rape was a woman's fault" (*Speak* 1987a, 5). Extending the understanding of rape, another feature reported from Ciskei where a woman filed a case against her former husband who tried to force her to have sex with her cousin, and being unsuccessful in this attempt, raped her in her house. The judge who heard the case ruled in the woman's favor by asserting that non-consensual sex within a marriage violates a woman's right to her body. The feature included helpful information on reporting and contact addresses of organizations assisting survivors (Keeton 1992). In this way the magazine's readers were introduced to complex understandings of coercive sexuality as a public-private concern resonating with similar strategies adopted by *Manushi* in India and *Sistren* magazine in Jamaica (Chapters 3 and 5).

Speak's connections between urban life, employment, infrastructure, sexual objectification, and violence are further extended in *Agenda*. Among the many articles which focus on women's lives in Durban, one on teenage pregnancy mentions that respondents "pointed to poverty, overcrowding, lack of recreational and educational facilities and to the fact that many mothers have to work in urban areas when asked why teenage pregnancies occur so frequently." In describing "lack of social provisions for teenagers in most African urban areas," the authors do not minimize other factors including value placed on childbearing, motherhood, and investment in patriarchal institutional structures (Preston-Whyte & Zondi 1989, 60, 61). Similarly, a feature on working class township families in the Durban area examines the dual effects of capitalism and apartheid on women in these families. Noting powerlessness in the face of sexual violence, the author takes location as a factor in her analysis though she does not consider the mutual impact of urban social conditions and gender roles as directly as other reports and articles (Campbell 1990, 1–22).

Agenda steadily advanced its critique of urban planners' lack of attention to structural connections between gender and power. In the early 1990s the collective participated in several workshops on women's development across South Africa which brought together NGOs, international organizations, political organizations, religious bodies, and trade unions to highlight how most planners "deal only with women's practical needs" ignoring power differentials between men and women, including sexual violence within and outside the family (Mayosi 1992, 81–82). Gine Zwart offers one of the clearest accounts of shifting understandings of development when she describes how a lack of analysis of gender led to some Zimbabwean NGOs adopting welfarist notions of growth focused on income generation projects that do not address women's position in society. Only recently have these approaches been challenged by "new" NGOs, some of which accomplish their goals through "the collection and dissemination of information" (1992, 21). Zwart's analysis is an example of the ways in which *Agenda*'s informational aims were a strident feminist critique of NGO-directed development.

A nuanced analysis of gender and power was crucial during this period as intra-African violence led to some areas becoming warzones. *Speak* had already initiated this crucial conversation, *Agenda* carried it forward. Wendy Annecke's report for *Agenda* about a workshop on the situation of women during the "war" between the Inkatha, ANC, and the South African Defense Force in Durban outlines how they are co-opted as providers, nurturers, and even as peacemakers in a violent situation not of their making. Women negotiate perilous infrastructures to provide food and shelter for the living and burial for the dead, "from the harrowing task of searching for the bodies of their kinsmen amongst the heap of bodies in the mortuaries…to the vigil and the graveside" (Annecke 1990, 14). Sexual assaults led to unwanted pregnancies and cases of men and women "dumping babies at hospitals and welfare organizations" (Annecke 1990, 19). On the same lines of intersectional locational feminist analysis, Beall and Todes' overview of the lived realities of Cato Manor (though published outside *Agenda*) in Durban is especially instructive. The authors note that the turmoil experienced by those living in the area in the 1990s was due to political conflict and social fragmentation leading to an increase in gendered crimes. The Cato Manor Development Authority conceptualized an integrated approach to development by involving women leaders in its Crime Prevention Strategy. With increased ownership of houses, emergence of an agricultural cooperative, and provision of services like schools and libraries, a model of gender analysis in equitable urban development slowly emerged (Beall & Todes 2004, 301–310).

Careful of the stereotyping of black masculinities during times of black on black, white on black, or black on white violence, Gqola's important work on the nightmare of rape in South Africa insists that we parse out the contexts in which specific racialized masculinities are asserted while holding perpetrators of gendered and sexualized atrocities accountable for their actions (2015, 79). Beryl Simelane' report for *Agenda* on Clermont Women's Organization describes the integration of gender and development perspectives in these times. Wresting control of the schools from KwaZulu authorities and restoring them to the Department of Education, generating employment opportunities through projects like candle-making and sewing, eradicating industrial dumping from the area, and ensuring road safety through negotiated repairs and construction of sidewalks were some of the ways this women's group regained control over the unsafe neighborhood (Simelane 1994, 95–97). Felicitous connections between urban and gender analysis in civic concerns such as health and transportation led to the success of the Claremont Women's Organization, a group whose trajectory illustrates the integration of civic feminism and feminist development. *Agenda* also critiqued development models narrowly focused on economic considerations by initiating a discussion about compulsory reproductive heterosexuality, albeit through circuitous means.

South African feminists describe that in the 1980s they were concerned with "trying to push feminism into the discourse for broader reasons of politics and policy and not just sexual politics," and that in response to the "ethnic and racial categorization and the apartheid pathologisation of black cultures... [they] steered clear of sexuality, polygamy, autonomy and choice" (Beall et al. 2011, 99–100). Phumelele Ntombela Nzimande, employed full time by *Speak* and an active participant in the Natal Organization of Women (NOW), mentions in a conversation that the magazine's coverage of "maternal health, rape, and battery and women's experiences on the shop floor" were well received by its blue collar readership but invited concerns from NOW members that these were "nonessential matters" that "might hinder the process of politicizing largely conservative women" (qtd. in Hassim 2006, 58). Perhaps it was the risk of alienating its readers which led to less attention to sexuality outside the heteronormative matrix in early numbers of *Speak*. From 1984 to 1991, *Speak*'s educational and civic emphasis led to a series of sex education articles for the "Health" section discussed later in this chapter, avoiding a direct focus on sexuality and choice.

Speak had introduced an analysis of sexual violence by including testimonies of rape and battery victims over the years. Given the readership of the magazine, it would not be surprising if the editors had decided to stop short of addressing sexual choice as this risked potential loss of readers. The articles published in the late 1990s are about women's decisions to remain outside the marital framework either within heterosexual or homosexual relationships. The "Healthbriefs" in the 1990s frequently contained information about female condoms which would give women more control over their sexuality and protect them from sexually transmitted diseases. *Speak* 56 raised the controversial matter of non-marital, nonreproductive sexuality by including an article about the relationship between Thenjiwe Mthintso and ANC activist Skenjana Roji (Gasa 1993, 26–27). From the early 1990s there was sporadic coverage of the lives of single women and lesbian women. Ntombi writes on the lives and fears of black lesbians in *Speak* 52 to dispel common misconceptions about lesbianism and masculinity (1993, 32). In 1994 the magazine published a feature on lesbian and gay marches in the country focusing on the daily struggles experienced by lesbians in mainstream society and gay solidarity networks (Telela 1994, 26–27). Printed in the Health section, this article is perhaps accidentally not included in the magazine's features page where all other contributions in the number are listed.

Agenda's discussion of the matter was more direct than *Speak*'s and can be traced to its 1991 number on "Sexual Politics." When the letters page began to be included in the journal, one of the first letters from Wendy Annecke, editor of the special number, addresses tolerance and acceptance of homosexuality in and around Durban. Annecke describes how she met a group of women living in a township just outside Durban who gossiped about male and female homosexuality. They did not merely describe homosexuality among married people, they offered critiques of gender and development when they listed specific reasons for preferring sexual relationships with other women rather than overly demanding partners of the opposite sex. In both cases women are aware that even as they are susceptible to homophobic violence, female relationships have a significant advantage over heterosexual liaisons in that there is no likelihood of the partners getting pregnant. Observing how they have accepted their homosexuality, the author calls for an analysis of shifting perspectives on sexual tolerance (Annecke 1991, 3). These discussions were one way of bridging civic feminism and feminist critiques of development. Another strategy was a broader focus on health and reproduction as the primary means of educating women about their sexualities.

Sexuality and (non)reproductivity

The impact of gender and power on reproductive sexuality is evident in South African debates over birth control and abortion. Conversations on abortion became lightning rods for control of women's choice during the 1970s. The formation of the South African Abortion Law Reform League in Cape Town in 1971 and the Abortion Law Reform Group in Durban in 1972 by white feminists indicated a strong push towards legalizing abortion. Passage of the 1975 Abortion and Sterilization Act sparked varying responses among nascent women's groups in the country as it connected the procedure to strict medical and psychological criteria (Klausen 2015). As with the apartheid regime's other measures to control black populations, the move evoked mixed reactions, not only because of the cultural valuation of motherhood, but also because of intense suspicion of the state's attempts to restrict black women's reproduction with the goal of creating a white Afrikaner nation. *Speak* and *Agenda*'s efforts at sex education, within and outside heterosexual reproductivity, can be read as responses to highly restrictive anti-abortion legislation passed in the 1970s and the pro-choice advocacy of progressive groups. These efforts eventually culminated in the hard-won passage of the 1996 Choice on Termination of Pregnancy (CTOP) Act allowing abortion on demand till the twelfth week of pregnancy and under other specific medical circumstances beyond the twelfth week.

Part of *Speak*'s mandate was to prioritize sexual health even as other civic matters continued to be widely covered. Its early articles on the topic included images, charts, and calendar dates to simplify predicting periods and ovulation, and a list of bodily changes accompanying menstruation. These were appropriate for the age-differentiated, multigenerational audience of women and girls that the magazine solicited as potential readers. Keeping in mind its varied audience, *Speak* presented information on pregnancy with hand-drawn illustrations in its early print runs when medical termination of pregnancy was still illegal. The first number carried a section on "methods of contraception" and the "pros and cons of each" so that "we will be in a better position to choose and decide what is best for ourselves" (*Speak* 1982, 5). The second number deals with the monthly "cycle" in an attempt to clarify menstrual health and indicate the days on which women are most likely to be ovulating and most fertile for pregnancy (*Speak* 1984a, 8–10).[8] While these may seem like obvious facts today, given the lack of information in schools and public health care clinics at the time, this was empowering knowledge for women.

Discussion on reproductive choices ensured that readers could take charge of their bodies by being vigilant about their health and available contraceptive options. The fifth number of the magazine carries a detailed article on intra-uterine contraceptive devices (IUCD) popularly called the "loop," and includes a description of the medical process by which it is inserted in the body. The editors were meticulous in pointing out the risks, benefits, and bodily symptoms as it is an invasive device requiring a minor medical procedure. Besides dispelling some of the popular myths associated with the process such as its impact on women's fertility, there is also a section on women's experience of using IUCDs which provides a first-person user-based versus a factual clinical health perspective (*Speak* 1984b, 15–17). Having cleared the ground for reproductive choices and sexual autonomy, the next number described the diaphragm as a birth control option that is less invasive than an IUCD and allows women some control during sex. As with the previous format of medical and first-person information, the pros and cons of the method are listed. A graphic strip with three panels addressed readership at multiple levels of literacy: men conversing with each other about their responsibility for birth control; a man and a woman in bed talking about women's preferred method of birth control; and a group of women chatting about diaphragms, condoms, and IUCDs while working (*Speak* 1984c, 21–23). Potential readers included girls at risk of teenage pregnancy and sexual abuse in Durban communities during the 1980s and older women unaware of contraceptive methods.

    Speak later introduced the topic of permanent birth control including vasectomy for men and hysterectomy for women. These images are more explicit though the description of the medical processes is thorough and uncomplicated. In addition, there are inset dialogue boxes with graphics in which women voiced their reasons for choosing various birth control methods in marital situations where they did not want additional the complications or expense of more children (*Speak* 1984d, 19–23). A four-page summative article brings together all the information by helpfully listing several contraceptive options (*Speak* 1985, 12–16). *Speak* 10 contains a report about a "Deadly Contraceptive," called Dalkon Shield, which posed risks to women who had opted for this IUCD (*Speak* 1986a, 17). In the same number, "Getting to know our bodies" informs readers of female health and reproduction by explaining functions of body parts during sexual intercourse with the aid of images (*Speak* 1986b, 25–27). From 1987 to 1988 the magazine included a series of photographic articles on pregnancy and health with the broad aim of demystifying the birth process.[9] This dual focus on birth control and healthy pregnancies was aimed at new readers since it reiterated information previously provided in *Speak*, a strategy that continued till the magazine shut down in 1994/1995. At the same time, the right to legal and safe abortions was voiced in the "Talk Back" section of *Speak* where several anonymous letters called for a ban on illegal abortions causing injuries or death. It is the subject of a detailed feature titled "A Woman's Choice" which narrates the experiences of a woman who had an illegal abortion in a back-street clinic in Soweto juxtaposed with the opinions of the Abortion Reform Group and a pro-life spokesperson (Telela 1993a, 18–19). These multigenerational, multi-literacy level, and multi-readerly efforts aimed to make readers aware of reproductive choices as a crucial aspect of sexual autonomy.

Agenda's first number appeared in 1987 coinciding with *Speak*'s civic feminist attention to women's sexual health. Discerning cultural factors influencing women's decisions, *Speak* had recruited men as potential allies to create a wider pro-choice platform. It included interviews with Indres Naidoo, former Robben Island prisoner and activist, on the status of women in the German Democratic Republic and availability of choices for contraception and safe abortions in that country (*Speak* 1992a, 14–16). Another article by Chris Diamond from the Abortion Reform Action Group confirmed that the crucial issue had secured male allyship (*Speak* 1992b, 24–25). Like *Speak, Agenda* sought to inform women about the range, variety, and multiple perspectives on reproductive choices but did so in the context of feminist debates about the ethical, medical, and social effects of these choices. *Agenda*'s multi-pronged efforts to carry forward the conversation about women's participation in the reproductive economy involved research on cultural factors influencing reproductive decisions, investigative medical accounts, and voices supporting choice. Research on teenage black mothers in Durban lists personal and cultural reasons which may influence their decision to give birth despite the availability of contraception. Among these are African families' valuation of motherhood, pressure from the partner, girls' fear of losing the ability to give birth, and, in some cases, the teenager's ability to continue her education after childbirth with her family's support. Raising important points about the lives of African teenagers in Durban, the study accounts for factors influencing their sexual expression (Preston-Whyte & Zondi 1989, 47–68). To assist readers in making informed decisions, *Agenda* reviewed Norplant, a controversial contraceptive, charting its use in the US and other developing nations and associated medical risks. The article concludes by sounding a warning about "coercive" uses of Norplant and vigilance against its potential use to "reduce growth" among black populations by "population planners" in South Africa (Bonnin 1991b, 20–22).

Agenda analyzed women's sexuality in a national and international framework, a worlding of South African women's concerns that enabled the collective and magazine contributors to connect with transnational feminist conversations. A two-page briefing in the second number describes the international day of action for women's health zeroing in on the availability of safe abortions (*Agenda* 1988, 81–83). Contributor Debby Bonnin frequently reported on international events on women's health. Documenting the first ever regional meeting of women and health in Africa (in 1989), organized by the Uganda Chapter of the Women's Global Network on Reproductive Rights, the writer sums up its main themes as "reproductive rights, community health, environmental health hazards, population policy, and AIDS" (Bonnin 1990, 31). She also comments on the surprising lack of discussion on abortion at this conference reiterating that delegates from various African countries can "impress upon their Governments the need to treat these issues seriously" (Bonnin 1990, 36). Similarly, the next report on the sixth international women and health meeting in the Philippines singles out "population policy" (1990). Her summative comment engages with the role of the state on the neglected area of women's health:

> The state is the arena of power, if we wish to move forward on women's health issues we need to engage with the source of power, but at the same time we do need to ensure that we don't become co-opted.
>
> (Bonnin 1991a, 31)

Later journal issues further reinforced this stand from legislative, sexual health, and public policy perspectives. In their article for a regular column, "Healthwatch," the authors place national population policies in an international framework of UN conferences on Environment and Development, Population and Development, and the World Plan for Population Action. They advocate a "reproductive health policy" which includes serious consideration of "violence against women along with more traditional issues such as maternal health, contraception and abortion, sexually transmitted diseases (STDs) and reproductive tract infections (RTSs)" (Pillay & Klugman 1994, 109).

The journal's special focus on Reproductive Rights positions choice as fundamental to sexuality and reproduction by invoking human rights guaranteed by the interim Constitution of South Africa (*Agenda* 1995). It includes articles on reproductive risks for women in the workplace and the need for legislation and control mechanisms to minimize such risks. One crucial legislative measure, the Termination of Pregnancy Bill, which amended the Interim Constitution, was in keeping with the equality clause outlawing discrimination on the grounds of pregnancy (O'Sullivan 1996). These demands on the state insert an important feminist critique of development, especially its lack of attention to women's sexual health. In making this critique *Agenda* continued the work *Speak* initiated by extending its mandate to include a range of controversial topics such as pornography, lesbianism, sex work, and sexually transmitted diseases including AIDS.

Sexual panics in the time of AIDS

As described in Chapter 6, while the Gay Association of South Africa recognized AIDS as a crisis, it did not address it in a racially inclusive manner. In contrast, black AIDS activists, among them Simon Nkoli and Zackie Achmat, recognized the need to address AIDS as a public health concern affecting people of all races. A similar urgency marked *Speak* and *Agenda*'s AIDS coverage. This provides a corrective to a claim in Mandisa Mbali's important work on AIDS activism that the South African women's movement's response to AIDS was "circumscribed," especially by comparison with that of the lesbian and gay movement, and though "some feminist publications covered the epidemic…women's participation around it was deferred because they did not identify with the issue" (2013, 6). *Speak* and *Agenda* are among the publications Mbali lists as having played a role in challenging AIDS-related sexism and popular representations of the pandemic (2013, 78, 90). This part of the chapter demonstrates how feminist collectives and their magazines dispelled a common perception of AIDS as a white gay male disease by educating women on its modes of transmission and means of prevention.

A crucial aspect of *Speak* and *Agenda*'s civic feminism was educating readers about increased incidence of heterosexual modes of AIDS transmission and risk of mother-to-child infection. *Speak* collaborated with governmental and non-governmental bodies including the National Progressive Primary Health Care Network and the Planned Parenthood Association of South Africa for some of its informational content. The collaborations were not uncritically acclamatory as the magazine often commented on the insufficiency of educational and prevention programs in the country. Even before its collaboration with the state and NGOs, *Speak* had initiated a public conversation on the topic with the column "AIDS: Let's Talk about It" (*Speak* 1988c, 10–11). Information about AIDS followed the pattern of sexual health education in the articles on pregnancy and reproduction. One article on the topic takes the form of "Who," "What," "How" questions to dispel popular misconceptions about transmission and spread (*Speak* 1990, 24–27). As the pandemic spread in the 1990s, the magazine stepped up its informational campaign.

In one of the last numbers published before the magazine ceased puclication, *Speak* did a feature article on a Masikhanyise, a women's group in Khayelitsha, supported by Planned Parenthood South Africa, whose members had been meeting for two years to discuss women's health, including teenage pregnancies, sexually transmitted diseases, child sexual abuse, and the spread of AIDS. Combining traditional civic matters such as income-generation with sexual health concerns, one of the members of the group articulated the explicitly feminist goal to "empower South African women" (*Speak* 1994b, 25). The Khayelitsha group had developed a community outreach program to make other women aware of sexual health. Even as the efforts of these community members were recognized, in other pieces *Speak* critiqued delayed governmental response to the crisis that had led to Transkei and other areas becoming epicenters of disease and death when migrant workers, too sick to work in the cities, came back to their homelands (*Speak* 1994c, 1994d).

Providing first-person readable accounts of AIDS, *Speak* excerpted a narrative from Noerine Kaleeba's book, *We All Miss You: AIDS in the Family*, about the disease's impact on the entire family (*Speak* 1992f, 20–22). Emphasizing incidence of male to female heterosexual transmission by including reports about women infected by their husbands, the magazine squarely placed the responsibility of transmission on men (Pandy 1993a, 18–19). Rather than blame and shame, it emphasized women's need to protect themselves before and after transmission. Two accounts of women living with AIDS, one a "respectably" married housewife and the other a prostitute, revealed that after being infected by their partners and/or clients, the women believed it best to keep their HIV positive status secret. Personalizing as well as publicizing the matter, *Speak* included information about the National AIDS program offices and graphics about safe sex using condoms in a non-judgmental reporting format (*Speak* 1994a, 24–25).

As in its demystification of the race-biology-sexuality-disease connection, *Speak* tried to dispel anxieties associated with AIDS testing. An article on AIDS was placed on the same page as an inset on how to report rape, helping readers make the connection between the increased incidence of sexual violence during this period and the possibility that raped women were infected with HIV (*Speak* 1992d, 21; 1992e, 29). The magazine also carried a feature on a person misdiagnosed with AIDS who later discovered that he was not HIV positive, perhaps as a way of encouraging its readers to secure reliable testing and proper medication should they test positive (*Speak* 1993b). From 1993 onwards the magazine conveyed information about transmission, symptoms, and early signs of AIDS in the form of a full-page infographic.

As in the case of women's sexual and reproductive processes, the accounts reached readers of various generations. *Speak* solicited opinions from students during the Congress of South African Students' (COSAS) launch of their campaign against AIDS; it reported on measures taken by the National Union of Mineworkers to ensure there was no discrimination against workers suffering from AIDS (Telela 1993b; *Speak* 1993c, 31). Various aspects of South African popular culture and traditional practices were pressed into service. Youth cultural icons – the famous Ugandan singer Philly Lutaya, who educated people about AIDS till he passed away in 1990, and the radio show host Shado Twala, an AIDS awareness advocate – were often profiled in articles (*Speak* 1991, 26–27; 1992c 5–7). For older and likely less literate audiences reliant on community structures rather than popular cultural traditions, the magazine included a photographic feature on *sangomas* (traditional healers, often identifying with composite masculine-feminine gender identities) in AIDS educational efforts. Ellen Elmendrop's photographs of the workshop depict *sangomas* being trained in the proper use of condoms so that they can convey the message of AIDS prevention to their clients (*Speak* 1993, 16–17).

Agenda too made it a matter of urgency to carry detailed articles on the topic, adopting civic feminist educational strategies on female condoms and comic strips about women's apprehensiveness regarding condoms. Drawing upon her experience as Manager at the AIDS Training and Information Center at the City Health Department in Durban, Vicci Tallis outlines what AIDS means for women by listing modes of transmission and infection, its course and symptoms, and safe sex options (1991, 4–9). From 1992 to 1995, *Agenda*'s Healthwatch column included articles about HIV risk factors and symptoms, connecting the incidence of the disease to power imbalances in sexual relations.

Part of the Agenda collective's efforts were directed towards scholarly research on AIDS to demand specific state-level interventions to prevent the already alarming spread of the disease in KwaZulu-Natal. Following the same format as its studies on teenage black mothers in Durban, another set of researchers conducted a study on two groups of unmarried heterosexual students to determine the incidence of AIDS in black and white populations. The study focused on the negotiation of safe sex practices among heterosexual populations including naturalization of sex as an uncontrollable drive, stigma attached to the use of condoms, and alternative non-penetrative forms of sexuality that diminish risk of transmission (Miles 1992, 14–27). Concluding that white women have more options for negotiating safe-sex relationships than black women, the researchers focused on hetero and homosexuality together to envisage new forms of non-rigid masculinities (Miles 1992, 25–26). Anna Strebel's interviews with black women living with AIDS exposed popular misconceptions including a fatalistic acceptance of post-transmission complications. Strebel found that many women, believing the virus is air or rain borne or even a matter of personal hygiene, are resigned to the possibility of being infected by male partners. For these women AIDS was not a "bio-medical" problem but rather "associated with the on-going struggles generated by their socio-economic and gender positions" and called for local, context-specific prevention programs (Strebel 1992, 60). These studies fulfilled important mandates for health awareness and disease prevention central to and going beyond state-supported post-colonial development imperatives at a time when AIDS activism in the country was in its early stages.

For both publications, worlding AIDS (like their efforts to world women's reproductive sexualities) involved placing it in a pan-African framework by including information on how countries such as Kenya, Zimbabwe, Namibia, and Botswana were handling or mishandling the crisis. This was one way in which they sought to make the South African government aware of urgently needed measures (Pandy 1993b, 24–25; *Speak* 1993d, 30; 1993e, 30). Facts and figures from UN bodies such as the World Health Organization were compiled to indicate that unless addressed as a priority, the disease was likely to claim millions of lives across the world; additionally, the UN Development Program's report on daily deaths of five hundred women in their teens and early twenties supported the call for scaling up the AIDS response (*Speak* 1993f, 31; 1994e, 34). In one piece, research from a Namibian magazine is cited to describe the different kinds of gynecological problems faced by infected women and to suggest measures that prevent infection (*Agenda* 1992). Much like the Health Briefs section in *Speak, Agenda*'s Healthwatch brought a pan-African and international perspective on the impact of HIV on women.

An analysis of sexuality within and outside reproductivity and efforts to educate women about STDs, especially AIDS, are common to both publications. The Agenda and Speak collectives sought to address serious gaps in civic and development delivery for women. Initially the publications did not directly address sexual diversity, though they recognized that constituencies such as lesbian women did not have a significant voice within the emerging women's movement (or established gay men's activism). *Speak*'s careful approach on these matters coincided and often overlapped with *Agenda*'s efforts. In the last year and a half of its publication, *Speak* carried informative articles about gay and lesbian activism. One of these was a detailed feature on GLOW president, Cecil Nyathi, who called for acceptance of gay men and lesbian women as "people of different races, cultures, religions, political ideas" while acknowledging that there are those who may not be as accepting (*Speak* 1992–1993, 10–11). Another was Rosalee Telela's piece on lesbian and gay marches which focused on black lesbians' experiences participating in these events. The article is about the common front gay men and lesbian women must present to combat sexism and homophobia while highlighting the differences between their tactics and thinking. Meghan Pillay, a member of GLOW, states how the

Lesbian Forum emerged out of GLOW, though some like her remain members of both organizations (Telela 1994, 26–27). While few and far between, these pieces reflect the magazine's commitment to looking at women's and LGBTQ+ concerns through and beyond the civics framework. *Agenda*'s coverage retained a similarly nuanced focus. Its 1991 number titled "Sexual Politics" included a detailed profile report of the Capetown-based Organization of Lesbian and Gay Activists (OLGA) and Louise Mina's piece titled "Questioning Heterosexism." In later years there were frequent articles on the gay and lesbian community including black lesbian identities. In bringing alternative sexualities to the forefront, albeit tentatively, these publications were shaping an environment in which non-discrimination would become one of the hallmarks of post-apartheid South Africa. Concluding our detailed conversation at her home in Mayfair, Johannesburg, Shamim Meer expressed the hope that "young lesbian media could use media like *Speak* today" (2012) to underline how emerging counterpublics can learn from those preceding them.

FIGURE 7.2 Photographs from an article on Gay Pride in *Speak* magazine. Courtesy of Shamim Meer and the magazine archive of Digital Imaging South Africa.

This chapter has examined similarities and differences in *Speak* and *Agenda*'s efforts to analyze gender and sexuality as South African social contradictions as central as race and class. Though *Speak*'s grassroots constituency and its early attention to women's safety, employment, education, and housing epitomized a traditional conception of civics, the collective and the magazine expanded this understanding to include women's health and sexuality. The Agenda collective critiqued overly economic notions of development, analyzing gender and power to become an effective successor of Speak's civic feminism. The approachable and scholarly, civic and developmental, endorsement and critique, proto- and radical feminism, race and class, health and choice are all central to continued and consistent emphases on gender, sexuality, and human rights in South Africa, and indeed in the world we inhabit. Disseminated by mainstream and alternative media, these ideas contributed to South Africa's world historic constitutional mandate promising a nation which did not discriminate based on race, sex, gender, or sexual orientation. Amid the larger successes of the anti-apartheid movement in the 1990s, and the constitutional-legislative successes for women and sexual minorities which announced a new South Africa, the contents of *Speak* and *Agenda* are reminders of how feminist locational counterpublics helped women regain sexual agency in the communities they inhabited in those troubled and violent times.

Notes

1 In 1996 *Agenda* brought out a special number on Women and the Media focused on concerns sidelined in the mainstream media and argued that women should be skilled at using print, audio, and video forms to represent themselves in post-apartheid South Africa.

2 These are not arbitrary dates. *Speak* ceased publication in 1994/1995. *Agenda* continues to be published and is an important venue for analysis of national policies impacting women. Gender and sexual equality advocacy by these and other collectives led to the formulation of the Equality Clause of the Bill of Rights in the South African Constitution in 1996. Section 9(3) of the Equality Clause reads: "The state may not unfairly discriminate directly or indirectly against anyone on one or more grounds, including race, gender, sex, pregnancy, marital status, ethnic or social origin, colour, sexual orientation, age, disability, religion, conscience belief, culture, language and birth."

3 Les Switzer and Mohamed Adhikari's edited collection *South Africa's Resistance Press* (2000) provides a detailed account of the history of anti-apartheid publications within South Africa. The collection largely focuses on trade union, student, and ANC-UDF publications, though select essays analyze how these publications covered women's issues.

4 These efforts included the Rural Women's Movement (1982) which enabled women from all over South Africa to have a voice in the drafting of the proposed constitution and to put their concerns on the national platform through the Natal Organization of Women (NOW) in 1983, the Congress of South African Trade Unions (COSATU) in 1985, and the South African Domestic Workers Union (SADWU) in 1987.

5 Women's testimonies were an important aspect of *Agenda*. The very first number included Dombi Khumalo's account of forcible eviction from her home, the violence directed at her family by the landowners who employed them, and their subsequent proletarianization (*Agenda* 1987a, 49–54).

6 Ineke van Kessel succinctly describes the civics movements in the context of the UDF: "Township based organizations of residents known as civic associations or civics made up an important part of the UDF's membership. During the 1980s, civics vacillated between different roles: watch dog bodies representing the interests of all township residents; political bodies aspiring to construct Charterist hegemony at the local level; brokers taking up individual problems and grievances of residents; organs of people's power; front organizations for the ANC, preparing to grab local power in the event of a seizure of power by the liberation movement. Sometimes a civic was formed as a means to an end, namely to provide residents with a vehicle to address township issues such as rents, transportation, crime, electricity…activists launched a civic in the belief that campaigns around rents or washing lines would provide a low threshold starting point from which residents could gradually be drawn into wider political struggles against the apartheid state." (2000, 150).

7 Seekings mentions sources of international funding which led to prioritization of a development oriented strategy. The funding was channeled through the Kagiso Trust which made European Commission funds available to anti-apartheid groups in South Africa (2000, 76–78).

8 There is some confusion in the digital curation of *Speak* since the second number is listed as published in 1982. The first page of the second available number indicates it was published in 1984. The digital archives do not contain numbers 3 and 4. After number 2, the next online number is *Speak* 5 which appeared in March 1984.

9 See for instance the articles: "I Am Pregnant: What Can go Wrong?" in *Speak* 20 (July–August 1988a): 20–22; "I Am Pregnant: How Can I Prepare for Labour" in *Speak* 21 (September–November 1988b): 20–23; "I Am Pregnant: What will Labor be Like?" in *Speak* 22 (December–January 1988–1989): 24–27.

CODA

Digital counterpublics and intergenerational listening

I learned and continue to learn to be feminist from the print counterpublics studied in this book. Through their struggles to combat sexual violence, secure reproductive choices, sexual health, and sexual freedom, feminist and queer media influenced and shaped the contemporary by expanding understandings of interactions between literature, society, politics, and history. As portals to activist worlds, these magazines, journals, newspapers, and newsletters offer a glimpse of future-oriented feminist-queer solidarities.

The transformation of print into the digital means that many more can step through these portals and participate, sometimes instantaneously, in shaping the direction of transformation. Forms of virtual assembly now replicate what print attempted through readers' contributions, feedback, opinions, reports, letters, sketches, and advertisements. We have seen these forms of physical and digital assembly and their transformative impact through the #MeToo, #BlackLivesMatter, and #RhodesMustFall activism in recent times. As these movements have taught us, transnational counterpublics negotiate multiple geographies, identities, and goals. Though such multiplicity evades easy definition, I want to locate feminist and queer as terms describing gender and sexuality but also moving beyond them. My working definition comes from an account of "queer indigeneity" in connection with feminized *hijra* subjectivities and quasi-kinship structures that I expressed in connection with postcolonial drama (Batra 2011). These formations can include cross-class, cross-caste, cross-race, and cross-geographic solidarities. We glimpse such solidarities when Caribbean gay identities are expressed in relation to Rastafarian beliefs and reggae aesthetics. We also see possible cohesions in recent acknowledgements that South Asian feminist and queer lives are multiply intersected by religious, caste, and class locations in 'third gender' identities of *hijras, aravanis, bhands,* and *kwajasarais*. Black, feminized, androgynous identities of *moffies, stabanes,* and *sangomas* in South Africa allow sightings of emerging solidarities. Feminist-Queer coalitions can be based

DOI: 10.4324/9781003170303-11

on myriad identity categories across classes; sexual safety and health; sex as pleasure and/or work; political and social identifications; emplacements in homes, clubs, bars, streets, trains, parks, public restrooms, community centers, drop-in centers, pride parades, conference venues; and creative expressions in various media.

The afterlives of print documenting women's, gay, lesbian, bisexual, and transgender lives online can be described as DigiFemQueer. Many organizations mentioned in this book have an active digital presence that sustains these identities and communities within a global context. J-FLAG's activity on social media compensates for the temporary unavailability of physical meeting spaces. It has maintained a closed Facebook group since 2014, and an open Facebook page "Friends of J-FLAG" since 2018 where there are vibrant discussions such as on the cancellation of the Montego Bay Pride celebrations in 2019 and a series of "asylum talks" on those seeking refugee status outside Jamaica in 2020. Feminist support by members of Sistren and the digital publications *OutCaribe* and *PrideJa* amplify these counterpublics. Humsafar Trust and Manushi continue their advocacy in India through their web presence and outreach activities, though their print media have ceased publication. Humsafar initiated the formation of the Integrated Network for Sexual Minorities (INFOSEM) to bring together 32 organizations working on lesbian, gay, bisexual, and transgender issues across the country for advocacy, capacity building, information dissemination, research, and resource mobilization. It also started a citizen journalism project to train writers on LGBTQ+ issues. Subsequently, there has been an explosion of online queer literary forums in India including *Scripts, Gaysi, Gaylaxy, Varta, Queer Chennai Chronicles*, and *In Plainspeak*. Following the demise of GASA and GLOW, Johannesburg- and Pretoria-based organizations Forum for Empowerment of Women (FEW) and OUT have provided advocacy, support, and services including OUT's recent 16 Days of Activism campaign on International Human Rights Day in December 2020. Similarly, the South African feminist collective Agenda's media, like that of its predecessor Speak, includes a journal, radio programming, and an active online presence. Even as feminist and queer communities form digital counterpublics, the forms in which they articulate human rights claims (a key concern in feminist and queer print media) within and beyond the nation await further analysis.

Large archival projects such as Digital Innovation South Africa (DISA) and the Digital Library of the Caribbean (DLoC) are examples of DigiFemQueer interventions. This book would not have been possible without the print sources archived in these projects. Even the limited corpus of such work examined in *Worlding Postcolonial Sexualities* allows mapping of key feminist and LGBTQ+ organizers, collectives, collaborations with state agencies and NGOs to record global South worldly interactions in furthering human rights claims. The critical nodes of such mapping include founding members and contributors; their personal, organizational, and institutional connections; catalogues of local descriptive terms in conversation with the expanding acronym LGBTQ+ (*dost, saheli, samlaingik, khush, moffie, stabane, sistren, bredren, battyman, buller, man royal, sodomite*), and records of feminist-queer interactions. The larger goal of such a mapping would be a sociography of global South second wave feminist-queer counterpublics. There is much work to be done.

In her pioneering work on African sexualities Sylvia Tamale mentions that research on sexuality is "likely to engage you in difficult and unpredictable ways" (2011, 46). Two such ways engaged me in the final stages of this work. One not entirely unpredictable direction has been a fortuitous involvement in digital humanities scholarship through the Orlando Project, a born-digital literary history of women's writing. As Orlando's trajectory demonstrates, the creation and analysis of content that intervenes in traditional literary or social histories is crucial to rewriting andro, hetero, and ethnocentric narratives.

The second unpredictable turn of this work came on a wintry morning in Portland this past December. Catching up on emails, I saw one from India written late the previous night. It was an anguished message from a father who described his daughter's struggles to learn about queer studies in an inhospitable academic, social, and familial context of right-wing populism and sexual conservatism. He asked if I would speak to his daughter (I call her A.) over the phone. When A. called late at night several days later, we talked about the books she had read as part of her English curriculum at the University of Delhi. I had studied and taught many of the same works, among them Ismat Chughtai's "Lihaaf," Judith Butler's *Gender Trouble*, Audre Lorde's *Zami*, Virginia Woolf's *Orlando*, and Jeanette Winterson's *Sexing the Cherry* in my years at the same university. In our hour-long conversation I learned about A.'s extended family threatening her with physical harm if she revealed her sexuality, her Delhi professor's suggestion that she pursue research on queer sexualities abroad, the trajectories of queer activism and literature in India, and shrinking safe spaces for those discovering their identities during COVID times. I shared with A. conditions of queer emergence 20 years ago when I was a student in Delhi and a similar inhospitable climate prevailed. I told her about a small bookstore in Connaught Place where I had purchased my copy of *Bombay Dost* and *Humjinsi* in the late 1990s and suggested she read the many Indian queer zines now available online. For that one hour we were two women learning about the making and remaking of history across continents, sexualities, and generations.

Reading and reconstructing history from scarcely remembered sources counters generational gaps in knowledge such that

> in an age where we recognize the right to be forgotten, we must also weigh the danger to both feminism and queer politics of hiding our history, forcing each new generation to start anew, with only the haziest stereotypes about previous generations to draw on for strength, or worse, to look on with derision, against the threat of confrontation, doxing, or violence to named [or future] activists.
>
> (Schwartz & Crompton 2018, 141)

Serendipitously, the completion of this book coincided with a critical intergenerational listening. A. embodies the next generation of feminist-queer thinkers, scholars, and activists. My decade of engagement with activist literature has come full circle as A. reaches out into the feminist-queer futures first imagined in late twentieth century print to create worlds of being, beholding, belonging, and doing.

BIBLIOGRAPHY

Primary magazines, newsletters, newspapers, and journals

Agenda, JSTOR, www.jstor.org/journal/agenpolianalyref.

Bombay Dost, Humsafar Trust Archives, Vakola, Mumbai.

Exit, Gay and Lesbian Memory in Action Archives, Johannesburg.

Jamaica Gaily News, Digital Library of the Caribbean, Caribbean International Resource Network, www.dloc.com/icirngfm.

Link/Skakel, Gay and Lesbian Memory in Action Archives, Johannesburg.

Manushi, Manushi, http://manushi-india.org/back-issues.htm.

Sistren, The Making of Caribbean Feminisms, University of the West Indies, St. Augustine, https://uwispace.sta.uwi.edu/dspace/handle/2139/45158.

Speak, Digital Innovation South Africa, http://disa.ukzn.ac.za/sp.

Secondary sources

Adler, Glenn and Jonny Steinberg. 2000. "Introduction." In *Comrades to Citizens: The South African Civics Movement and the Transition to Democracy*, edited by Glenn Adler and Jonny Steinberg, 1–25. New York: Palgrave Macmillan. http://ebookcentral.proquest.com/lib/ttu/detail.action?docID=203596.

Agarwal, Deepa. 1995a. "Follow Up: Yielding to Pressure? Recent Developments in the Hamida Case." *Manushi* 89: 42.

Agarwal, Deepa. 1995b. "Hamida's Nightmare." *Manushi* 88: 20–27.

Agarwal, Deepa. 1998. "Judgements Galore: Yet Justice Eludes a Child Victim of Rape." *Manushi* 106 (May–June): 27–31.

Agenda. 1987a. "Lifestory: Dombi Khumalo's Story." *Agenda* 1: 49–54. www.jstor.org/stable/4547911.

Agenda. 1987b. "Speak." *Agenda* 1: 24. www.jstor.org/stable/4547903.

Agenda. 1988. "Briefing: International Day of Action for Women's Health." *Agenda* 2: 81–83. www.jstor.org/stable/4065702.

Agenda. 1992. "Health Watch: HIV Symptoms in Women." *Agenda* 13: 3–4. www.jstor.org/stable/4065603.

Agenda. 1995. "Reproductive Rights." *Agenda* 27: 1–128. www.jstor.org/stable/i386159.

Agenda. 1996. "Women's Sexuality." *Agenda* 28: 1–130. www.jstor.org/stable/i386314.

Agnes, Flavia. 1993. "The Anti-Rape Campaign: The Struggle and the Setback." In *The Struggle against Violence,* edited by Chaya Datar. 99–150. Calcutta: Stree Press.

AIDS Bhedbhav Virodhi Andolan (ABVA). 1991. *Less Than Gay: A Citizens' Report on the Status of Homosexuality in India.* New Delhi: AIDS Bhedbhav Virodhi Andolan (AIDS Anti-Discrimination Movement). https://docs.google.com/file/d/0BwDlipuQ0I6ZMXVmNWk0ajdqWEU/edit.

Akhter, Afreen. 2008. "Sistren: The Vanguard of Popular Theater in Jamaica." *Signs: Journal of Women in Culture and Society* 33. 2: 431–436. https://doi.org/10.1086/521058.

Alexander, M. Jacqui. 2005. "Erotic Autonomy as a Politics of Decolonization: Feminism, Tourism, and the State in the Bahamas." In *Pedagogies of Crossing: Meditations on Feminism, Sexual Politics, Memory, and the Sacred,* 21–65. Durham: Duke University Press.

Alexander, M. Jacqui and Chandra T. Mohanty. 2010. "Cartographies of Knowledge and Power." In *Critical Transnational Feminist Praxis,* edited by Amanda Lock Swarr and Richa Nagar. 23–45. Albany: State University of New York Press.

Amita, Naseem and Preeti. 1991. "Dear Sisters." *Bombay Dost* 1. 1: 7–8.

Anamika. 1986. "Letters: Trikon." *Anamika* 1. 2: 2.

Annecke, Wendy. 1990. "Women and the War in Natal." *Agenda: Empowering Women for Gender Equity* 7: 12–20. www.jstor.org/stable/4065495.

Annecke, Wendy. 1991. "Letters." *Agenda* 11: 2–4. www.jstor.org/stable/4547962.

Apter, Emily. 2010. "'Women's Time' in Theory." *Differences: A Journal of Feminist Cultural Critique* 21. 1: 1–18.

Aquarius. 1978. "Personally Speaking." *Jamaica Gaily News* 2. 1 (September 15): 5.

Arondekar, Anjali. 2009. *For the Record: On Sexuality and the Colonial Archive.* Durham: Duke University Press.

Arondekar, Anjali and Geeta Patel. 2016. "Area Impossible: Notes toward an Introduction." *GLQ: A Journal of Lesbian and Gay Studies* 22. 2: 151–171. www.muse.jhu.edu/article/613184.

Ashok. 1995. "Saif Sex." *Bombay Dost* 4. 1: 8.

Bacchetta, Paola. 2002. "Rescaling Transnational 'Queerdom': Lesbian and 'Lesbian' Identitary Positionalities in Delhi in the 1980s." *Antipode: A Radical Journal of Geography* 34. 5: 947–973. https://doi.org/10.1111/1467-8330.00284.

Backwash, Jimmy. 1983. "Fag Hag Theory is Challenged." *Link/Skakel* (August): 3.

Bailey, Robert. 1998. *Gay Politics, Urban Politics.* New York: Columbia University Press.

Barnes, Natasha. 2006. *Cultural Conundrums: Gender, Race, Nation, and the Making of Caribbean Cultural Politics.* Ann Arbor: University of Michigan Press.

Bassnett, Susan. 1993. "Beyond the Frontiers of Europe: Alternative Concepts of Comparative Literature." In *Comparative Literature: A Critical Introduction,* 31–47. Oxford: Blackwell.

Batra, Kanika. 2010. "'Our Own Gayful Rest: A Postcolonial Archive." *Small Axe: A Caribbean Journal of Criticism* 14. 1: 46–59. https://muse.jhu.edu/article/374388/pdf.

Batra, Kanika. 2011. *Feminist Visions and Queer Futures in Postcolonial Drama.* New York: Routledge.

Batra, Kanika. 2016a. "Creating a Locational Counterpublic: *Manushi* and the Articulation of Human Rights and Sexuality from Delhi, India." *Signs: Journal of Women in Culture and Society* 42. 1: 845–867. www.journals.uchicago.edu/doi/pdf/10.1086/685118.

Batra, Kanika. 2016b. "Worlding Sexualities under Apartheid: From Gay Liberation to a Queer Afropolitanism." *Postcolonial Studies* 19. 3: 1–16. https://doi.org/10.1080/13688790.2016.1222857.

Batra, Kanika. 2018. "Transporting Metropolitanism: Road-Mapping Feminist Solutions to Sexual Violence in Delhi." *Journal of Postcolonial Writing* 54. 3: 387–397. https://doi.org/10.1080/17449855.2018.1461979.

Baxi, Upendra. (2002) 2008. *The Future of Human Rights*. 3rd edn. New Delhi: Oxford University Press.

Beall, Jo and Alison Todes. 2004. "Gender and Integrated Area Development Projects: Lessons from Cato Manor, Durban." *Cities* 21. 4: 301–310. www.elsevier.com/locate/issn/02642751.

Beall, Jo, Owen Crankshaw and Susan Parnell, eds. 2002. *Uniting a Divided City: Governance and Social Exclusion in Johannesburg*. London: Earthscan.

Beall, Jo, Shireen Hassim and Alison Todes. 2011. "We are all Radical Feminists now: Reflections on 'A Bit on the Side.'" *Transformation: Critical Perspectives on Southern Africa* 75: 95–106. https://doi.org/10.1353/trn.2011.0002.

Beavon, Keith. 2005. *Johannesburg: The Making and Shaping of a City*. Pretoria: University of South Africa Press.

Bechdel, Allison. 2012. *Are You My Mother: A Comic Drama*. New York: Houghton Mifflin.

Benhabib, Seyla. 2011. *Dignity in Adversity: Human Rights in Troubled Times*. Cambridge: Polity Press.

Bernal, Victoria and Inderpal Grewal. 2014. "Introduction." In *Theorizing NGOs: States, Feminisms, and Neoliberalism*, edited by Victoria Bernal and Inderpal Grewal, 1–18. Durham: Duke University Press.

Berry, Chris, Fran Martin and Audrey Yue. 2003. "Introduction: Beep-Click-Link." In *Mobile Cultures: New Media in Queer Asia*, 1–20. Durham: Duke University Press.

Bhaiya, Abha. 1992. "Letters to Manushi: Beyond Reproduction." *Manushi* 72 (September–October): 42.

Bombay Dost. 1990a. "Editorial: Out of the Closet!" *Bombay Dost* 1. 2 (October–December): 3.

Bombay Dost. 1990b. "Review: Out of the Shadows 'Veeru Dada.'" *Bombay Dost* 1. 2 (October–December): 19–20.

Bombay Dost. 1991a. "Review: Mast Kalandar." *Bombay Dost* 1. 1 (July–September): 15.

Bombay Dost. 1991b. "Editorial: Fight the Pandemic." *Bombay Dost* 1. 2 (October–December): 3.

Bombay Dost. 1991c. "The World." *Bombay Dost* 1. 1(July–September): 9.

Bombay Dost. 1992a. "First National Conference on AIDS." *Bombay Dost* 1. 3–4 (January–June): 11.

Bombay Dost. 1992b. "Editorial: In the Thick of It." *Bombay Dost* 1. 3–4 (January–June): 3.

Bombay Dost. 1993a. "Editorial: Structural Reforms." *Bombay Dost* 2. 3 (August–September): 3.

Bombay Dost. 1993b. "Editorial: New Voices." *Bombay Dost* 2. 1–2 (January–June): 5.

Bombay Dost. 1994a. "Attention Advertisers!" *Bombay Dost* 3. 1 (January–March): 5.

Bombay Dost. 1994b. "Local News: South Asian Gay Conference." *Bombay Dost* 3. 1 (January–March): 18.

Bombay Dost. 1995a. "Yellamma's Night." *Bombay Dost* 4. 1: 16.

Bombay Dost. 1995b. "A Strange Wedding." *Bombay Dost* 4. 2: 8–9.

Bombay Dost. 1996a. "Untitled." *Bombay Dost* 5. 1: 11.

Bombay Dost. 1996b. "Khush Khat." *Bombay Dost* 5. 2–3: 22.

Bombay Dost. 1996c. "Sexual Health Problems." *Bombay Dost* 5. 2–3: 16.

Bombay Dost. 1997. "Khush Chhokris." *Bombay Dost* 5. 4: 18.

Bombay Dost. 1998. "Khush Khat." *Bombay Dost* 6. 2–3: 21.

Bonnin, Debby. 1990. "1st Regional Meeting of Women and Health in Africa." *Agenda* 6: 31–36. www.jstor.org/stable/4065539.

Bonnin, Debby. 1991a. "Sixth International Women and Health Meeting." *Agenda* 9: 29–32. www.jstor.org/stable/4547948.

Bonnin, Debby. 1991b. "Wonder Contraceptive or Danger?" *Agenda* 11: 20–22. www.jstor.org/stable/4547968.

Bonnin, Debby. 2004. *Understanding the Legacies of Political Violence: An Examination of Political Conflict in Mpumalanga Township, KwaZulu-Natal, South Africa.* Crisis States Research Centre Working Papers Series 1, 44. London: Crisis States Research Centre, London School of Economics and Political Science. 1–19. http://eprints.lse.ac.uk/28220/.

Bose, Brinda. (2000) 2007. "The Desiring Subject: Female Pleasure and Feminist Resistance in Deepa Mehta's *Fire.*" In *The Phobic and the Erotic: The Politics of Sexualities in Contemporary India,* edited by Brinda Bose and Subhabrata Bhattacharya, 437–450. London: Seagull Books.

Botha, Henk. 2013. "Exit: Memories of the Early Years," www.exit.co.za/frmArticle.aspx?art=41. Accessed June 31, 2013.

Braganza, Rose Ann. 1984. "The Courageous Women of Babubigha." *Manushi* 22: 13.

Bremner, Lindsay. 2000. "Reinventing the Johannesburg Inner City." *Cities* 17. 3: 185–193. https://doi.org/10.1016/S0264-2751(00)00013-5.

Brodber, Erna. 1975. *A Study of the Yards of Kingston.* Working Papers 9. Mona: Institute of Social and Economic Research, University of West Indies.

Bronze. 1980. "Short Story." *Jamaica Gaily News* (September 26): 4.

Brown, Trevor. 1990. "On Location with 'Miss Amy and Miss May.'" *Sistren* 12. 1: 17–18.

Buddies. 1983. "Buddies." *Link/Skakel* (January): 3.

Bunch, Charlotte. 1990. "Women's Rights as Human Rights: Toward a Re-Vision of Human Rights." *Human Rights Quarterly* 12: 486–498.

Bundy, Colin. 2000. "Survival and Resistance: Township Organizations and Non-violent Direct Action in Twentieth Century South Africa." In *Comrades to Citizens: The South African Civics Movement and the Transition to Democracy,* edited by Glenn Adler and Jonny Steinberg, 26–51. New York: Palgrave Macmillan. http://ebookcentral.proquest.com/lib/ttu/detail.action?docID=203596.

Bureau of Women's Affairs (Gender Affairs) and The Gender Advisory Committee. 2010. *National Policy for Gender Equality (NPGE).* Kingston: Bureau of Women's Affairs.

Burton, Antoinette. 2005. *Archive Stories: Facts, Fictions and the Writing of History.* Durham: Duke University Press.

Cameron, Edwin. 2005. *Witness to AIDS.* London: IB Tauris.

Campaign for Lesbian Rights (CALERI). 1999. *Khamosh, Emergency Zaari Hai, Lesbian Emergence: Campaign for Lesbian Rights, A Citizen's Report.* New Delhi: CALERI.

Campbell, Catherine. 1990. "The Township Family and Women's Struggles." *Agenda* 6: 1–22. www.jstor.org/stable/4065536.

Candace. 1991. "Exploring the Myth: Women Want to Feel Pain During the Sex Act." *Sistren* 13. 2–3: 21.

Carnegie, Charles V. 2014. "The Loss of the Verandah: Kingston's Constricted Postcolonial Geographies." *Social and Economic Studies* 63. 2 (June): 59–85. www.jstor.org/stable/24384087.

Carnegie, Charles V. 2017. "How Did There Come to Be a 'New Kingston'?" *Small Axe: A Caribbean Journal of Criticism* 21. 3: 138–151. https://muse.jhu.edu/article/676007.

The Caribbean IRN. 2020. *Launch of the Digital Archive of the Jamaica Gaily News.* YouTube video, 2:11:41. www.youtube.com/watch?v=azaF5FLIHxk.

CAS. 1993. "Say No to Norplant." *Sistren* 15. 2–3: 32–33.

Cave, D. Michelle and Joan French. 1995. "Sexual Choice as a Human Rights Issue." *CAFRA Newsletter.* 17–19.

CEDAW-WROC. 2008. *Rights a di Plan, wid CEDAW in wi Han': CEDAW for Jamaicans*. Kingston: Women's Resource and Outreach Center and the United Nations Development Fund for Women.

Chakrabarty, Dipesh. 2000. "Subaltern Studies and Postcolonialism." *Nepantla: Views from South* 1. 1: 9–32. www.muse.jhu.edu/article/23873.

Chakravarty, Debjani. 2004. "Karan Razdan's *Girlfriend*: A Caricature of Lesbian Love." *Manushi* 146: 35–36.

Chandrasekaran, Padma, Gina Dallabetta, Virginia Loo, Sujata Rao, Helene Gayle and Ashok Alexander. 2008. "Containing HIV/AIDS in India: The Unfinished Agenda." *The Lancet Infectious Diseases* 6. 8: 508–521.

Chang Larry. 2008. Personal Communication with Author.

Chang, Larry. 2011. "Genesis of the Jamaica Gay Freedom Movement Archive." Locating Caribbean LGBT Histories. *sx salon* 6 (August 2011). http://smallaxe.net/wordpress3/discussions/2011/08/30/genesis-of-the-jamaica-gay-freedom-movement-archive/#more-170.

Chang, Larry. 2012. Interview with Thomas Glave. YouTube video. www.youtube.com/watch?v=PvzmGsF57vw.

Charanji, Kavita. 1992. "The Difficulties of Redressal." *Manushi* 68 (January–February): 16.

Chaturvedi, Asha. 1988. "Letters to Manushi: Why Not?" *Manushi* 46 (May–June): 23.

Cheah, Pheng. 2016. *What is a World: On Postcolonial Literature as World Literature*. Durham: Duke University Press.

Chernis, Linda. 2016. "Guest Post: Archiving an Icon-GALA's Simon Nkoli Collection by Linda Chernis." (November 11). LGBTQ+ Archives, Libraries, Museums and Special Collections, "Without Borders" Conference, June 22–24, London. http://lgbtqalms.co.uk/2016/11/11/guest-post-archiving-an-icon-galas-simon-nkoli-collection-by-linda-chernis/.

Chevannes, Barry. 2001. *Learning to be a Man: Culture, Socialization, and Gender Identity in Five Caribbean Communities*. Mona: University of the West Indies Press.

Chevannes, Barry. 2003. "The Role of the Street in the Socialization of Caribbean Males." In *The Culture of Gender and Sexuality in the Caribbean*, edited by Linden Lewis, 215–233. Gainesville: University Press of Florida.

Chin, Matthew. 2019a. "Constructing 'Gaydren' The Transnational Politics of Same-Sex Desire in 1970s and 1980s Jamaica." *Small Axe: A Caribbean Journal of Criticism* 23. 2: 17–33. https://muse.jhu.edu/article/731021.

Chin, Matthew. 2019b. "Tracing 'Gay Liberation' through Postindependence Jamaica." *Public Culture* 31. 2: 323–341. https://doi.org/10.1215/08992363-7286849.

Chin, Matthew. 2020. Personal Communication with Author.

Chin, Staceyanne. 2000. *The Other Side of Paradise: A Memoir*. New York: Scribner.

Chin, Timothy S. 1999. "Jamaican Popular Culture, Caribbean Literature, and the Representation of Gay and Lesbian Sexuality in the Discourses of Race and Nation." *Small Axe* 5 (March): 14–33.

Clarke, Colin. 2006. *Decolonizing the Colonial City: Urbanization and Stratification in Kingston, Jamaica*. Oxford: Oxford University Press.

Coburn, Thomas. 1995. "Sita Fights While Ram Swoons." *Manushi* 90 (September–October): 5–16.

Cohen, Lawrence. 2011. "Song for Pushkin." In *Law like Love: Queer Perspectives on Law*, edited by Arvind Narrain and Alok Gupta, 510–529. New Delhi: Yoda Press.

Conway, Daniel. 2009. "Queering Apartheid: The National Party's 1987 "Gay Rights" Election Campaign in Hillbrow." *Journal of Southern African Studies*, 35. 4: 849–863. https://doi.org/10.1080/03057070903313210.

Cooper, Carolyn. 1989. "Writing Oral History: Sistren Theatre Collective's *Lionheart Gal*." *Kunapipi* 11. 1: 49–57. https://ro.uow.edu.au/kunapipi/vol11/iss1/8.

Cooper, Carolyn. 2004a. "'Lyrical Gun': Metaphor and Role-Play in Jamaican Dancehall Culture." In *Sound Clash: Jamaican Dancehall Culture at Large*, 145–178. New York: Palgrave Macmillan.

Cooper, Carolyn. 2004b. *Soundclash: Jamaican Dancehall Culture at Large*. New York: Palgrave Macmillan.

Cooper, Frederick. 1994. "Conflict and Connection: Rethinking Colonial African History." *American Historical Review* 99. 5: 1516–1545. https://doi.org/10.1086/ahr/99.5.1516.

Cruz-Malawe, Arnaldo and Martin F. Manalansan, eds. 2002. *Queer Globalizations: Citizenship and the Afterlife of Colonialism*. New York: New York University Press.

Currier, Ashley. 2012. *Out in Africa: LGBT Organizing in Namibia and South Africa*. Minneapolis: University of Minnesota Press.

Currier, Ashley and Thérèse Migraine-George. 2016. "Queer Studies / African Studies: An (Im)possible Transaction?" *GLQ* 22. 2: 281–305. https://muse.jhu.edu/article/613192.

Cvetkovich, Ann. 2003. *An Archive of Feelings: Trauma, Sexuality, and Lesbian Public Cultures*. Durham: Duke University Press.

Dasgupta, Rohit K. 2017. *Digital Queer Cultures in India: Politics, Intimacies and Belonging*. London: Routledge.

Dave, Naisargi N. 2010. "To Render Real the Imagined: An Ethnographic History of Lesbian Community in India." *Signs: Journal of Women in Culture and Society* 35. 3: 595–619. https://doi.org/10.1086/648514.

Dave, Naisargi N. 2012. *Queer Activism in India: A Story in the Anthropology of Ethics*. Durham: Duke University Press.

Davidson, Gerry and Ron Nerio. 1995. "*Exit*: Gay Publishing in South Africa." In *Defiant Desire: Gay and Lesbian Lives in South Africa*, edited by Mark Gevisser and Edwin Cameron, 225–231. New York: Routledge.

Debabrata, Roma. 1998. "When Police Act as Pimps: Glimpses into Child Prostitution in India." *Manushi* 105 (March–April): 27–31.

de Boeck, Filip. 2002. "Kinshasa: Tales of the 'Invisible City' and the Second World." In *Under Siege: Four African Cities: Freetown, Johannesburg, Kinshasa, Lagos*, edited by Okwui Enwezor et al, 243–286. Ostfildern: Hatje Cantz.

Deeptipriya. 1985. "Challenging a Masculinist Culture: Women's Protest in St. Stephen's College." *Manushi* 28 (May–June): 32–35.

Demaro. 2019. *Mi Readi*. Dir. Tony Vallés. YouTube video, 2:43. www.youtube.com/watch?v=C7kHrP_cbc4.

D'Emilio, John. 1998. *Sexual Politics, Sexual Communities: The Making of a Homosexual Minority in the United States, 1940–1970*, 2nd edn. Chicago: University of Chicago Press.

Derrida, Jacques. 2006. *Archive Fever: A Freudian Impression*, trans. Eric Prenowitz. Chicago: University of Chicago Press.

Desai, Jigna. 2002. "Homo on the Range: Mobile and Global Sexualities." *Social Text* 20. 4: 65–89. www.muse.jhu.edu/article/38470.

Dewan, Renu. 1986. "Letters to Manushi: Not Passive Acceptance." *Manushi* 32 (January–February): 26.

Ditsie, Bev. 2019. "A Love Letter to my Queer Family." *Daily Maverick*, October 24. www.dailymaverick.co.za/article/2019-10-24-a-love-letter-to-my-queer-family/.

Donnell, Allison. 2007. "Feeling Good? Look Again! Feel Good Movies and the Vanishing Points of Liberation in Deepa Mehta's *Fire* and Gurinder Chadha's *Bend it Like Beckham*." *Journal of Creative Communications* 2. 1–2: 43–55. https://doi.org/10.1177/097325860700200203.

Dost Team. 1995. "To Drag or Not to Drag." *Bombay Dost* 4. 2: 6–7.

Dube, Siddharth. 2000. *Sex, Lies, and AIDS*. New Delhi: Harper Collins.

Eekhoff, Jo. 1991. "Mothers, Sons, and Police." *Sistren* 13. 1: 22.

Elmendrop, Ellen. 1993. "Sangomas Fight AIDS." *Speak* 52 (August): 16–17. https://disa. ukzn.ac.za/sites/default/files/pdf_files/SpAug93.pdf.

Esteves, Lesley and Ashwini Sukthankar. 1996. "Chhokri." *Bombay Dost* 5. 2–3: 33.

Exit. 1984. "International Body Welcomes SA Gays." *Exit* (August): 1.

Exit. 1985. "Law Affects All." *Exit* (October): 5.

Exit. 1986a. "Gasa on Nkoli." *Exit* (March–April): 1.

Exit. 1986b. "R42000 in One Night." *Exit* (May): 1.

Exit. 1986c. "Fund Drive is Proof of Unity." *Exit* (May): 8.

Exit. 1986d. "'Gay Plague' Knocked." *Exit* (August–September): 1.

Exit. 1987a. "Election was Gay Victory." *Exit* (June–July): 1.

Exit. 1987b. "Hillbrow can be Key for Rights." *Exit* (May/June): 1.

Exit. 1988. "Glow Celebrates Pride." *Exit* (June–July): 9.

Exit. 1989. "Glow Celebrates 1st Year with Big Rally." *Exit* (January–March): 3.

Fernandez, Bina, ed. 1999. *Humjinsi: A Resource Book of Lesbian, Gay and Bisexual Rights in India*. New Delhi: India Center for Human Rights and Law.

Ford-Smith, Honor. 1989. *Ring Ding in a Tight Corner: A Case Study of Funding and Organizational Democracy in Sistren, 1977–1988*. Toronto: Women's Program ICAE.

Ford-Smith, Honor. 1991. "Teens in Action: Young Jamaican Women Find Solutions." *Sistren* 13. 1: 12–13.

Ford-Smith, Honor. 1993a. "The Value of an Angry Woman: The Importance of Una Marson." *Sistren* 15. 1–2: 24.

Ford-Smith, Honor. 1993b. "Una's Achievement: Her Life." *Sistren* 15. 3–4: 26–27.

Ford-Smith, Honor. 1994. "Marson: Her Isolation." *Sistren* 16. 2–3: 29–30.

Ford-Smith, Honor. 1997. *Ring Ding in a Tight Corner: Sistren, Collective Democracy, and the Organization of Cultural Production*. Toronto: Sister Vision Press.

Francis-Hinds, Suzanne. 1990. "A Cameo Comes to Live." *Sistren* 12. 1: 16–17.

Fraser, Nancy. 1997. *Justice Interruptus: Critical Reflections on the "Postsocialist" Condition*. New York: Routledge.

Fraser, Nancy. 2007. "Transnationalizing the Public Sphere: On the Legitimacy and Efficacy of Public Opinion in a Post-Westphalian World." European Institute for Progressive Cultural Politics. www.buildingglobaldemocracy.org/node/1771.

Fraser, Nancy. 2014. "Publicity, Subjection, Critique: A Reply to My Critics." In *Transnationalizing the Public Sphere*, edited by Kate Nash, 129–156. Oxford: Wiley.

Freeman, Elizabeth. 2010. *Time Binds: Queer Temporalities, Queer Histories*. Durham: Duke University Press.

French, Joan. 2020. Personal Communication with Author.

Fruend, Bill. 2002. "City Hall and the Direction of Development." In *(D)urban Vortex: South African City in Transition*, edited by Bill Freund and Vishnu Padayachee, 11–41. Pietermaritzburg: University of Natal Press.

Gajjala, Radhika. 2004. *Cyber Selves: Feminist Ethnographies of South Asian Women*. Walnut Creek: AltaMira Press-Rowman Littlefield.

Gandhi, Nandita and Nandita Shah. 1993. *The Issues at Stake Theory and Practice in the Contemporary Women's Movement in India*. New Delhi: Kali for Women.

Gasa, Nomboniso. 1993. "Bitter-Sweet Memories." *Speak* 56 (December): 26–27. https:// disa.ukzn.ac.za/sites/default/files/pdf_files/SpDec93.pdf.

Gay Duncan, B. 1978. [Extracts from Joan Ross Article]. *Jamaica Gaily News* 16 (March 31): 5–6.

Gay Freedom Movement. n.d.a. "Gay Freedom Movement Fact Sheet." *GFM Archive*. Caribbean International Resource Network. https://ufdc.ufl.edu/AA00002984/00001.

Gay Freedom Movement. n.d.b. "Gay Freedom Movement." *GFM Archive*. Caribbean International Resource Network. https://ufdc.ufl.edu/AA00002992/00001.

Gay Freedom Movement. n.d.c. "Gay Rights are Human Rights." *GFM Archive*. Caribbean International Resource Network. https://ufdc.ufl.edu/AA00002985/00001.

Gay Freedom Movement. 1980. "Constitution of the Gay Freedom Movement of Jamaica." *GFM Archive*. Caribbean International Resource Network. 1–10. https://ufdc.ufl.edu/AA00002982/00001.

Gay Freedom Movement. 1981a. "Gays in Jamaica: A Position Paper." *GFM Archive*. Caribbean International Resource Network. 1–26. https://ufdc.ufl.edu/AA00001485/00001.

Gay Freedom Movement. 1981b. "Handwritten Notes and Agenda for IGA Conference1981." *GFM Archive*. Caribbean International Resource Network. https://ufdc.ufl.edu/AA00001418/00001.

Gay Freedom Movement. 1981c. "Draft Report on IGA 1981." *GFM Archive*. Caribbean International Resource Network. https://ufdc.ufl.edu/AA00003026/00001.

Gevisser, Mark. 1995. "A Different Fight for Freedom: A History of South African Lesbian and Gay Organisation from the 1950s to the 1990s." In *Defiant Desire: Gay and Lesbian Lives in South Africa*, edited by Mark Gevisser and Edwin Cameron, 14–86. New York: Routledge.

Gevisser, Mark and Edwin Cameron, eds. 1995. *Defiant Desire: Gay and Lesbian Lives in South Africa*. New York: Routledge.

Ghosh, Shohini. 2010. "The Wonderful World of Queer Cinephilia." *Bioscope: South Asian Screen Studies* 1. 1: 17–20. https://journals.sagepub.com/doi/pdf/10.1177/097492760900100104.

Gikandi, Simon. 2011. "Foreword: On Afropolitanism." In *Negotiating Afropolitanism: Essays on Borders and Spaces in Contemporary African Literature and Folklore*, edited by Jennifer Wawrzinek and J. K. S. Makokha, 9–11. Amsterdam: Rodopi.

Ginger. 1977. "Politics and Us." *Jamaica Gaily News* (November 25): 1.

Glave, Thomas. 2000. "Toward a Nobility of the Imagination: Jamaica's Shame (An Open Letter to the People of Jamaica)." *Black Renaissance* 2. 3: 77. https://search.proquest.com/docview/215532566?accountid=7098.

Glave, Thomas, ed. 2008. *Our Caribbean: A Gathering of Lesbian and Gay Writing from the Antilles*. Durham: Duke University Press.

Glave, Thomas. 2013. *Among the Bloodpeople: Politics and Flesh*. New York: Akashic.

Gopinath, Gayatri. 2005a. *Impossible Desires: Queer Diasporas and South Asian Public Cultures*. Durham: Duke University Press.

Gopinath, Gayatri. 2005b. "Local Sites/Global Contexts: The Transnational Trajectories of *Fire* and 'The Quilt.'" In *Impossible Desires: Queer Diasporas and South Asian Public Cultures*, 131–160. Durham: Duke University Press.

Gopinath, Gayatri. 2018. *Unruly Visions: The Aesthetic Practices of the Queer Diaspora*. Durham: Duke University Press.

Goswami, Namita. 2008. "Autophagia and Queer Nationality: Compulsory Heteroimperial Masculinity in Deepa Mehta's *Fire*." *Signs* 33. 2: 343–369. https://doi.org/10.1086/521052.

Gqola, Pumla Dineo. 2015. *Rape: A South African Nightmare*. Auckland Park: Melinda Ferguson Books. http://search.ebscohost.com.libe2.lib.ttu.edu/login.aspx?direct=true&db=nlebk&AN=1240044&site=ehost-live.

Gray, Obika. 2004. *Demeaned but Poor: The Social Power of the Urban Poor in Jamaica*. Jamaica: University of the West Indies Press.

Green, Marcus. 2002. "Gramsci Cannot Speak: Presentations and Interpretations of Gramsci's Concept of the Subaltern." *Rethinking Marxism* 14. 3: 1–24. https://doi.org/10.1080/089356902101242242.

Green, Sharon L. 2004. "Sistren Theatre Collective: Struggling to Remain Radical in an Era of Globalization." *Theatre Topics* 14. 2: 473–495. https://doi.org/10.1353/tt.2004.0017.

Grewal, Inderpal and Caren Kaplan. 2001. "Global Identities: Theorizing Transnational Studies of Sexuality." *GLQ: A Journal of Lesbian and Gay Studies* 7. 4: 663–679. www.muse.jhu.edu/article/12186.

Grover, Vrinda et al. 2013. "Dear Sisters (and Brothers?) at Harvard: Letter from Indian Feminists Vrinda Grover, Mary E. John, Kavita Panjabi, Shilpa Phadke, Shweta Vachani, Urvashi Butlia and Others, To Their Siblings at Harvard." *Kafila* (February 20). http://kafila.org/2013/02/20/dear-sisters-and-brothers-at-harvard/.

Gupta, Alok. 2005. "*Englishpur ki Kothi*: Class Dynamics and the Queer Movement in India." In *Because I Have a Voice: Queer Politics in India*, edited by Arvind Narrain and Gautam Bhan, 123–142. New Delhi: Yoda Press.

Gutzmore, Cecil. 2004. "Casting the First Stone: The Policing of Homo/Sexuality in Jamaican Popular Culture." *Interventions* 6. 1: 118–134. https://doi.org/10.1080/1369801042000185697.

Habermas, Jürgen. (1961) 1991. *The Structural Transformation of the Public Sphere: An Inquiry into a Category of Bourgeois Society*. Boston: MIT Press.

Halberstam, Jack. 2014. "Introduction." In *Reclaiming Afrikan: Queer Perspectives on Sexual and Gender Identities*, edited by Zethu Matabeni, 12–15. Athlone: Modjaji Books.

Halberstam, Judith. 2005. *In a Queer Time and Place: Transgender Bodies, Subcultural Lives*. New York: New York University Press.

Hall, Stuart. 1980. "Race, Articulation, and Societies Structured in Domination." In *Sociological Theories: Race and Colonialism*, 305–345. Paris: UNESCO.

Hall, Stuart. 1988. "Gramsci and Us." In *The Hard Road to Renewal: Thatcherism and the Crisis of the Left*, 161–173. London: Verso.

Hall, Stuart. 1996. "On Postmodernism and Articulation: An Interview with Stuart Hall." In *Stuart Hall: Critical Dialogues in Cultural Studies*, edited by David Morley and Kuang Hsing-Chen, 131–150. London: Routledge.

Hamilton, Carolyn, Verne Harris and Graeme Reid. 2002. "Introduction." In *Refiguring the Archive*, 7–18. Cape Town: David Philip Publishers – New Africa Books.

Hansen, Thomas Blom. 2001. *Wages of Violence: Naming and Identity in Postcolonial Bombay*. Princeton: Princeton University Press.

Harneker, Zaidi. 1986. "She Still Wanted to Scream." *Speak* 12 (October–December): 10–11. https://disa.ukzn.ac.za/sites/default/files/pdf_files/SpOct86.pdf.

Haskar, Nandita. 2005. "Human Rights Lawyering: A Feminist Perspective." In *Writing the Women's Movement: A Reader*, edited by Mala Khullar, 131–151. New Delhi: Zubaan.

Hassim, Shireen. 2006. *Women's Organizations and Democracy in South Africa: Contesting Authority*. Madison: University of Wisconsin Press.

Hawley, John, ed. 2001. *Postcolonial Queer*. Ser. Explorations in Postcolonial Studies. Albany: SUNY Press.

Haynes, Jonathan. 2007. "Nollywood in Lagos, Lagos in Nollywood Films." *Africa Today* 54. 2: 131–150. www.jstor.org/stable/27666895.

Heller, Patrick and Libhongo Ntlokonkulu. 2001. *A Civic Movement or a Movement for Civics? The South African National Civic Organisation (SANCO) in the Post-Apartheid Period*. Research Report no. 84. Social Policy Series. Johannesburg: Center for Policy Studies. 1–64.

Hemmings, Clare. 2011. *Why Stories Matter: The Political Grammar of Feminist Theory*. Durham: Duke University Press.

Heron, Taitu. 2003. "Plantalogical Politics: Battling for Space and the Jamaican Constitution." In *Living at the Borderlines: Nationalism, Identity and Survival in the Eastern Caribbean*, edited by Cynthia Barrow-Giles and Don Marshall, 493–516. Kingston: Ian Randle Publishers.

Higonnet, Margaret. 1994. "Comparative Literature on the Feminist Edge." In *Comparative Literature in the Age of Multiculturalism*, edited by Charles Bernheimer, 155–164. Baltimore: Johns Hopkins University Press.

Hoad, Neville. 2007. *African Intimacies: Race, Homosexuality, and Globalization*. Minneapolis: University of Minnesota Press.

Hoad, Neville, Karen Martin and Graeme Reid, eds. 2005. *Sex and Politics in South Africa*. Cape Town: Double Storey.

Hope, Donna P. 2000. *Inna Di Dancehall: Popular Culture and the Politics of Identity in Jamaica*. Kingston: University of the West Indies Press.

Hope, Donna P. 2010. *Man Vibes: Masculinities in the Jamaican Dancehall*. Kingston: Ian Randle Publishers.

ILGA. 2015. "Jamaica Ready for its First Pride Ever." *LGBulleTIn* 8 (July 25). https://ilga.org/lgbulletin-8-week-lgbti-news-around-world-july-25-3-2015.

Imma, Z'étoile. 2017. "Black, Queer, and Precarious Visibilities: Simon Nkoli's Activist Image in South Africa's *Exit* Newspaper." *Callaloo* 40. 3: 61–74. https://doi.org/10.1353/cal.2017.0120.

Jagori. 2004. "Living Feminisms: Jagori, A Journey of 20 Years." www.jagori.org/sites/default/files/publication/Living%20Feminisms.pdf.

Jamaica Council for Human Rights. 1981. *Citizens' Rights: Police Power-JCHR*. GFM Archive. Caribbean International Resource Network. https://ufdc.ufl.edu/AA00002997/00001.

Jamaica Gaily News. 1977. "In the News." *Jamaica Gaily News* 6 (November 11): 4.

Jamaica Gaily News. 1978a. "Speakeasy Attack." *Jamaica Gaily News* 29 (October 13): 1.

Jamaica Gaily News. 1978b. "Lesbian Row Ends in Stabbing." *Jamaica Gaily News* 23 (July 21): 1.

Jamaica Gaily News. 1978c. "DJ Held for Buggery." *Jamaica Gaily News* 2 (January 20): 1.

Jamaica Gaily News. 1978d. "Freed of Buggery Charge." *Jamaica Gaily News* 19 (May 12): 1.

Jamaica Gaily News. 1978e. "Gay Man Killed." *Jamaica Gaily News* 25 (August 18): 1.

Jamaica Gaily News. 1978f. "Editorial." *Jamaica Gaily News* 31 (November 10): 3.

Jamaica Gaily News. 1978g. "Editorial." *Jamaica Gaily News* 23 (July 21): 3.

Jamaica Gaily News. 1978h. "Editorial." *Jamaica Gaily News* 32 (November 24): 3.

Jamaica Gaily News. 1978i. "Youth Group Proposed," *Jamaica Gaily News* 29 (October 13): 1.

Jamaica Gaily News. 1978j. "Youth Group Launched." *Jamaica Gaily News* 30 (October 27): 1, 3.

Jamaica Gaily News. 1978k. "Health Clinic to Open Nov. 4," *Jamaica Gaily News* 30 (October 27): 1.

Jamaica Gaily News. 1978l. "Clinic Opens." *Jamaica Gaily News* 31 (November 10): 1.

Jamaica Gaily News. 1978m. "The Test is Best," *Jamaica Gaily News* 28 (September 29): 1.

Jamaica Gaily News. 1978n. "Editorial" *Jamaica Gaily News* 19 (May 12): 3.

Jamaica Gaily News. 1978o. "Editorial." *Jamaica Gaily News* 26 (September 1): 3.

Jamaica Gaily News. 1978p. "NPM Thinks Gays Sick." *Jamaica Gaily News* 31 (November 10): 2.

Jamaica Gaily News. 1979a. "Editorial." *Jamaica Gaily News* 42 (April 27): 1.

Jamaica Gaily News. 1979b. "Speakeasy Fracas." *Jamaica Gaily News* 43 (May 11): 1.

Jamaica Gaily News. 1979c. "VD Clinic Reopened." *Jamaica Gaily News* 38 (March 9): 1.

Jamaica Gaily News. 1979d. "You Don't Say!" *Jamaica Gaily News* 37 (February 23): 2.

Jamaica Gaily News. 1980a. "Suicide Attempts: At Home and Abroad." *Jamaica Gaily News* 56 (January 19): 2.

Jamaica Gaily News. 1980b. "GFM Mobay Gets Own Centre." *Jamaica Gaily News* 59 (April 4): 2.

Jamaica Gaily News. 1980c. "GFM/JPA Meet Again." *Jamaica Gaily News* 70 (November 23): 1, 11.

Jamaica Gaily News. 1980d. "Is Homosexuality a Way of Life." *Jamaica Gaily News* 60 (April 18): 1.

Jamaica Gaily News. 1980e. "Letter to the Editor." *Jamaica Gaily News* 70 (November 23): 12.

Jamaica Gaily News. 1981a. "Editorial: Where do we go from here?" *Jamaica Gaily News* 72 (March 15): 7.

Jamaica Gaily News. 1981b. "New Club Soon and...." *Jamaica Gaily News* 73 (May 22): 1.

Jamaica Gaily News. 1982. "Editorial." *Jamaica Gaily News* 76 (July 3): 7.

Jamaica Gaily News. 1984a. GFM/Nurses Talk," *Jamaica Gaily News* 77 (January): 2, 11.

Jamaica Gaily News. 1984b. "Marshall's Club Reopens as Bar." *Jamaica Gaily News* 77 (January): 2.

Jamaica Gaily News. 1984c. *Jamaica Gaily News* 79 (April–May): 1–12.

Jamaica Gaily News. 1984d. *Jamaica Gaily News* 80 (June): 1–12.

The Jamaica Task Force Committee for Comprehensive Sexuality Education. 2008. *Jamaican Guidelines for Comprehensive Sexuality Education: Pre-School through Age 24*. Kingston: Famplan Jamaica-Seicus. https://hivhealthclearinghouse.unesco.org/sites/default/files/resources/bie_jamaica_guidelines_siecus.pdf.

Jameson's. 1983. "Jameson's." *Link/Skakel* (August): 3.

Jaquette, Jane S. 2017. "Women/Gender and Development: The Growing Gap between Theory and Practice." *Studies in Comparative International Development* 52. 2: 242–260. https://doi.org/10.1007/s12116-017-9248-8.

Ja Will. 1978a. "Pan Di Scene, Iya." *Jamaica Gaily News* 23 (July 21): 6.

Ja Will. 1978b. "Pan Di Scene, Iya." *Jamaica Gaily News* 27 (September 15): 6.

Ja Will. 1978c. "Pan Di Scene, Iya." *Jamaica Gaily News* 28 (September 29): 2.

J-FLAG. 2016. *The Road Towards Sustainable Development: A National Focus on Human Rights, Economic and Social Justice*. http://equalityjamaica.org/assets/human_rights_call_to_action.pdf.

J-FLAG et al. 2016. *Human Rights Violations Against Lesbian, Gay, Bisexual, and Transgender (LGBT) People in Jamaica: A Shadow Report submitted for Consideration at the 118th Session of the Human Rights Committee*. http://equalityjamaica.org/assets/jamaica_lgbt_report_september_2016.pdf.

Johnson, Colin. 1980. "Maddams Re-opens." *Jamaica Gaily News* 60 (April 18): 3, 9.

Jojdand, Nikhil. 2008. *Mahacharacha*. Vakola, Mumbai: Humsafar.

Jolly, Susie. 2000. "'Queering Development: Exploring the Links Between Same-Sex Sexualities, Gender, and Development." *Gender & Development* 8. 1: 78–88. https://doi.org/10.1080/741923414.

Joseph, Ammu. 2006. "Women's Magazines: Style over Substance." In *Whose News? The Media and Women's Issues*, edited by Ammu Joseph and Kalpana Sharma, 204–231. New Delhi, London: Sage.

Kalonji, Sizzla. 2015. *Sizzla 'Bun' Gays, Government and the System*. YouTube video, 12:26. www.youtube.com/watch?v=07slF5kS3HU.

Kannabiran, Kalpana. 2002. "A Ravished Justice: Half a Century of Judicial Discourse on Rape." In *De-Eroticizing Assault: Essays on Modesty, Honor, and Power*, edited by Kalpana Kannabiran and Vasantha Kannabiran, 104–169. Calcutta: Stree Press.

Kapur, Ratna. (2005) 2012. *Erotic Justice: Law and the New Politics of Postcolonialism*. London: Glass House Press; Portland: Cavendish Press.

Karani, Nitin. 1998a. "Life's Not Just a Party." *Bombay Dost* 6. 1: 14.

Karani, Nitin. 1998b. "Report: Need for Coalition." *Bombay Dost* 6. 2–3: 34–35.

Katrak, Ketu. 2006. *The Politics of the Female Body: Postcolonial Women Writers*. New Brunswick: Rutgers University Press.

Katyal, Akhil. 2016. *The Doubleness of Sexuality: Idioms of Same-Sex Desire in Modern India*. New Delhi: New Text.

Keeton, Claire. 1992. *Speak* 40 (June): 19–22. https://disa.ukzn.ac.za/sites/default/files/pdf_files/SpJun92.pdf.

Kempadoo, Kamala. 2004. *Sexing the Caribbean: Gender, Race and Sexual Labor*. New York: Routledge.

Kempadoo, Kamala. 2009. "Caribbean Sexuality: Mapping the Field." *Caribbean Review of Gender Studies* 3 (November): 1–24. https://sta.uwi.edu/crgs/november2009/journals/Kempadoo.pdf.

Khan, Sultan. 1994. "Some Neat Gay-Bashing." *Bombay Dost* 3. 2: 8.

Khayal. 1986. "Nairobi: South Asian Lesbians at Nairobi." *Anamika* 1. 2 (March): 3.

Khayal and Utsa. 1985. "A Letter from Us." *Anamika* 1. 1 (May): 1–2.

Kishwar, Madhu. 1990. "Why I Do Not Call Myself a Feminist." *Manushi* 61: 2–8.

Kishwar, Madhu. 1992a. "Sex Harassment and Slander as Weapons of Subjugation." *Manushi* 68 (January–February): 2–15.

Kishwar, Madhu. 1992b. "Follow Up Report on a Case of Sexual Harassment in Delhi University." *Manushi* 69 (March–April): 19–20.

Kishwar, Madhu. 1992c. "Letters to Manushi." *Manushi* 7: 40.

Kishwar, Madhu. 1997. "Destroying Minds and Skills: The Dominance of Angreziyat in Our Education." *Manushi* 102: 21–29.

Kishwar, Madhu. 1998. "Naïve Outpourings of a Self-Hating Indian: Deepa Mehta's *Fire*." *Manushi* 109 (November–December): 3–14.

Kishwar, Madhu. 1999a. "Responses to Manushi." *Manushi* 112 (May–June): 5–11.

Kishwar, Madhu. 1999b. "Responses to Manushi: More Ire on *Fire*" *Manushi* 114 (September–October): 38–44.

Kishwar, Madhu and Ruth Vanita. 1987. "Using Women as a Pretext for Repression: The Indecent Representation of Women (Prohibition) Bill." *Manushi* 38: 2–8.

Klausen, Susanne M. 2015. *Abortion Under Apartheid: Nationalism, Sexuality, and Women's Reproductive Rights in South Africa*. New York: Oxford University Press.

Krouse, Matthew, ed. 1993. *The Invisible Ghetto: Lesbian and Gay Writing from South Africa*. Johannesburg: The Gay Men's Press-Congress of South African Writing.

Kruger, Loren. 2013. *Imagining the Edgy City: Writing, Performing, and Building Johannesburg*. Oxford: Oxford University Press.

Kulshreshtha, Indu. 1983. "Letters to Manushi: Holi Hooliganism." *Manushi* 18 (August–September): 28.

Kumar, Arvind. 1987. "Letters." *Anamika* 1. 3 (June): 3.

La Font, Suzanne. 2001. "Very Straight Sex: The Development of Sexual Morés in Jamaica." *Journal of Colonialism and Colonial History* 2. 3. http://muse.jhu.edu/journals/journal_of_colonialism_and_colonial_history/v002/2.3lafont.html#FOOT9.

Lago Collective. 1987. "Misplaced." *Exit* (July–August): 2.

Lalwani, Nikita. 2014. "India's First Gay Magazine Struggles to Survive." https://blogs.wsj.com/indiarealtime/2014/02/03/indias-first-gay-magazine-struggles-to- survive/.

Lampart, Camille. 1987. "Feminism in Jamaica: Major Strength, Major Dilemma." *Sistren* 9. 3: 13.

Landau, Loren. 2006. "Transplants and Transients: Idioms of Belonging and Dislocation in Inner-City Johannesburg." *African Studies Review* 49. 2: 125–145. www.jstor.org/stable/20065243.

Lanser, Susan. 2014–2015. "Comparatively Lesbian: Queer/Feminist Theory and the Sexuality of History." The 2014–2015 Report on the State of the Discipline of Comparative

Literature. http://stateofthediscipline.acla.org/entry/comparatively-lesbian-queerfeminist-theory-and-sexuality-history-0.

Lawes, Carol. 1986–1987. "*Lionheart Gal* 'Hilarious.'" *Sistren* 8. 3: 10, 16.

Lazarus, Latoya. 2013. "Working with Marginalized and 'Hidden' Populations: Researchers' Anxieties and Strategies for Doing Less Harmful Research." *Caribbean Review of Gender Studies* 7 (March): 1–22. http://sta.uwi.edu/crgs/december2013/journals/CRGS%20_7_Lazarus.pdf.

Levy, C. 1980. "Letters: Mampala Morgan." *Jamaica Gaily News* 70 (November 23): 12.

Lewis, Emma. 2017. "'Tambourine Army' Gathers Recruits as Jamaicans' Anger Over Child Sexual Abuse Grows." *Global Voices* (February 7). https://globalvoices.org/2017/02/07/tambourine-army-gathers-recruits-as-jamaicans- anger-over-child-sexual-abuse-grows/.

Lewis, Linden. 2003. "Exploring the Intersections of Gender, Sexuality, and Culture in the Caribbean: An Introduction." In *The Culture of Gender and Sexuality in the Caribbean*, edited by Linden Lewis. Gainesville: University Press of Florida.

Link/Skakel.1982a. "Gays Link Up." *Link/Skakel* (May): 1–2.

Link/Skakel. 1982b. "Dial Pink." *Link/Skakel* (May): 2.

Link/Skakel. 1983. "Whites Only." *Link/Skakel* (December): 10.

Link/Skakel. 1984. "Saturday Group Notice." *Link/Skakel* (June–July): 3.

Link/Skakel. 1985. "Exit *Link/Skakel* Enter *Exit*." *Link/Skakel* (July): 1.

Livermon, Xavier. 2012. "Queer(y)ing Freedom: Black Queer Visibilities in Postapartheid South Africa." *GLQ: A Journal of Lesbian and Gay Studies* 18. 2–3: 297–323. www.muse.jhu.edu/article/472154.

Lloyd, Libby. 1991. "Danger! Nightshift." *Speak* 37: 20–22. https://disa.ukzn.ac.za/sites/default/files/pdf_files/Spn3791.pdf.

Lorde, Audre. 1991. "Celebration." *Sistren* 13. 2–3: 17.

Lorentz, Christopher. 1987. "Discrimination Abhorrent." *Exit* (July–August): 2.

Lothian, Alexis and Amanda Phillips. 2013. "Can Digital Humanities Mean Transformative Critique?" *Journal of e-Media Studies* 3. 1: 1–25. https://citeseerx.ist.psu.edu/viewdoc/download?doi=10.1.1.673.6424&rep=rep1&type=pdf.

Lotter, Karen. 1982. "Is There a Lesbian Identity." *Link/Skakel* (November): 10.

Lotter, Karen. 1989. "Back in Africa: Simon Nkoli Reports Back on ILGA Conference and His Trip Overseas." *Exit* (November): 7.

Lourenco Marques Restaurant. 1983. "Lourenco Marques Restaurant." *Link/Skakel* (July): 9.

Lugones, María. 2007. "Heterosexualism and the Colonial/Modern Gender System." *Hypatia* 22. 1: 186–219. www.jstor.org/stable/4640051.

Maharaj, Brij. 1996. "The Historical Development of the Apartheid Local State in South Africa: The Case of Durban." *International Journal of Urban and Regional Research* 20. 4: 587–600. https://onlinelibrary.wiley.com/doi/pdf/10.1111/j.1468-2427.1996.tb00337.x.

Making of Caribbean Feminisms WI Special Collection. Alma Jordan Library. The University of the West Indies, St. Augustine. http://uwispace.sta.uwi.edu/dspace/handle/2139/45158.

Mampala Morgan. 1980. "Suss-uration." *Jamaica Gaily News* 71 (December 21): 5

Mampala Morgan. 1981a. "Suss-uration." *Jamaica Gaily News* 74 (September 4): 5.

Mampala Morgan. 1981b. "Suss-uration." *Jamaica Gaily News* 76: 8.

Mampala Morgan. 1981c. *Jamaica Gaily News* 72 (March 15): 5, 12.

Mampala Morgan. 1981d. "Suss-uration." *Jamaica Gaily News* 75 (October 16): 5.

Manalansan, Martin. 2003. *Global Divas: Filipino Gay Men in the Diaspora*. Durham: Duke University Press.

Mandy, Nigel. 1984. *A City Divided: Johannesburg and Soweto*. New York: St. Martin's Press.

Manushi. 1997. "Follow Up: Hamida goes Home." *Manushi* 98: 33–34.

Manushi. 1999. "Responses to Manushi." *Manushi* 112: 2–11.

Martin, Yasmina. 2020. "'Now I Am Not Afraid': Simon Nkoli, Queer Utopias and Transnational Solidarity." *Journal of Southern African Studies*, 46. 4: 673–687. https://doi.org/10.1080/03057070.2020.1780022.

Massad, Joseph A. 2007. "Re-Orienting Desire: The Gay International and the Arab World." In *Desiring Arabs*, 160–190. Chicago: University of Chicago Press.

Matebeni, Zethu. 2011. "Exploring Black Lesbian Sexualities and Identities in Johannesburg." PhD diss., University of the Witwatersrand.

Maxwell, Shakira. 2012. "Fighting a Losing Battle? Defending Women's Reproductive Rights in Twenty-First Century Jamaica." *Social and Economic Studies* 61. 3: 95–115. www.jstor.org/stable/41803769.

Maylam, Paul. 1995. "Explaining the Apartheid City: 20 Years of South African Urban Historiography." *Journal of Southern African Studies*. Special Issue: Urban Studies and Urban Change in Southern Africa. 21. 1: 19–38. www.jstor.org/stable/2637329.

Mayosi, Nomfundo. 1992. "Utilising Development and Political Process to Entrench the Rights of Women." *Agenda* 15: 81–82. www.jstor.org/stable/4065590.

Mbali, Mandisa. 2013. *South African AIDS Activism and Global Health Politics*. Houndmills: Palgrave Macmillan.

Mbembe, Achille. 2002. "The Power of the Archive and its Limits." In *Refiguring the Archive*, edited by Carolyn Hamilton, Verne Harris and Graeme Reid, 19–27. Cape Town: David Philip – New Africa.

Mbembe, Achille. 2004. "Afropolitanism." In *Africa Remix: Contemporary Art of a Continent*, trans. Laurent Chauret, 26–29. Ostfildern: Hatje Cantz.

Mbembe, Achille and Sarah Nuttall, eds. 2008. *Johannesburg: The Elusive Metropolis*. Durham and London: Duke University Press.

McHardy, Diana. 1987. "From Our Mailbox." *Sistren* 9. 2: 10.

Meer, Shamim. 1998. "Introduction." In *Women Speak: Reflections on our Struggles, 1982–1997*, 9–18. Cape Town: Kwela Books – Oxfam GB.

Meer, Shamim. 2012. Conversation with Kanika Batra. Mayfair, Johannesburg.

Menon, Nivedita. 2012. *Seeing Like a Feminist*. New Delhi: Zubaan-Penguin Books.

Menon, Nivedita. 2013a. "'The Impunity of Every Citadel is Intact': The Taming of the Verma Committee Report, and Some Troubling Doubts." *Kafila* (February 3). http://kafila.org/2013/02/03/the-impunity-of-every-citadel-is-intact-the-taming-of-the-verma-committee-report-and-some-troubling-doubts/.

Menon, Nivedita. 2013b. "Harvard to the Rescue!" *Kafila* (February 16). http://kafila.org/2013/02/16/harvard-to-the-rescue/.

Michael. 1982a. "You and the Law." *Link/Skakel* (October): 7.

Michael. 1982b. "You and the Law 2." *Link/Skakel* (November): 7.

Michael. 1982c. "You and the Law 3." *Link/Skakel* (December): 7.

Michael. 1983a. 'You and the Law 4." *Link/Skakel* (January): 9.

Michael. 1983b. 'You and the Law 5." *Link/Skakel* (February): 11.

Michael. 1983c. "You and the Law 8." *Link/Skakel* (June): 11.

Milady. 1979a. "Girl Talk." *Jamaica Gaily News* 44 (May 25): 6, 7.

Milady. 1979b. "One Last Memory." *Jamaica Gaily News* 45 (June 8): 4.

Milady. 1979c. "One Last Memory." *Jamaica Gaily News* 46 (June 29): 2.

Miles, Lesley. 1992. "Women, AIDS, Power and Heterosexual Negotiation: A Discourse Analysis." *Agenda*, 15: 14–27. www.jstor.org/stable/4065579.

Miller, Alice M. and Carole S. Vance. 2004. "Sexuality, Human Rights, and Health." *Health and Human Rights* 7. 2: 5–15.

Miller, Kei. 2015. "If a Gay Man Screams in the Caribbean and a White Man isn't there to Hear Him, Has He Still Made a Sound?" https://underthesaltireflag.com/2015/07/13/if-a-ga

y-man-screams-in-the-caribbean-and-a-white-man-isnt-there-to-hear-him-has-he-still-ma de-a-sound/.

Mills, Charles. 1997. "'Smadditizin.'" *Caribbean Quarterly* 43. 2 (June): 54–68.

Mina, Louisa. 1991. "Questioning Heterosexism: A Dead Debate or a Valid Challenge?" *Agenda* 11: 57–65. www.jstor.org/stable/4547979.

Mishra, Ram Manohar, Madhulika Dube, Damodar Sahu, Niranjan Saggurti and Arvind Pandey. 2012. "Changing Epidemiology of HIV in Mumbai: An Application of the Asian Epidemic Model." *Global Journal of Health Science* 4. 5: 100–112. www.ncbi.nlm.nih. gov/pmc/articles/PMC4776940/.

Mkhuma, Zinghisa. 1992. "Taxi Talk" *Speak* 41 (July): 32. https://disa.ukzn.ac.za/sites/defa ult/files/pdf_files/SpJul92.pdf.

Moghadam, Valentine M. 2005. *Globalizing Women: Transnational Feminist Networks*. Baltimore: Johns Hopkins University Press.

Mohammed, Patricia. 2000. "Considerations in the Construction of Gender-Related Development Indicators for Jamaica." In *The Construction of Gender Development Indicators for Jamaica*, 1–8. Kingston: Planning Institute for Jamaica, United Nations Development Program, and the Canadian International Development Agency.

Mohanty, Chandra Talpade. 2003. *Feminism without Borders: Decolonizing Theory, Practicing Solidarity*. Durham: Duke University Press.

Molyneux, Maxine and Shahra Razavi, eds. 2002. *Gender Justice, Development, and Rights*. Oxford: Oxford University Press.

Molyneux, Maxine and Shahra Razavi. 2005. "Beijing Plus Ten: An Ambivalent Record on Gender Justice." *Development and Change* 36. 6: 983–1010.

Morgan, Ruth, Charl Marais and Joy Rosemary Wellbeloved, eds. 2009. *Trans: Transgender Life Stories from South Africa*. GALA: Fanele-Jacana.

Morris, Alan. 1999. *Bleakness and Light: Inner-City Transition in Hillbrow, Johannesburg*. Johannesburg: Witwatersrand University Press.

Mukhopadhyay, Maitrayee and Shamim Meer. 2008. "Gender, Rights, and Development." In *Gender, Rights and Development: A Global Sourcebook*, 11–25. No. E50–1158. Amsterdam: Royal Tropical Institute.

Munro, Brenna M. 2012. *South Africa and the Dream of Love to Come: Queer Sexuality and the Struggle for Freedom*. Minneapolis: University of Minnesota Press.

Mwangi, Evan. 2014. "Queer Agency in Kenya's Digital Media." *African Studies Review*, 57. 2: 93–113. https://doi.org/10.1017/asr.2014.49.

Nagar, Richa. 2014. *Muddying the Waters: Coauthoring Feminisms across Scholarship and Activism*. Urbana: University of Chicago Press.

Nagar, Richa and Saraswati Raju. 2003. "Women, NGOs and the Contradictions of Empowerment and Disempowerment: A Conversation." *Antipode* 35. 1: 1–13. https:// doi.org/10.1111/1467-8330.00298.

Nagar, Richa and Amanda Lock Swarr. 2010. "Introduction: Theorizing Transnational Feminist Praxis." *Critical Transnational Feminist Praxis*, edited by Amanda Lock Swarr and Richa Nagar 1–20. Albany: State University of New York Press.

"Name withheld." 1985. "Letters to Manushi: Resisting Molestation." *Manushi* 30 (September–October): 25.

Narrain, Arvind and Gautam Bhan. 2005. "Introduction." In *Because I Have a Voice: Queer Politics in India*, edited by Arvind Narrain and Gautam Bhan, 1–29. New Delhi: Yoda Press.

Nash, Jennifer C. 2013. "Practicing Love: Black Feminism, Love-Politics, and Post-Intersectionality." *Meridians* 11. 2: 1–24. https://doi.org/10.2979/meridians.11.2.1.

Nettleford, Rex. 1972. *Identity, Race, and Protest in Jamaica*. New York: William Morrow.

Nettleford, Rex. 1979. *Caribbean Cultural Identity, The Case of Jamaica: An Essay in Cultural Dynamics*. Studies on Social Process and Change. Los Angeles: Center for Afri-American Studies and UCLA Latin American Center.

Nettleford, Rex. (2001) 2005. "The Cultural Aspects and Societal Implications of Human Rights Legislation, Particularly in the Caribbean Context." In *Selected Speeches*, edited by Kenneth Hall, 26–39. Kingston: Ian Randle.

Nicol, Julia. 1991. "Organization of Lesbian and Gay Activists." *Agenda* 11: 45–46.

Nkambule, Sebenzile Samkelisiwe. 2018. "Of Bravery and Invisibility: Black Lesbian Activism in South Africa between 1980 and 2016." MA thesis, University of Pretoria.

Nkoli, Simon. 1988. "Nkoli Answers Progressive Gay." *Exit* (June–July): 2.

Nkoli, Simon. 1990. 'Simon Nkoli writes an Open Letter to Nelson Mandela – Reprinted from New York's *Village Voice*." *Exit* (July–August): 16.

Ntombi. 1993. "Taxi Talk." *Speak* 52 (August): 32. https://disa.ukzn.ac.za/sites/default/files/pdf_files/SpAug93.pdf.

O'Connor, Florizelle. 1991. "From Our Mailbag." *Sistren* 13. 2–3: 40.

Olcott, Jocelyn. 2012. "Empires of Information: Media Strategies for the International Women's Year 1975." *Journal of Women's History* 24. 4: 24–48. https://muse.jhu.edu/article/492519.

Oloka-Onyango, Joseph and Sylvia Tamale. 1995. "The Personal is Political, or Why Women's Rights are Indeed Human Rights: An African Perspective on International Feminism." *Human Rights Quarterly* 17: 691–731. https://muse.jhu.edu/article/13504.

Omotoso, Yewande and Rebecca Fasselt. 2015. "'I'm not Afropolitan — I'm of the Continent': A Conversation with Yewande Omotoso." *The Journal of Commonwealth Literature* 50. 2: 1–23. https://journals.sagepub.com/doi/pdf/10.1177/0021989414552922.

Ong, Aihwa. 2011. "Introduction: Worlding Cities or, the Art of Being Global." In *Worlding Cities: Asian Experiments and the Art of Being Global*, edited by Ananya Roy and Aihwa Ong, 1–25. Chichester: Wiley-Blackwell.

Osinubi, Taiwo Adetunji. 2016. "Queer Prolepsis and the Sexual Commons: An Introduction." *Research in African Literatures* 47. 2 (Summer): vii–xxiii. www.jstor.org/stable/10.2979/reseafrilite.47.2.01.

O'Sullivan, Michelle. 1996. "Legaleye: The Termination of Pregnancy Bill Faces a Contested Passage." *Agenda* 30: 79–83. www.jstor.org/stable/4065786.

Panalal, Rupande. 1990. "When a Poor Woman Gets Raped." *Manushi* 60: 34–36.

Pandey, Gyanendra. 2006. "In Defense of the Fragment." In *Routine Violence: Nations, Fragments, Histories*, 16–35. Stanford: Stanford University Press.

Pandy, Thoraya. 1993a. "AIDS: Rights and Responsibilities." *Speak* 50 (June): 18–19. https://disa.ukzn.ac.za/sites/default/files/pdf_files/SpJun93.pdf.

Pandy, Thoraya. 1993b. "Act Against AIDS Now!" *Speak* 47 (March): 24–25. https://disa.ukzn.ac.za/sites/default/files/pdf_files/SpMar93.pdf.

Parnell, Susan and Alan Mabin. 1995. "Rethinking Urban South Africa." *Journal of Southern African Studies* 21. 1: 39–61. www.jstor.org/stable/pdf/2637330.pdf.

Pathak, Ila and Amina Amin. 1990. "How IWAG Dealt with a Rapist." *Manushi* 58: 37–38.

Patton, Cindy and Beningo Sanchez-Eppler, eds. 2000. *Queer Diasporas*. Durham: Duke University Press.

Payne, Robert. 2014. *The Promiscuity of Network Culture: Queer Theory and Digital Media*. New York: Routledge.

Pettman, Jan Jindy. (1996) 2004. *Worlding Women: A Feminist International Politics*. London and New York: Routledge.

Phadke, Shilpa. 2013. "Traversing the City: Some Gendered Questions of Access in Mumbai." In *Transforming Asian Cities: Intellectual Impasse, Asianizing Space, and Emerging*

Translocalities, edited by Nihal Perera and Wing-Shing Tang, 177–189. Oxford: Routledge.

Phadke, Shilpa, Sameera Khan and Shilpa Ranade. 2011. *Why Loiter?: Women and Risk on Mumbai Streets*. New Delhi: Penguin Books.

Pike, Phillip. 2002. *Songs of Freedom: Compelling Stories of Courage and Hope by Jamaican Gays and Lesbians*. Toronto: Jahloveboy Productions.

Pillay, Navi and Barabara Klugman. 1994. "Healthwatch: Developing Population Policies." *Agenda* 21: 107–113. www.jstor.org/stable/4065832.

Poison Pudi. 1997. "Mumbai Masala." *Bombay Dost* 5. 1: 19.

Poison Pudi. 1998a. "Mumbai Masala." *Bombay Dost* 4. 4: 11.

Poison Pudi. 1998b. "Purr…Fect Parties." *Bombay Dost* 6. 2–3: 4.

Povinelli, Elizabeth. 2011. "The Woman on the Other Side of the Wall: Archiving the Otherwise in Postcolonial Digital Archives." *differences: A Journal of Feminist Cultural Studies* 22. 1: 146–171. https://doi.org/10.1215/10407391-1218274.

Powell, Patricia. 1994. *A Small Gathering of Bones*. Oxford: Heinemann.

Powell. Patricia. 1998. *Pagoda*. Orlando: Harvest-Harcourt.

Powell, Patricia. 2003. *A Small Gathering of Bones*. Boston: Beacon.

Preston-Whyte, Eleanor and Maria Zondi. 1989. "To Control Their Own Reproduction: The Agenda of Black Teenage Mothers in Durban." *Agenda* 4: 47–68. www.jstor.org/stable/4547930.

Puri, Jyoti. 2002. *Woman, Body, Desire in Post-Colonial India: Narratives of Gender and Sexuality*. New York: Routledge.

Puri, Jyoti. 2011. "GenderQueer Perspectives: Sameness and Difference in Sections 375/6 and 377 of the Indian Penal Code." In *Law Like Love: Queer Perspectives on Law*, edited by Arvind Narrain and Alok Gupta, 203–227. New Delhi: Yoda Press.

Quayson, Ato. 2010. "Signs of the Times: Discourse Ecologies and Street Life on Oxford St., Accra." *City and Society* 22. 1: 72–96. https://doi.org/10.1111/j.1548-744X.2010.01031.x.

Ramesh and Prakash. 1996. "Humsafar ki Aawaz." *Bombay Dost* 5. 2–3: 16.

Raka, Ray. 2000. *Fields of Protest: Women's Movements in India*. Minneapolis: University of Minnesota Press.

Rao, R. Raj. 2017. *Criminal Love? Queer Theory, Culture, and Politics in India*. New Delhi: Sage Publications.

Rape Crisis. 1986. "Rape." *Speak* 10 (February–April): 13–15. https://disa.ukzn.ac.za/sites/default/files/pdf_files/SpFeb86.pdf.

Ratti, Rakesh. 1993. *A Lotus of Another Color: An Unfolding of South Asian Gay and Lesbian Experience*. New York: Alyson Books.

Rege, Arati. 1999. "A Decade of Lesbian Hulla Gulla." In *Humjinsi: A Resource Book of Lesbian, Gay, & Bisexual Rights in India*, edited by Bina Fernandez, 92–94. Mumbai: India Center for Human Rights and Law.

Reid, Graeme. 2013. *How to be a Real Gay: Gay Identities in Small-Town South Africa*. Durban: University of KwaZulu-Natal Press.

Reid, Graeme and Teresa Dirsuweit. 2002. "Understanding Systemic Violence: Homophobic Attacks in Johannesburg and its Surrounds." *Urban Forum* 13. 3: 99–126. https://link.springer.com/content/pdf/10.1007/s12132-002-0010-5.pdf.

Robertson, James. 2010. *The Humsafar Trust, Mumbai, India: Empowering Communities of Men who Have Sex with Men to Prevent HIV*. USAID-AIDSTAR-One. https://pdf.usaid.gov/pdf_docs/Pnadx301.pdf.

Robinson, Dee. 1995. "Marginally Female." *Sistren* 17. 2: 13.

Robinson, Tracy. 2007. "A Loving Freedom: A Caribbean Feminist Aesthetic." *Small Axe* 11. 3: 118–129. https://muse.jhu.edu/article/224207.

Robinson, Tracy. 2011. "Our Imagined Lives." In *Sex and the Citizen: Interrogating the Caribbean*, edited by Faith Smith, 201–241. Charlottesville: University of Virginia Press.

Robotham, Don. 1998. *Vision and Volunteerism: Reviving Volunteerism in Jamaica*. Grace Kennedy Foundation. http://gracekennedy.com/lecture/GKF1998Lecture.pdf.

Rogers, Alice and Mia Thomson. 1993. "10th Anniversary of WCC." *Sistren* 15. 3–4: 16–17.

Roper, Danielle and Traci-Ann Wint. 2020. "The Tambourine Army: Sonic Disruptions and the Politics of Respectability." *Small Axe: A Caribbean Journal of Criticism* 24. 2: 35–52. https://muse.jhu.edu/article/762555.

Ross-Frankson, Joan. 1985. "Women on the Streets: The Sporting Life." *Sistren* 7. 3 (December): 3–12.

Ross-Frankson, Joan. 1986. "Women on the Streets 2: Begging a Living." *Sistren* 8. 1 (April): 3–4.

Ross-Frankson, Joan. 1987. "Women Speak Out: Exploding the Myth of Domestic Bliss." *Sistren* 9. 1: 3, 12.

Ross-Frankson, Joan. 1989a. "Caribbean Women's Movement: Stronger and Broader." *Sistren* 11. 1: 18.

Ross-Frankson, Joan. 1989b. "Editorial: Our Bodies: Our Right!" *Sistren* 11. 2: 5.

Ross-Frankson, Joan. 1989c. "Birthing Pains at Victoria Jubilee." *Sistren* 11. 3: 8–13.

Ross-Frankson, Joan. 2020. Conversation with Kanika Batra. May. Lubbock, Texas, via Zoom.

Row Kavi, Ashok. 1992a. "Report: Solidarity in Asia." *Bombay Dost* 1. 3–4 (January–June): 13–14.

Row Kavi, Ashok. 1992b. "We're ILGA Members." *Bombay Dost* 1. 5–6 (July–December): 7, 14.

Row Kavi, Ashok. 1996. "Our Own Home." *Bombay Dost* 5. 2–3: 15.

Row Kavi, Ashok. 1998a. "Bombay Parties: Then and Now." *Bombay Dost* 6. 1: 13–14.

Row Kavi, Ashok. 1998b. "Report: We Exist!" *Bombay Dost* 6. 2–3: 27.

Row Kavi, Ashok. 2008. Conversation with Kanika Batra. June. New Delhi.

Row Kavi, Ashok. 2011. "*Kothis* versus Other MSM: Identity versus Behavior in the Chicken and Egg Paradox." In *The Phobic and the Erotic: The Politics of Sexuality in Contemporary India*, edited by Brinda Bose and Subhabrata Bhattacharya, 391–398. Oxford: Seagull Books.

Roy, Ananya. 2011. "Urbanisms, Worlding Practices and the Theory of Planning." *Planning Theory* 10. 1: 6–15. https://journals.sagepub.com/doi/pdf/10.1177/1473095210386065.

Roy, Sandip. 2003. "From Khush List to Gay Bombay: Virtual Webs of Real People." In *Mobile Cultures: New Media in Queer Asia*, edited by Chris Berry, Fran Martin, Audrey Yue, 180–200. Durham: Duke University Press.

Rydström, Jens. 2005. "Solidarity – With Whom? The International Gay and Lesbian Rights Movement and Apartheid." In *Sex and Politics in South Africa*, edited by Neville Hoad, Karen Martin and Graeme Reid, 34–49. Cape Town: Double Storey.

Said, Edward. 1993. *Culture and Imperialism*. London: Chatto & Windus.

Sakshi. 1995. "Violence in our Lesbian Lives." *Bombay Dost* 4. 2: 17

Sangtin Writers and Richa Nagar. 2006. *Playing with Fire: Feminist Thought and Activism Through Seven Lives in India*. Minneapolis: University of Minnesota Press.

Saunders, Kriemild. 2002. "Introduction: Towards a Deconstructive Post-Development Criticism." In *Feminist Post Development Thought: Rethinking Modernity, Post-Colonialism and Representation*, edited by Kriemild Saunders. London: Zed Books.

Saunders, Patricia. 2003. "Is Not Everything Good to Eat Good to Talk: Sexual Economy and Dancehall Music in the Global Marketplace." *Small Axe* 7. 1: 95–115. https://doi.org/10.1215/-7-1-95.

Schwartz, Michelle and Constance Crompton. 2018. "Remaking History: Lesbian Feminist Historical Methods in the Digital Humanities." In *Bodies of Information Intersectional Feminism and the Digital Humanities*, edited by Elizabeth Losh and Jacqueline Wernimont, 131–156. Minneapolis and London: University of Minnesota Press. https://dhdebates.gc. cuny.edu/read/untitled-4e08b137-aec5-49a4-83c0-38258425f145/section/ 5c06c277-b9c1-4caf-a81c-a6c201e08a5a#ch09.

Scott, David. 2004. *Conscripts of Modernity: The Tragedy of Colonial Enlightenment.* Durham: Duke University Press.

Scott, David. 2017. "'Seeing False Images of Ourselves': Rex Nettleford's *Mirror Mirror* in the Wake of the 1960s." *Small Axe* 21. 3: 152–166. https://muse.jhu.edu/article/676008.

Scott, David and Rex Nettleford. 2006. "'To be Liberated from the Obscurity of Themselves': An Interview with Rex Nettleford." *Small Axe* 10. 2: 97–246. https://doi.org/10. 1215/-10-2-97.

Seekings, Jeremy. 1991. "Gender Ideology and Township Politics in the 1980s." *Agenda* 10: 77–88. www.jstor.org/stable/4065458.

Seekings, Jeremy. 2000. "The Development of Strategic Thought in South Africa's Civic Movements, 1977–90." In *Comrades to Citizens: The South African Civics Movement and the Transition to Democracy*, edited by Glenn Adler and Jonny Steinberg. New York: Palgrave Macmillan. 52–85. http://ebookcentral.proquest.com/lib/ttu/detail.action?docID=203596.

Sen, Gita and Caren Grown. 1987. *Development, Crises, and Alternative Visions: Third World Women's Perspectives.* New York: Monthly Review Press.

Sen, Gita and Marina Durano, eds. 2014. *The Remaking of Social Contracts.* London: Zed Books.

Shaggy. 2015. Interview with Sway. March 4. https://13thstreetpromotions.com/2015/03/ 05/new-video-realsway-interviews-direalshaggy/.

Shah, Chayanika. 2005. "The Roads that E/Merged: Feminist Activism and Queer Understanding." In *Because I Have a Voice: Queer Politics in India*, edited by Arvind Narrain and Gautam Bhan, 143–154. New Delhi: Yoda Press.

Shah, Svati P. 2015. "Queering Critiques of Neoliberalism in India: Urbanism and Inequality in the Era of Transnational 'LGBTQ' Rights." *Antipode* 47. 3: 635–651. http s://doi.org/10.1111/anti.12112.

Shahni, Pramesh. 2008. *Gay Bombay: Globalization, Love and (Be)longing in Contemporary India.* New Delhi: Sage.

Sharma, Parvez. 1994. "Emerging from the Shadow" *Bombay Dost* 3. 3 (September–October): 10, 15.

Sheller, Mimi. 2012. *Citizenship from Below: Erotic Agency and Caribbean Freedom.* Durham: Duke University Press.

Shewani, Amina. 1985. "Letters to Manushi: Resisting Molestation." *Manushi* 28 (May–June): 24.

Sikand, Yoginder. 1995. "A Cross-Dressing Saint." *Bombay Dost* 4. 2: 11.

Silvera, Makeda. 1992. "Man Royals and Sodomites: Some Thoughts on the Invisibility of Afro-Caribbean Lesbians." In *Piece of My Heart: A Lesbian of Color Anthology*, edited by Makeda Silvera, 14–26. Toronto: Sister Vision.

Simelane, Beryl. 1994. "Holding Hands in Clermont." *Agenda* 20: 95–97. www.jstor.org/sta ble/4065878.

Simone, Abdoumaliq. 2004. "On the Worlding of African Cities." *African Studies Review* 44. 2: 15–41. www.jstor.org/stable/pdf/525573.pdf.

Sistren. 1985a. "Sista Ansa A Chat 'Bout De Decade." *Sistren* 7. 2 (May–August): 1, 12.

Sistren. 1985b. "Sista Ansa An Granny Chat Bout Peace." *Sistren* 7. 3 (December): 4.

Sistren. 1986a. "Sistren Movements: Sistren Research." *Sistren* 8. 1 (April): 10.

Sistren. 1986b. "Woman Time Long Time: The 1980s Meet the 1930s." *Sistren* 8. 2 (August–September): 16.

Sistren. 1986/1987. "Setting a Fine Example." *Sistren* 8. 3 (December–January): 11.

Sistren. 1987. "Your Bottom Line is Beautiful When you Make it in Jamaica." *Sistren* 9. 1: 1.

Sistren. 1989a. "The Daddies that Do." *Sistren* 11. 3: 15.

Sistren. 1989b. "Yes, Jamaican Men Can Be Loving Parents!" *Sistren* 11. 3: 14.

Sistren. 1989c. "Building Confidence in Non-Traditional Jobs." *Sistren* 11. 1: 14–15.

Sistren. 1990. "Let's Rope in the Men!" *Sistren* 12. 1: 5.

Sistren. 1991a. "Sistren Research Update." *Sistren* 13. 1: 25–26.

Sistren. 1991b. "The Pauline Mullings Story." *Sistren* 13. 2–3: 46.

Sistren. 1991c. "Sister Lillian Speaks on Intimate Relationships." *Sistren* 13. 2–3: 17.

Sistren. 1991d. "Women on Being Woman: Women and Sexuality." *Sistren* 13. 2–3: 38.

Sistren. 1991e. "AIDS/HIV Infections on the Increase." *Sistren.* Special Issue: Women, Sexuality, and Health. 13. 2–3: 29.

Sistren. 1993a. "Can I call you Sister." *Sistren* 15. 1–2: 34.

Sistren. 1993b. "Health Update: Say No to Norplant!" *Sistren* 15. 3–4: 32–33.

Sistren. 1993c. "Health Update." *Sistren* 15. 1–2: 25.

Sistren. 1994. "Health Update." *Sistren* 16. 1–2: 27.

Sistren. 1995a. "Can I call you Sister: Bev. Hanson Raps with Uncle Barry." *Sistren* 17. 2: 10–12.

Sistren. 1995b. "Health Update." *Sistren* 17. 1–2: 25.

Sistren with Honor Ford-Smith. 1987. *Lionheart Gal: Life Stories of Jamaican Women.* Toronto: Sister Vision Press.

Sistren Theatre Collective. 2001. "QPH." In *Postcolonial Plays: An Anthology,* edited by Helen Gilbert, 153–178. London and New York: Routledge.

Slack, Jennifer Daryl. 1996. "The Theory and Method of Articulation in Cultural Studies." In *Stuart Hall: Critical Dialogues in Cultural Studies,* edited by David Morley and Kuang Hsing-Chen, 113–129. London: Routledge.

Slaughter, Joseph. 2007. *Human Rights, Inc: The World Novel, Narrative Form, and International Law.* Fordham: Fordham University Press.

Smikle, Patrick. 1994. "Louise Fraser Bennett…Against Slackness, Lewdness and Gun Lyrics… But." *Sistren* 16. 1–2: 16–17.

Smith, Ann. 1982a. "New Look at Social Lesbianism." *Link/Skakel* (November): 4.

Smith, Ann. 1982b. "Lesbian Role Playing." *Link/Skakel* (December): 11.

Smith, Ann. 1984. "GASA Group for Women Proposed." *Link/Skakel* (February): 6.

Smith, Ann. 1986. "Simon Part of a Greater Problem." *Exit* (March–April): 5.

Smith, Ann. 2005. "Where was I in the Eighties?" In *Sex and Politics in South Africa,* edited by Neville Hoad, Karen Martin and Graeme Reid, 58–63. Cape Town: Double Storey.

Smith, Donna. 2020. *Launch of the Digital Archive of the Jamaica Gaily News.* YouTube video, 2:11:41. www.youtube.com/watch?v=azaF5FLIHxk.

Smith, Faith Lois, ed. 2011. *Sex and the Citizen: Interrogating the Caribbean.* Charlottesville: University of Virginia Press.

Smith, Faith Lois. 2015. "Introduction: Sexing the Citizen." In *Sex and the Citizen: Interrogating the Caribbean,* edited by Faith Smith, 1–19. Charlottesville: University of Virginia Press.

Smith, Karina. 2008. "Narratives of Success, Narratives of Failure: The Creation and Collapse of Sistren's 'Aesthetic Space.'" *Modern Drama* 51. 2: 234–258. https://doi.org/10.3138/md.51.2.234.

Smith, Karina. 2013. "From Politics to Therapy: Sistren Theatre Collective's Theatre and Outreach Work in Jamaica." *New Theatre Quarterly* 29. 1: 87–97. https://doi.org/10.1017/S0266464X13000080.

Smith, Michael Garfield, Roy Augier, and Rex Nettleford. 1967a. "The Rastafari Movement in Kingston, Jamaica: Part I." *Caribbean Quarterly* 13. 3: 3–29. www.jstor.org/stable/pdf/40653024.pdf.

Smith, Michael Garfield, Roy Augier, and Rex Nettleford. 1967b. "The Rastafari Movement in Kingston, Jamaica: Part II." *Caribbean Quarterly* 13. 4: 3–14. www.jstor.org/stable/pdf/40653036.pdf.

Soske, Jon. 2018. *Internal Frontiers: African Nationalism and the Indian Diaspora in Twentieth-Century South Africa.* Johannesburg: Wits University Press.

Speak. 1982. "Health." *Speak* 1 (May): 5. https://disa.ukzn.ac.za/sites/default/files/pdf_files/Spn182.pdf.

Speak. 1984a. "Health: Our Cycle." *Speak* 2: 8–10. https://disa.ukzn.ac.za/sites/default/files/pdf_files/Spn282.pdf.

Speak. 1984b. "Our Health: The IUCD/The Loop." *Speak* 5 (March): 15–17. https://disa.ukzn.ac.za/sites/default/files/pdf_files/SpMar84.pdf.

Speak. 1984c. "Health: The Diaphragm and the Condom." *Speak* 6 (July): 21–23. https://disa.ukzn.ac.za/sites/default/files/pdf_files/SpJul84.pdf.

Speak. 1984d. "Health: Sterilization-Permanent Contraception for Men and Women." *Speak* 7 (December): 19–23. https://disa.ukzn.ac.za/sites/default/files/pdf_files/SpDec84.pdf.

Speak. 1985. "Health: Chart on Contraception." *Speak* 8 (April): 12–16. https://disa.ukzn.ac.za/sites/default/files/pdf_files/SpApr85.pdf.

Speak. 1986a. "Deadly Contraceptive." *Speak* 10 (February–April): 17. https://disa.ukzn.ac.za/sites/default/files/pdf_files/SpFeb86.pdf.

Speak. 1986b. "Our Health: Getting to Know Our Bodies." *Speak* 10 (February–April): 25–27. https://disa.ukzn.ac.za/sites/default/files/pdf_files/SpFeb86.pdf.

Speak. 1987a. "No to Rape Say Port Alfred Women." *Speak* 13 (January–March): 3–5. https://disa.ukzn.ac.za/sites/default/files/pdf_files/SpJan87.pdf.

Speak. 1987b. "We are not Toys!" *Speak* 14 (March–May): 5. https://disa.ukzn.ac.za/sites/default/files/pdf_files/SpMar87.pdf.

Speak. 1988a. "I Am Pregnant: What Can go Wrong?" *Speak* 20 (July–August): 20–22. https://disa.ukzn.ac.za/sites/default/files/pdf_files/SpJul88.pdf.

Speak. 1988b. "I Am Pregnant: How Can I Prepare for Labour." *Speak* 21 (September–November): 20–22. https://disa.ukzn.ac.za/sites/default/files/pdf_files/SpSep88.pdf.

Speak. 1988c. "AIDS: Let's Talk about It." *Speak* 20 (July–August): 10–11. https://disa.ukzn.ac.za/sites/default/files/pdf_files/SpJul88.pdf.

Speak. 1988–1989. "I Am Pregnant: What will Labor be Like?" *Speak* 22 (December–January): 24–27. https://disa.ukzn.ac.za/sites/default/files/pdf_files/SpDec88.pdf.

Speak. 1990. "Understanding AIDS." *Speak* 28: 24–27. https://disa.ukzn.ac.za/sites/default/files/pdf_files/Spn2890.pdf.

Speak. 1991. "Today it's Me, Tomorrow it's Someone Else." *Speak* 35: 26–27. https://disa.ukzn.ac.za/sites/default/files/pdf_files/Spn3591.pdf.

Speak. 1992a. "A Conversation with Indres Naidoo." *Speak* 38: 14–16. https://disa.ukzn.ac.za/sites/default/files/pdf_files/Spn3892.pdf.

Speak. 1992b. "Abortion: Campaigning to Change the Law." *Speak* 42 (August): 24–25. https://disa.ukzn.ac.za/sites/default/files/pdf_files/SpAug92.pdf.

Speak. 1992c. "Nomshado Twala: The Person Behind the Voice." *Speak* 41 (July): 5–7. https://disa.ukzn.ac.za/sites/default/files/pdf_files/SpJul92.pdf.

Speak. 1992d. "Advice: Reporting Rape." *Speak* 40 (June): 21. https://disa.ukzn.ac.za/sites/default/files/pdf_files/SpJun92.pdf.

Speak. 1992e. "Advice: AIDS Tests." *Speak* 40 (June): 29. https://disa.ukzn.ac.za/sites/default/files/pdf_files/SpJun92.pdf.

Speak. 1992f. "We all miss you: A Story about AIDS in the Family." *Speak* (August): 20–22. https://disa.ukzn.ac.za/sites/default/files/pdf_files/SpAug92.pdf.

Speak. 1992g. "Women Behind the Wheel." *Speak* 44 (October): 24–25.

Speak. 1992h. "Taxi Talk" *Speak* 39 (May): 32. https://disa.ukzn.ac.za/sites/default/files/pdf_files/SpMay92.pdf.

Speak. 1992i. "Abortion: Campaigning to Change the Law." *Speak* 42 (August): 24–25. https://disa.ukzn.ac.za/sites/default/files/pdf_files/SpAug92.pdf.

Speak. 1992–1993. "Gay and Proud." 46 (December–January): 10–11. https://disa.ukzn.ac.za/sites/default/files/pdf_files/SpDec92.pdf.

Speak. 1993a. "Behind the Wheel to Save Lives," *Speak* 47 (March): 22–23. https://disa.ukzn.ac.za/sites/default/files/pdf_files/SpMar93.pdf.

Speak. 1993b. "'I thought I had AIDS': Mandala Hlatshwayo Tells His Story." *Speak* 48 (April): 24–25. https://disa.ukzn.ac.za/sites/default/files/pdf_files/SpApr93.pdf.

Speak. 1993c. "Health Briefs: Bosses and Workers Agree." *Speak* 55 (November): 31. https://disa.ukzn.ac.za/sites/default/files/pdf_files/SpNov93.pdf.

Speak. 1993d. "Health Briefs: AIDS Spreading Like Wild Fire." *Speak* 51 (July): 30. https://disa.ukzn.ac.za/sites/default/files/pdf_files/SpJul93.pdf.

Speak. 1993e. "Health Briefs: AIDS-Botswana in Trouble." *Speak* 52 (August): 30. https://disa.ukzn.ac.za/sites/default/files/pdf_files/SpAug93.pdf.

Speak. 1993f. "Health Briefs: Four Million Women Will Die of AIDS." *Speak* 55 (November): 31. https://disa.ukzn.ac.za/sites/default/files/pdf_files/SpNov93.pdf.

Speak. 1994a. "Learning to Live with AIDS." *Speak* 57 (August): 24–25. https://disa.ukzn.ac.za/sites/default/files/pdf_files/SpFeb94.pdf.

Speak. 1994b. "Throwing Light on our Lives." *Speak* 63: 24–25. https://disa.ukzn.ac.za/sites/default/files/pdf_files/SpAug94.pdf.

Speak. 1994c. "HIV and AIDS: Need for New Prevention Plan." *Speak* 59 (April): 22–23. https://disa.ukzn.ac.za/sites/default/files/pdf_files/SpApr94.pdf.

Speak. 1994d. "Home to Die." *Speak* 60 (May): 28–29. https://disa.ukzn.ac.za/sites/default/files/pdf_files/SpMay94.pdf.

Speak. 1994e. "Health Briefs: AIDS is Growing Fastest Among Young Women." *Speak* 59 (April): 34. https://disa.ukzn.ac.za/sites/default/files/pdf_files/SpApr94.pdf.

Spivak, Gayatri Chakravarty. 1985. "The Rani of Sirmur: An Essay in Reading the Archives." *History and Theory* 24. 3: 247–272. www.jstor.org/stable/2505169.

Spivak, Gayatri Chakravarty. 1988. "Can the Subaltern Speak?" In *Marxism and the Interpretation of Culture*, edited by Cary Nelson and Laurence Grossberg, 271–313. Basingstoke: Macmillan.

Spivak, Gayatri Chakravarty. 2005. "Scattered Speculations on the Subaltern and the Popular." *Postcolonial Studies* 8. 4: 475–486.

Spivak, Gayatri Chakravarty. 2012. "The New Subaltern: A Silent Interview." In *Mapping Subaltern Studies and the Postcolonial*, edited by Vinayak Chaturvedi, 324–340. London: Verso.

Sridhar. 1998. "Party Etiquette: Have a Ball!" *Bombay Dost* 6. 1: 10–12.

Srilata, K. 1999. "The Story of the 'Up-Market' Reader: *Femina's* 'New Woman' and the Normative Feminist Subject." *Journal of Arts and Ideas* 32–33: 61–72.

Srivastava, Neelam and Baidik Bhattacharya, eds. 2012. *The Postcolonial Gramsci*. New York: Routledge.

Steedman, Carolyn. 2002. *Dust: The Archive and Cultural History*. New Brunswick: Rutgers University Press.

Stein, Marc. 2004. *City of Sisterly and Brotherly Loves: Lesbian and Gay Philadelphia, 1945–1972*. Chicago: University of Chicago Press.

Stoler, Ann Laura. 2009. *Along the Archival Grain: Epistemic Anxieties and Colonial Common Sense*. Princeton: Princeton University Press.

Strebel, Anna. 1992. "'There's Absolutely Nothing I Can Do, Just Believe in God': South African Women with AIDS." *Agenda* 12: 50–62. www.jstor.org/stable/4065478.

Stud Barn. 1984. "Stud Barn." *Link/Skakel* (June–July): 10.

Sukthankar, Ashwini. 1997. *Facing the Mirror: Lesbian Writing in India*. New Delhi: Penguin.

Sultan. 1992. "Hijra or High Camp?" *Bombay Dost* 1. 5–6: 16.

Sunder Rajan, Rajeswari. (2000) 2002. "The Story of Draupadi's Disrobing: Meanings for our Times." In *Mapping Histories: Essays Presented to Ravinder Kumar*, edited by Ravinder Kumar and Neera Chandoke, 39–60. London: Anthem Press.

Swarr, Amanda Lock. 2012a. "Paradoxes of Butchness: Lesbian Masculinities and Sexual Violence in Contemporary South Africa." *Signs: Journal of Women in Culture and Society* 37. 4: 961–986. https://doi.org/10.1086/664476.

Swarr, Amanda Lock. 2012b. *Sex in Transition: Remaking Gender and Race in South Africa*. Albany: State University of New York Press.

Swarr, Amanda Lock and Richa Nagar. 2004. "Dismantling Assumptions: Interrogating 'Lesbian' Struggles for Identity and Survival in India and South Africa." *Signs: Journal of Women in Culture and Society* 29. 2: 491–516. www.jstor.org/stable/10.1086/378573.

Switzer, Les and Mohamed Adhikari. 2000. *South Africa's Resistance Press: Alternative Voices in the Last Generation under Apartheid*. Vol. 74. Athens: Ohio University Press.

Tafari Ama, Imani. 1987. "Teens Respond to Rape in Community." *Sistren* 9. 3: 4.

Tafari Ama, Imani. 1989. "Action Packed Teens." *Sistren* 11. 3: 6.

Tallis, Vicki. 1991. "Aids: What Does It Mean for Women?" *Agenda* 9: 4–9. www.jstor.org/stable/4547942.

Tamale, Sylvia. 2011. "Researching and Theorising Sexualities in Africa." In *African Sexualities: A Reader*, edited by Sylvia Tamale, 11–36. Cape Town: Pambazuka Press.

Team Culture Lab. 2019. "The Role of Caste in the LGBTQ Community." The Godrej India Culture Lab (blog) (February 5). https://indiaculturelab.org/blog/the-role-of-caste-in-the-lgbtq-community/.

Telela, Rosalee. 1993a. "Abortion: A Woman's Choice." *Speak* 51 (July): 18–19. https://disa.ukzn.ac.za/sites/default/files/pdf_files/SpJul93.pdf.

Telela, Rosalee. 1993b. "Condoms: A Weapon Against AIDS." *Speak* 55 (November): 20–21. https://disa.ukzn.ac.za/sites/default/files/pdf_files/SpNov93.pdf.

Telela, Rosalee. 1994. "No Wo(man)'s Land." *Speak* 65: 26–27. https://disa.ukzn.ac.za/sites/default/files/pdf_files/SpOct94.pdf.

Tellis, Ashley. 2012. "Disrupting the Dinner Table: Re-Thinking the 'Queer Movement' in Contemporary India." *Jindal Global Law Review* 4. 1: 142–156.

Thadani, Giti. 1998. *Sakhiyani: Lesbian Desire in Ancient and Modern India*. London: Cassell.

Thadani, Giti. 2011. *Project Bolo: A Collection of Oral Histories of LGBT Persons*. Solaris Pictures-United Nations Development Program. YouTube video, 31:14. www.youtube.com/watch?v=uT_QuqAJ8kw.

Thapalyal, Abha, Prabha Rani and Ruth Vanita. 1987. "A Study of Twenty Cases." *Manushi* 40: 18–24.

Thapan, Meenakshi. 2004. "Embodiment and Identity in Contemporary Indian Society: *Femina* and the 'New' Indian Woman." *Contributions to Indian Sociology* 38. 3: 411–444.

Thomas, Deborah. 2011. *Exceptional Violence: Embodied Citizenship in Transnational Jamaica*. Durham: Duke University Press.

Thomas, V. R. 1977. "A Reader's Comments." *Jamaica Gaily News* 3 (October 7): 6.

Tickner, J. Ann. 2001. *Gendering World Politics: Issues and Approaches in the Post-Cold War Era*. New York: Columbia University Press.

Todes, Allison. 1995. "Gender in Metropolitan Development Strategies: The Case of Durban." *Cities* 12. 5: 327–336. https://doi.org/10.1016/0264-2751(95)00071-S.

Trikon. 1987. "Letters." *Trikon* (June): 3.

Tucker, Andrew. 2009. *Queer Visibilities: Space, Identity and Interaction in Cape Town.* Chichester: Wiley-Blackwell.

Vahed, Goolam and Thembisa Waetjen. 2010. *Gender, Modernity & Indian Delights: The Women's Cultural Group of Durban, 1954–2010.* Capetown: HSRC Press.

Vaid, Urvashi. 1995. *Virtual Equality: The Mainstreaming of Gay and Lesbian Liberation.* New York: Anchor-Doubleday.

van der Laagen, Hans. 1983. "Fag Hags and Sex." *Link/Skakel* (June–July): 3.

Vanita, Ruth. 1987. "Can the Police Reform Husbands? The Crimes Against Women Cell, Delhi." *Manushi* 40 (May–June): 12–18.

Vanita, Ruth. 2002a. "*Dosti* and *Tamanna*: Male-Male Love, Difference, and Normativity in Hindi Cinema." In *Everyday Life in South Asia*, edited by Diane P. Mines and Sarah Lamb, 146–158. Bloomington: Indiana University Press.

Vanita, Ruth. 2002b. *Queering India: Same-Sex Love in Indian Culture and Society.* New York: Routledge.

Vanita, Ruth. 2004. "Born to Two Mothers, the Hero Bhagiratha: Female-Female Love and Miraculous Birth in Hindu Texts." *Manushi* 146: 22–33.

Vanita, Ruth. 2005. "The Sita Who Smiles: Wife as Goddess in the *Adbhut Ramayana.*" *Manushi* 148: 32–39.

Vanita, Ruth. 2007. "Lesbian Studies and Activism in India." *Journal of Lesbian Studies* 11. 3–4: 243–253. https://doi.org/10.1300/J155v11n03_07.

Vanita, Ruth and Saleem Kidwai. 2001. *Same Sex Love in India: Readings from Literature and History.* New York: Palgrave.

van Kessel, Ineke. 2000. *Beyond Our Wildest Dreams: The United Democratic Front and the Transformation of South Africa.* Charlottesville and London: University of Virginia Press.

van Zyl, Mikki and Melissa Steyn, eds. 2008. *Performing Queer: Shaping Sexualities 1994–2004*, Vol 1. Cape Town: Kwela Books.

Varghese, Sudha. 1997. "Justice Denied: The Suspicious Death of Deepa Murmu." *Manushi* 98: 17–19.

Verma, Ruchi, Abhijeet Shekhar, Sharmistha Khobragade, Rajatashuvra Adhikary, Bitra George, Banadalkoppa M. Ramesh and Virupax Ranebennur. 2010. "Scale-up and Coverage of Avahan: A Large-Scale HIV-Prevention Programme Among Female Sex Workers and Men Who Have Sex with Men in Four Indian States." *Sexually Transmitted Infections* 86. 1: i76–i82. http://dx.doi.org/10.1136/sti.2009.039115.

Vernon, R. N. 1977. "Letter." *JGN* 3 (October 7): 7.

Versey, Farzana. 1994. "A Gay Life, Indeed." *Bombay Dost* 3. 2 (June–August): [back cover].

Vikram. 1999. "White Out: The White Party and After." *Bombay Dost* 7. 1: 18–19.

Visser, Gustav. 2010. "Leisurely Lesbians in a Small City in South Africa." *Urban Forum* 21. 2: 171–185. www.africabib.org/htp.php?RID=332736512.

Vladislavic, Ivan. 2006. *Portrait with Keys: The City of Johannesburg Unlocked.* New York: Norton Press.

Vladislavic, Ivan. (2001) 2014. *The Restless Supermarket.* Claremont: David Phillip.

Wainaina, Binyavanga. 2011. *One Day I Will Write about this Place.* Minneapolis: Graywolf Press.

Warner, Michael. 1993. "Introduction." In *Fear of a Queer Planet: Queer Politics and Social Theory*, edited by Michael Warner. Sexual Politics 6, xvii–xxi. Minnesota: University of Minnesota Press.

Warner, Michael. 2002. *Publics and Counterpublics.* New York: Zone Books.

Wedderburn, Judith and Members of Women's Media Watch. 2015. Conversation with Kanika Batra. Kingston, Women's Media Watch. July.

Williams, Lawson. 2000. "Homophobia and Gay Rights Activism in Jamaica," *Small Axe* 7 (March): 106–111.

Williams, Paulette. 1990. "AIDS: Our Babies at Risk." *Sistren* 12. 2–3: 26.

Wilson, Rob, Sandeep Banerjee, Frank Schulze-Engler, Zahi Zalloua, Ming Xie and Ranjan Ghosh. 2019. "More than Global? A Roundtable Discussion." *New Global Studies* 13. 1: 125–158. www.degruyter.com/document/doi/10.1515/ngs-2019-0008/html. Wits Gay Movement. 1987.

Women's Resource and Outreach Center (WROC) and the United Nations Development fund for Women (UNIFEM). 2008. *Rights a di Plan, Wid CEDAW in Wi Han': CEDAW for Jamaicans*. Kingston: WROC.

Wynter, Sylvia. 1990. "Beyond Miranda's Meanings: Un/silencing the 'Demonic Ground' of Caliban's 'Woman.'" In *Out of the Kumbla: Caribbean Women and Literature*, edited by Carole Boyce Davies and Elaine Savory Fido, 355–372. Trenton: Africa World Press.

Wynter, Sylvia and David Scott. 2000. "The Re-Enchantment of Humanism: An Interview with Sylvia Wynter." *Small Axe* 8: 119–207. https://serendipstudio.org/oneworld/system/files/WynterInterview.pdf.

Zabus, Chantal. 2013. *Out in Africa: Same-Sex Desire in Sub-Saharan Literatures and Cultures*. Melton: James Currey.

Zwart, Gine. 1992. "Women in Development to Gender and Development, More than a Change in Terminology?" *Agenda* 14: 16–21. www.jstor.org/stable/4547992.

INDEX

Printed in the United States
by Baker & Taylor Publisher Services